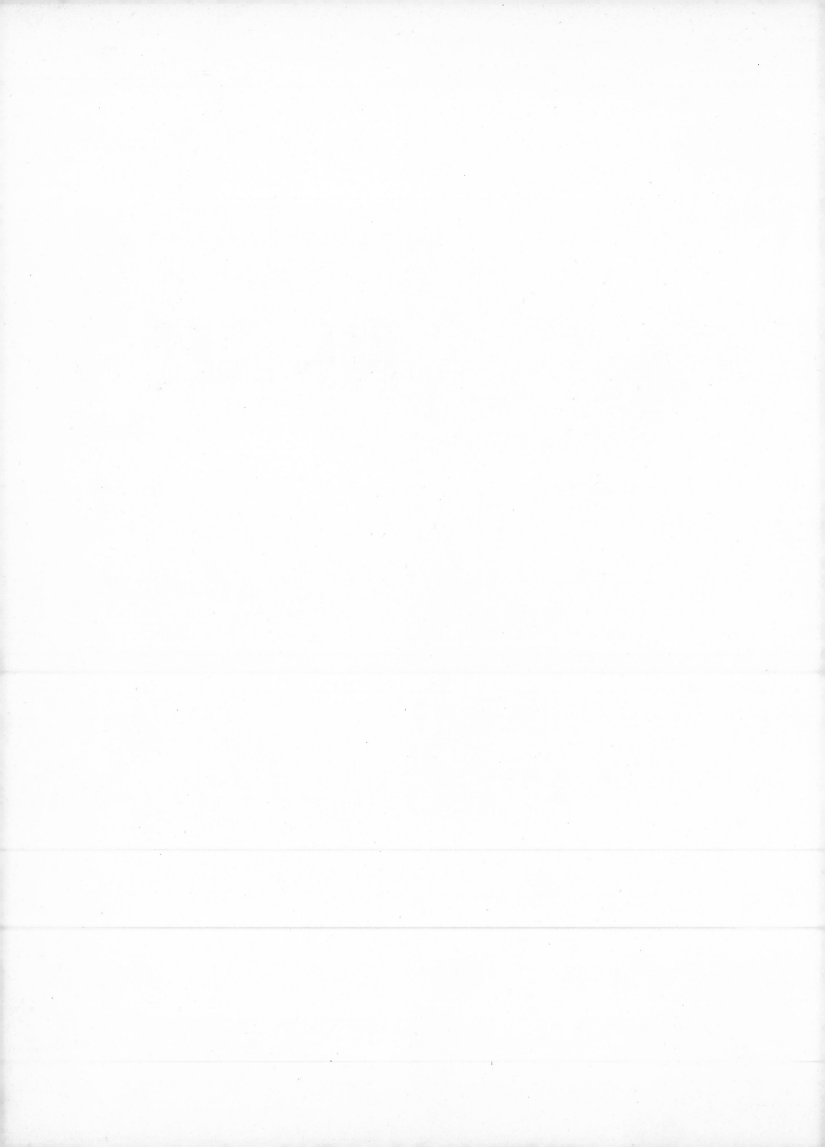

AFRICA
History of a Continent

Endpapers : The Asante Yam Festival, from Bowdich's
Mission from Cape Coast Castle to Ashantee (1819)

AFRICA

History of a Continent

Basil Davidson

with photographs by Werner Forman

Spring Books
London·New York·Sydney·Toronto

Other books about Africa by Basil Davidson

Old Africa Rediscovered
Black Mother: The African Slave Trade
The African Past: Chronicles from Antiquity to Modern Times
The Growth of African Civilization: West Africa AD 1000-1800
Guide to African History
A History of West Africa to 1800
A History of East and Central Africa to the late 19th Century

Contemporary affairs
Report on Southern Africa
The African Awakening
Which Way Africa? The Search for a New Society
The Liberation of Guiné: Aspects of an African Revolution
In the Eye of the Storm: Angola's People

Other books about Africa illustrated by W. and B. Forman
Benin Art with Philip Dark
Afro-Portuguese Ivories with William Fagg
Egyptian Art with Milada Vilimkova and Mohammed Abd-ur-Rahman
Photographic Methods for the Identification of Egyptian Works of Art
by Werner Forman

© Copyright 1966, 1972 by Basil Davidson
Design of illustrations by Bedrich Forman

Original edition published 1966 by George Weidenfeld and Nicolson Ltd., London
This revised edition published 1972 by
The Hamlyn Publishing Group Limited
London · New York · Sydney · Toronto
Hamlyn House, Feltham, Middlesex, England

Printed in Italy by Arnoldo Mondadori Editore Officine Grafiche, Verona

ISBN 0 600 30083 8

Contents

1 Old Myths: New Truths

An introduction to the study of African history from the earliest times – Africa's importance for the development of early types of hominid and of *homo sapiens* – The 'green Sahara', 5000–2000 BC, as a cradle of early cultures – Some consequences of Saharan desiccation – Beginnings of the African Iron Age north and south of the Sahara

2 Ancient Glories

Origins of Ancient Egypt, its growth and achievement – Links of Pharaonic Egyptians with neighbouring peoples – Emergence and history of the kingdoms of Kush on the Middle Nile, Napata and Meroe; and of Axum in Ethiopia – The old civilization of the Berbers – Punic and Roman North Africa and early links with West Africa

3 The Factors of Growth

Development and diversity of community life in ancient times south of the Sahara – Growth and importance of trading centres – Further evolution of Iron Age political systems – History of some of the largest of these systems in western and central-southern Africa up to the sixteenth century – The Christian kingdoms of Nubia and Ethiopia – Rise and early consequences of Islam

4 Tropical Achievement

The great 'middle period' of the African Iron Age and its many cultures and political systems throughout Africa south of the Sudan – The kingdoms of the Rift Valley, of the stone-building peoples of the central-southern plateau, of the Luba-Lunda and other Congo states, and of the peoples of West Africa in the sixteenth century

5 New Encounters

North Africa from AD 1100 until the European raids of the fifteenth and sixteenth centuries and the somewhat later Ottoman conquests – East Africa and its city-states along the coast during the early years of Portuguese discovery – West Africa and the coming of the European sea-traders – Growth and consequences of the Atlantic slave trade

6 Towards Crisis

General outline of the history of the seventeenth and eighteenth centuries – Emergence of new states in the forest and coastal lands of West Africa; in the Niger delta; in Oyo, Dahomey and Asante – The Western Sudan after 1600 – The Bambara states – The Muslim revival movement both in Western and Eastern Sudan up to the 1890s – East Africa, including Madagascar, after the Portuguese ravages – South Africa and the Zulu empire – The condition of Africa in the nineteenth century

7   Conquest and Colonial Rule

Geographical exploration of inner Africa – New missionary endeavours – Rise of European imperialism and its meaning for Africa – Rivalries for African possessions: from coastal encroachment to the continental 'scramble' and full-scale invasion – Brief history of the colonial period in the first two of its three main phases: 1900–20 and 1920–45

8   Towards Liberation

The forerunners of modern African independence movements, north and south of the Sahara, before 1945 – Outline of the third main phase of the colonial period after 1945 – Growth of nationalism and the emergence of independent states – The legacy of the past and new problems of economic and social transition

It is our duty to proceed from what is near to what is distant, from what is known to that which is less known, to gather the traditions from those who have reported them, to correct them as much as possible and to leave the rest as it is, in order to make our work help anyone who seeks truth and loves wisdom.

Abu'l-Rayhan Muhamad al-Biruni, AD 973–1050

1 Old Myths: New Truths

*An introduction to the study of African history from the earliest times –
Africa's importance for the development of early types of hominid and of
homo sapiens – The 'green Sahara', 5000–2000 BC, as a cradle of early
cultures – Some consequences of Saharan desiccation – Beginnings of the
African Iron Age north and south of the Sahara*

Africa's Place in History

Not long ago, while writing about the African past, an elderly scholar of the West African city of Bobo-Dyulasso recalled the downfall of the Ummayad Caliphate, and opined that Africa had changed since then. Considering that the downfall of the Ummayad Caliphate had occurred a thousand years earlier, this was no small understatement; but the mufti of Bobo, concerned to argue that African history was both long and very intricate, was perfectly aware of the fact. He went on to rub it in. As a further warning to anyone who should think it easy to write African history, he observed that any attempt to bring together the events of the last thousand years would be like trying to trap wind in a sieve, for 'everybody who attained to distinction spared no effort at extinguishing the flame of his rival . . . [and] everybody was in contradiction with the others . . . [while] many a year would drag on fruitlessly because of the numerous quarrels and wars among them.' In saying this, of course, the learned mufti was rather at the other extreme of overstatement. Yet the warning is a useful one, for it is true that scholarship is only at the beginning of a deep understanding of the African past. Much remains to be discovered. Much remains to be agreed.

It is none the less already possible to know a great deal about African history. Whether in the field of scientific archaeology, the study of languages or the movement of ideas, the assembly of historical tradition or the elucidation of records written by Africans, Europeans, Asians and Americans, fruitful labour and

learning in several countries over the past few decades have produced a large body of explanatory work, and have proved that the writing of African history need be neither the repetition of romantic legend nor the mere listing of faceless names and battles long ago. These historical advances have swept away some old myths and established some new truths. The seductively agreeable belief so dear to nineteenth-century Europe that all in Africa was savage chaos before the coming of the Europeans may still linger here and there, but not among historians concerned with Africa. The happy conviction of the conquerors that they were bringing civilization to peoples against whom the Gates of Eden had barely closed may still have its adherents, yet not among those who have looked at the evidence. Far from being a sort of Museum of Barbarism whose populations had stayed outside the laws of human growth and change through some natural failing or inferiority, Africa is now seen to possess a history which demands as serious an approach as the history of any other continent. What we now have, more and more clearly, is the bodying forth of a broad and vivid process of human development.

Pessimist though he was, the mufti of Bobo rightly conceived his problem in terms of a very long span of years. And this process of development may now in fact be seen as a continuum evolving with no decisive break from the pastoral populations of the green Sahara five thousand years ago, or still earlier from the rise of agriculture in the valley of the Nile, or even, though very mistily now, still earlier again from Stone Age peoples of the most remote antiquity. Anyone who might try to explain everything that has happened since then would undoubtedly be trapping wind in a sieve; but this, after all, is true of other continents besides Africa, and the writing of history would in any case become a hopeless venture if it involved explaining everything. What now exists for Europe is a fairly solid outline of the past that is filled with interesting and meaningful detail, and divided for the sake of convenience into a number of fairly well accepted periods. It is this kind of outline and periodization, though as yet with far less detail and definition, that is now beginning to exist for the very different history of Africa as well.

The book that follows here is not, of course, an attempt to offer anything approaching a complete review of what is known and thought about the African past. No such effort could succeed within a single volume unless this were to be a mere catalogue of facts and hypotheses; and even then the treatment would have to be unreadably dense. Besides, there is already beginning to be available a number of good histories of single countries or regions; a brief list of some of them will be found further on. This means that the specialist and even the non-specialist will find many omissions in these pages. I am well aware of them myself. They will be forgiven, I hope, for the sake of clarity and readability within a short volume designed to offer a continental view of the past. What follows here, accordingly, is an attempt to trace a broad outline of African growth and change over some twenty centuries, to present a general and yet reasonably chronological survey of those years, as well as to suggest the long-range historical explanation of Africans and their development which modern scholarship can now increasingly reveal, and which, in the measure that it can be well done, may really 'help anyone who seeks truth and loves wisdom'.

The winning of this new view of Africa, historical Africa, has been compared with the nineteenth century's geographical exploration of the 'unknown continent'; and there is something to be said for the comparison. For a long time now, labouring in solitude and often in great obscurity, many good enthusiasts have given themselves to the task of African historical exploration. Like the pioneering travellers of old, they tend to vanish for months or even years, unnoticed and unsung, forgotten by all but their families and their friends, only to return suddenly one day with an effect of glamour and discovery that must be much the same as the impression made by Mungo Park, a hundred and fifty years ago, when he came home from West Africa and told his London audience that he had seen the

Niger flowing to the east and not the west. Only last year, as I was beginning to write this book, a modern Mungo Park who is otherwise a French archaeologist of many years' experience arrived on my doorstep in the middle of the morning, actually from Waterloo Station in the heart of London and not the heart of Africa, yet bringing with him all the same the gleam and glint of distant places, and the news that beneath the ruins of a certain West African site, a medieval city of the Western Sudan, there lay a neolithic settlement no smaller than one kilometre square. And a year later, as I was finishing this book, there came a letter from Central Africa with another piece of news still more exciting in its context: 'Have you heard', it laconically remarked, 'that Hamo Sassoon in Tanzania has a date for Engaruka of AD 1450?' Thanks to many such pioneers, the truths of old Africa at last take firm and rounded shape.

This enfolds the whole continent. A rigid dividing of Africa into historical regions can be useful for purposes of detailed study; it will no longer satisfy a balanced view of the past. For while it is true that the Sahara has long placed a barrier between northern Africa and the rest of the continent, and that the great rain forests, further south, have sometimes done the same in relation to central-southern Africa, it is also true that all these regions really belong together, and that what is particular to each of them is general to them all in their foundation and emergence. So that there can be little more sense in studying southern Africa in separation from central and northern Africa than in trying to understand northern Europe apart from central and southern Europe. This is not of course to deny the obvious fact that some of Africa's large regions have developed in ways distinctive from those of other regions. Yet the essential truths and probabilities yielded by research over the past few decades repeatedly insist on two great underlying themes, manifest or hidden, concerning all African development no matter what the region may be. These themes are unity and continuity of cultural growth among them all, and from an immense depth of time.

10

The Peopling of a Continent

If the learned mufti of Bobo had trouble with the last thousand years, this is nothing to the jungle of tentative terminology in which the description of the Stone Age is still ensnared. Fossils and artifacts of a great variety of types have been labelled after the sites of their first discovery, and the labels then attached to similar types of fossils and artifacts no matter how much distance may lie between. So we have lately had the Kenya Aurignacian, for example, after a typesite in Europe, and now we have the Kenya Capsian after a typesite in Tunisia; and such examples could be repeated many times over. This is bad enough. But the confusion has long become worse confounded by necessary revision and reservation to the point where any detailed survey of the Palaeolithic, however simplified, requires a long list of special terms. No doubt the prehistorians could not have worked in any other way, for they have been faced with the interesting fact that palaeolithic men lived in closely related cultures over very wide areas of the globe. Lately, however, a synthesis has begun to emerge even here.

Ironically enough, given Africa's more or less complete historical eclipse in recent times, Africa is now seen to have played a part of crucial importance in framing this synthesis of early human development. Thanks largely to the African evidence, several large and even revolutionary alterations have been made to the simple scheme of nineteenth-century anthropology. It used to be said that man and the apes had developed from a common ancestor, and that one of the tasks of anthropology would be to find the essential 'missing link' between the two. It used to be thought that *homo sapiens* was the first tool-maker, and that it was precisely this capacity to think well enough to make tools which differentiated him from his less successful relatives. Now it seems clear, on the contrary, that *homo sapiens* was in fact the tardy product of natural selection from a large number of different types of manlike ancestors, or hominids, and that some of these hominids were themselves skilled in the manufacture and use of simple stone tools and weapons. The general picture at present is one of technical development among manlike creatures that begins nearly two million years ago, spreads gradually across the world, and leads by definable stages to the disappearance of all these hominids, one after another, and the sole survival of *homo sapiens*. But

Opposite: Among the richest in the world, the rock arts of Africa bear witness to slow but fruitful centuries of Stone Age growth. While the once green Sahara has more painting and engraving than any other part of Africa, these arts are found in almost every region. A few surviving Stone Age peoples, such as the Bushman of southern Africa, practised rock painting until recent times. This painting, showing huntsmen and a man drawing in a net, is from the Tassili n'Ajjer mountains in the Central Sahara

the earliest available evidence of tool-making hominids lies in the upland country of north-western Tanganyika. Africa was apparently the mother of tool-making man.

Of these ingenious East African hominids the most advanced was evidently a creature about four feet six inches in height, capable of running fast and using his (its?) arms for throwing missiles, whom the anthropologists have named *Australopithecus africanus*. He and his somewhat stouter fellow-hominid, *Australopithecus robustus*, were certainly not apes, for they could do things that apes have not been able to do; but they were not much like *homo sapiens* either, having massive heads and beetling features that were more like those of apes than men. They lived in small groups in dry grassland country not much different from that of inland Tanganyika today; but through many centuries they spread to many places, and types of *Australopithecus* are known from Asia as well as from different parts of Africa. They survived mainly by collecting vegetables, yet they could also hunt, kill and cut up animals; and among their inventory of tools there are pointed stones which may have been used to harden the tips of primitive hoes.

If the hominid types ancestral to *homo sapiens* had already appeared in these early times, they had to share their world with many strange relations. We catch a fossilized glimpse of these as the anthropologists work down the ages. After about a million years the quantity of stone tools has vastly increased; and they are being used by a wide variety of more or less manlike creatures. The most frequent of these tools is called a hand-axe: in appearance it is a large oval of chipped flint which may weigh anything up to several pounds and must have required a powerful, but also skilful hand to use it. Hand-axe folk are known to have inhabited the whole of the continent but for the rain-forest zones of the Congo and western Africa, as well as many countries outside Africa.

Technical improvement remains snail-slow, but it continues. The later stages of the hand-axe millennia are times of great increase and spread of human or proto-human occupation. They reach a crucial point of change, at least so far as Africa is concerned, about 50,000 years ago with the emergence of populations who have learned how to make fire, who live in caves or rock shelters, know how to carry burdens, and are equipped with better tools, notably choppers and scrapers. These heavy-browed Sangoans spread across most of Africa south of the Sahara. But the interesting

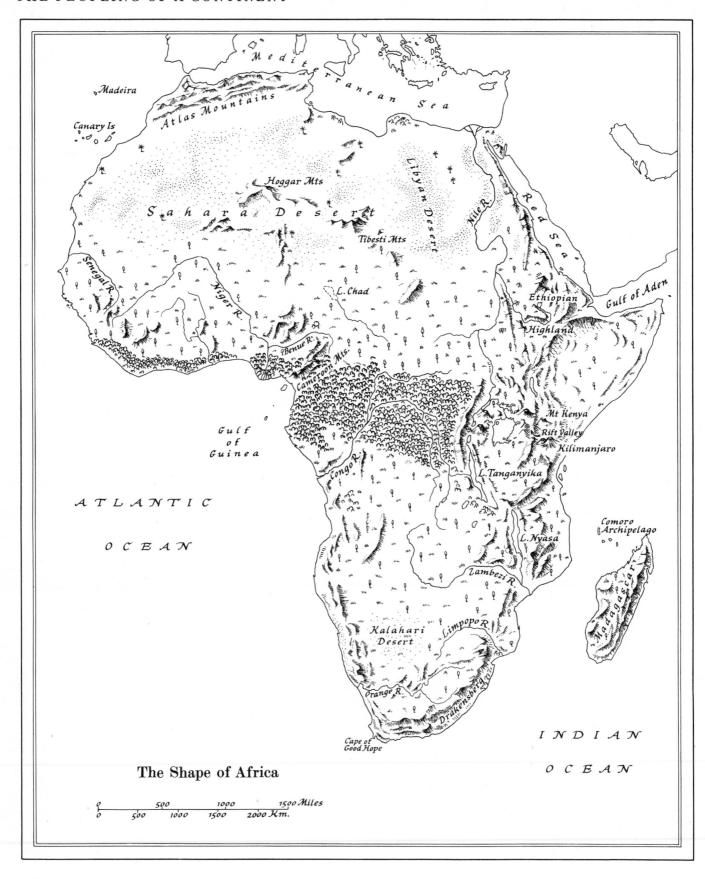

The Shape of Africa

point here, perhaps, is that several major regional variations are already present even 40,000 years ago. The Sangoans occupied neither the extreme south nor the lands to the north of the Sahara. The extreme south remained at an earlier phase of technical development, while the north was replenished by another heavy-browed type of man, the Neanderthal who, like the Sangoan, disappeared after the Middle Stone Age.

They disappeared, that is to say, as types; yet it is also clear, as in Europe and elsewhere, that they were partially ancestral to *homo sapiens*, who makes his bow, once more after processes of natural selection during an immensely long time, about 35,000 years ago. By the time the Middle Stone Age comes to an end, soon after 10,000 BC, *homo sapiens* in one form or another is everywhere predominant. The Bushman form has

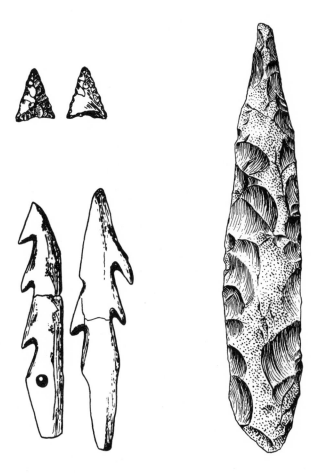

Stone Age craftsmanship from eastern Africa: (*top left*) Magosian hollow-based arrowheads; (*bottom left*) bone fishing harpoon and spearhead, Shaheinab, near Khartoum; and (*right*) Lupemban lancehead, Yala Alego, Kenya

taken over in the extreme south of Africa; the Sangoans and their like have been everywhere displaced by the 'Negro' form; while the Neanderthals and neighbours in North Africa have given way to incoming settlers from other Mediterranean lands who are also a form, or rather two forms, of early man. All these new folk, certainly much mingled in their further procreation, are recognizably human in ways that the older types were not: they bury their dead with care and have some use for paint and decoration. They live in larger groups, and begin to solve the problems of regulating community life among comparatively great numbers of people.

The regional variations, one may note, continued through these transformations: as between north and centre-south no doubt partly because the Saharan belt remained uninhabitable, much as it is today, throughout a great deal of the Middle Stone Age. But at some time after 10,000 BC, the climate of the Sahara grew cooler and less dry. Pastures appeared. Rivers flowed. The land became fertile. This marked another turning point, and may be regarded as a highly progressive period in African prehistory. Some of the peoples of North Africa, known as Aterian, pushed southward into this welcoming Sahara, while others in central-west Africa probably pushed northward; and throughout the Saharan region there began an interchange of peoples, ideas and equipment that was accompanied by a corresponding impulse towards the improvement of tools and techniques.

This spread and mingling of peoples through the wide plains of the Sahara continued in later times. Between about 5500 and 2500 BC there occurred a 'wet phase', the Makalian, which was evidently very favourable to the fruitful mixing and multiplication of peoples, tropical types from the south and Mediterranean types from the north; and for about three thousand years the Sahara teems with life. The rivers of its temperate and pleasant climate are wide, reliable and many, and are filled with many varieties of fish. Its hillsides are covered with forests of oak, cypress and other handsome trees. Its grassland plains are alive with wild game. Its peoples raise great herds of horned cattle. And towards 3500 BC, while their neighbours in the Nile Valley have already learned how to grow food by regular tilling and sowing and irrigation, these Saharans also embark on primitive agriculture. With this the Sahara becomes the cradle of farming cultures of the Neolithic or New Stone Age; and the growth of early African civilization has passed another large landmark in development.

Briefly, then, three central points emerge. In the first place, Africa has been a continent of very early and perhaps decisive importance for the development of those types of hominid who possessed the evolutionary potential that was fully realized in *homo sapiens*. Secondly, the human stocks of Africa (as elsewhere, by variety of selection) have developed out of hominid types which had existed in Africa for upwards of two million years. Thirdly, the basic physical variations ancestral to those of today took shape at least 35,000 years ago. By the dawn of the Neolithic, soon after 5000 BC, Africa is therefore populated by Bushman-types in the far south, by 'Negro-types' in the bulk of the continent, and by a mingling of North African, Mediterranean, or Near Eastern types in the north and north-east.

Any such brief statement, perhaps needless to say, implies great simplification of the facts. It is clear from blood-group analysis, for example, that Bushman and 'Negro' have partly derived from the same stocks, though by no means clear when or how this derivation took place, or precisely what the ancestral stocks looked like. It is similarly clear that the familiar attribution of the term 'white' to the North African and Nile Valley stocks (as of the term 'black' to the others) is merely a latter-day mystification of the racialist sort. Those old Cro-Magnon Europeans and 'Caucasoids' who came into North Africa some 12,000 years ago were quite surely far from blonde, and any notion that they were European in the modern sense of the word can be safely dismissed. What one needs to hold in mind is the gradual crystallization of a few main stocks out of an extremely complex process of natural selection through tens of thousands of years, this process being itself the sequence to another and immensely longer period of selection among a wide range of hominids who were not apes, but who were not fully-fledged men either. With this crystallization of human types there also came, little by little, a gradual emergence of specialization in the use of tools and weapons, as one or other branch of humanity adjusted itself to the particular environment in which it lived. The almost universal hand-axe of a million years ago gave way, in short, to a far better armoury of tools and weapons wielded by different types of men for different purposes in different places. By the dawn of the Neolithic this diversification was already far advanced.

In the Heart of Africa

What Desmond Clark has lately called the 'feedback relationship' between biological evolution and cultural change was certainly present in Stone Age times. Favourable conditions enabled this or that group to develop improved techniques for getting food: in doing so, they changed their way of life. In changing it, they themselves gradually became different from their ancestors, handier, more skilful, better able to think and to act by thought. Putting it another way, one can say that progress requires a fruitful interaction of environment and invention, of men's relations with nature and men's relations with each other.

In Old Stone Age times the rate of progress was as quietly slow as countless ages. With the coming of early farming and settlement, the pace enormously quickened. Just how quickly the biological-cultural feedback could now operate is suggested by the astonishing speed of social and technical advance in the Nile Valley. Long sunk beneath the waters of the Nile and its lakes and marshes, the land of Egypt began to emerge some ten thousand years ago. Only by about 8000 BC, in some recent words of H. W. Fairman, did there begin 'that deposition of alluvium over the deep-lying water-laid gravels and silts that resulted eventually in the formation of the real, habitable Egypt; it can hardly be much more than 7000 years ago that this process of deposition had reached the stage that continuous areas of land began slowly to form in and emerge from the swamps and marshes', and human settlement became possible.

Yet by 4000 BC the descendants of these earliest settlers in this 'new' land of Egypt were already cultivating regular crops. By 3500 BC they had formed themselves into early states. By 3200 there came the unification of Lower and Upper Egypt and the beginnings of a brilliant urban civilization. All the essential foundations of Pharaonic Egypt, whether material or intellectual, were now already in existence; and soon after 2600 the Pharaoh Cheops could order the building of the Great Pyramid at Gizeh, 756 feet square at the base and one of the greatest structures the world has ever seen. The time-span from *Australopithecus africanus* with his earliest tools to neolithic man with his farming is not much less than two million years; yet not much more than two thousand years separate the earliest farmers who settled along the river Nile from the

Opposite: Bushman painting of a hunter with bow and arrows, from Rhodesia

Above and below: Stone Age rock engravings, discovered in 1954 at In Settane in the Tassili n'Ajjer, showing a bull and a giraffe (Sandstone blocks, $15\frac{1}{4} \times 31\frac{1}{2}$ in. and $19\frac{3}{4} \times 20\frac{1}{2}$ in.)

Above: Acheulian hand-axe, about ten inches long, from Isimila Korongo in Tanganyika
Opposite: Three Kudu bulls from a Rhodesian rock painting

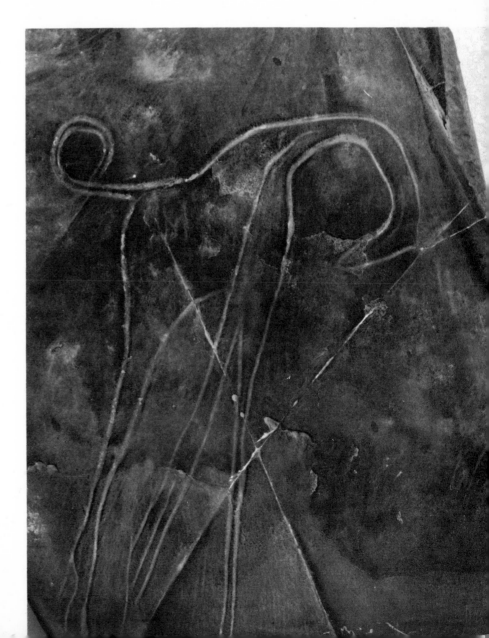

mathematically precise builders of the monuments of Egypt.

This same process, though with less startling results than along the uniquely beneficent banks of the Nile, was present elsewhere. The peopling of Africa with most of the ancestors of its modern inhabitants, from the far south to the far north, was more or less complete by two thousand years ago. In considering how it took place, and how the feedback between biological evolution and cultural change worked to make it possible, the green Sahara and Sudan of the temperate Makalian Phase (c. 5500-2500 BC) is a helpful place to begin. There are two reasons why it is helpful. The first is that the green Sahara and Sudan were evidently the first African region outside the confines of the Nile where early farming was practised on any scale. The second is that it was probably from this green though desiccating region that many techniques of farming were carried southward for adaptation in the rest of the continent.

Egypt remains something of a special case in this respect as in others. This was partly because of its proximity to earlier farming cultures in the Near East but even more because of its unparalleled advantage in the Nile floods. Yet from the standpoint of African development Egypt clearly belongs to the Saharan-Sudanese region of the Makalian Phase. Its earliest recognizable farmers, those of the Tasian Culture, were close neighbours of the Middle Nile, while the next farming culture, the Badarian, seems quite certainly to have consisted of peoples who had come into the Nile region from the west or south-west. 'The peopling of pre-dynastic Egypt', to quote Fairman again, 'must have been largely the result of the desiccation of the Sahara.' The ancient Egyptians belonged, that is, not to any specific Egyptian region or Near Eastern heritage but to that vast community of peoples who lived between the Nile and the Atlantic Ocean, shared a common 'Saharan-Sudanese culture', and drew their reinforcements from the same great source; even though, as time went by, they also absorbed a number of wanderers from the Near East. Herodotus saw the matter very clearly when travelling through Egypt not long after 450 BC, for he had no difficulty in concluding that Egypt's cultural origins lay in continental Africa. On the subject of circumcision, for example, he remarked that 'as between the Egyptians and the Ethiopians [by which he meant the peoples we call African], I should not like to say which learned from the other . . .', a remarkably up-to-date statement of

the case. Here in this ancient community of cultures between the Atlantic and the Nile, one may indeed trace the ground-stratum of many obscure but persistent unities of thought and attitude among African peoples now living far apart and apparently in total isolation from each other. Thus it was not simple diffusion from Pharaonic Egypt, but still earlier diffusion from the Saharan-Sudanese community, which can probably explain why the ram and the python should be symbols of religion all round the Sahara and far beyond it, or why many related social attitudes and institutions should be present among widely separated African peoples.

True enough, the 'Saharans' of the Nile Valley developed farming somewhat earlier than their western neighbours, perhaps drawing on the technical advances of their Near Eastern neighbours as well as inventing methods of their own. The feedback worked more slowly in the far plains of the Sahara. Yet the difference was not so very great. We already have a Carbon-14 date (this isotope of carbon loses radioactivity at a measurable rate, and so provides a broadly reliable means of dating ancient materials in which it is present) for a fully neolithic site in the central Sahara – that of Meniet in what is now the far south of Algeria – for as early as 3450 BC, with a tolerance of 150 years either way; and earlier dates may yet appear. So far, however, it must be said that other Carbon-14 dates for Saharan farming are ranged around 3000 BC. They indicate relatively large populations in the Sahara who lived in a neolithic way at this time. These peoples engraved and painted beautifully on stone and have left great galleries of pictures of themselves, their gods, their cattle and the game they knew.

In this period, accordingly, there were many peoples in this wide region who were genotypically of stocks native to continental Africa, North Africa and the Nile Valley, and who undoubtedly possessed a close affinity in material and spiritual culture. But they lived in a land with no future for themselves. Earlier even than 2500 BC the Sahara began to lose rainfall, rivers and rich pastures, and its capacity for supporting large and stable populations. There occurred a steady movement of Saharan peoples into more favourable lands nearby. The migrants who went northward out of the Sahara merged with those populations of Mediterranean type, themselves the distant product of long mingling between Mediterranean newcomers and Aterian natives, who were already in North African

Opposite: The Niger, greatest river of western Africa, as it flows through the grasslands of the Western Sudan near Timbuktu

lands; and after 2000 BC there emerged the strong group of peoples whom we know as Berber, a term which properly applies only to the languages they speak, and not to any specific physical characteristic. Firmly established along the North African littoral, among the mountains of Morocco and far southward into the fringes of the Sahara, these Berbers also made contact with Bronze Age neighbours in Spain; partly through this contact, they entered a Bronze Age of their own. By the thirteenth century, if not earlier, the Egyptian rulers had to face the invasion of Libyan Berbers who were well equipped with bronze swords, spears and even body-armour. Skilled horsemen, these North Africans were expert in the use of the war chariot and also, possibly, of the merchant cart. How soon they began trading across the Sahara we do not yet know, but the available evidence suggests that Berber chariots drawn by horses or donkeys were traversing the Sahara by several well-marked trails from Morocco to the Senegal river and beyond, and from Tunisia through the central Sahara to the middle waters of the Niger, by about 500 BC.

Those Saharans who pushed eastward into the good lands of the Nile came up against stiff Egyptian resistance. At least two of the pharaohs of the Nineteenth Dynasty (c. 1308-1194) – and there must have been many earlier cases – were obliged to meet the threat of Saharan invasion. The second of these, Merenptah (1224-1214), even had to face a regular coalition between several Berber peoples and five groups of 'peoples of the sea' who included, judging by their name Akawasha, some of those famous Achaeans who ruled Mycenean Greece. In a great battle at Pi-yer, a place lying in or near the delta of the Nile, Merenptah's army slew 6000 Libyans as well as many of their allies, and took 9000 prisoners. Even if the inscriptions exaggerate, the clash was obviously a memorable one. Behind it lay the driving pressures of an arid land, again recorded in one of Merenptah's inscriptions where he reviles the invading Berbers for having come to Egypt 'in search of food for their mouths'. The invasions continued as Egypt grew weaker. After 950 BC a line of Libyan princes grew powerful enough to impose their rule on Upper Egypt for nearly two hundred years.

There was a third movement of dispersal. Other Saharans edged their way southward into the heart of the continent and mingled with the peoples whom they found there. Stock-raising cultures emerged on the Ethiopian plateau and in East Africa. The Sudanese fringes of the south-western Sahara began to support a neolithic way of life which was in many ways the product of local experiment and invention. Here in western Africa new crops were cultivated, possibly sorghum and rice, together with a number of other crops such as Guinea yams and melons, while in Ethiopia the early type of cereal called *eleusine* began to be grown. Little by little, new habits of cultivation moved southward to the verge of the dense forests of the tropical rain belt; but here there came a pause. Regular farming appeared in the forestland only at a much later date, perhaps little earlier than 500 BC; and it is not difficult to see why. Given the richness and variety of fruit and edible vegetables in the forestlands, Stone Age hunting and food-collecting folk could still live as well as neolithic farmers, and with less labour for their pains, without growing any food. For them, there could be little incentive to supplementing the abundance of nature. Not until populations greatly expanded did this easy-going situation alter.

Beginning in about 500 BC or soon after, though for reasons as yet far from clear, this expansion among long-established people was soon associated with another development of critical importance, the gradual replacement of stone by iron for essential weapons and tools. Once iron had appeared, the whole perspective was changed. Iron-pointed spears were an armament that could take small groups of wandering men through unknown country they had never dared or cared to enter before. Iron-tipped hoes were a big improvement on stone cultivators in lands where the tsetse fly – evidently present in much of central-southern Africa since the earliest times of man's appearance – forbade the use of draught animals. Iron-shod axes could master the forestland as stone tools had never done. With the spreading use of iron, peoples also spread, and populations grew. Taking its rise some two thousand years ago, early iron-working laid the foundation of the Africa we know today.

The appearance of iron-working, and its closely associated phenomena of early farming and population growth throughout most of Africa south of the Sahara, began at different times in different regions. North of the Sahara, as we shall see, the use of iron became general in the Nile Valley after about 500 BC and was quite extensively used in the Berber lands, in Kush on the Middle Nile, and in the rising state of Axum in north-eastern Ethiopia. By 200 BC, or possibly a little

Opposite top: Rock painting from the Tassili n'Ajjer. Herodotus tells us that it was the Libyans who taught the Greeks to harness four horses to a chariot. But who taught the Libyans to paint a chariot hurtling along with horses at the 'flying gallop' associated with Greek art?
Bottom: Rock painting from Oran. Berber horses such as these were famous in antiquity for their good looks and staying-power. Probably they were bred from horses first brought to Egypt by Asians during the second millennium BC

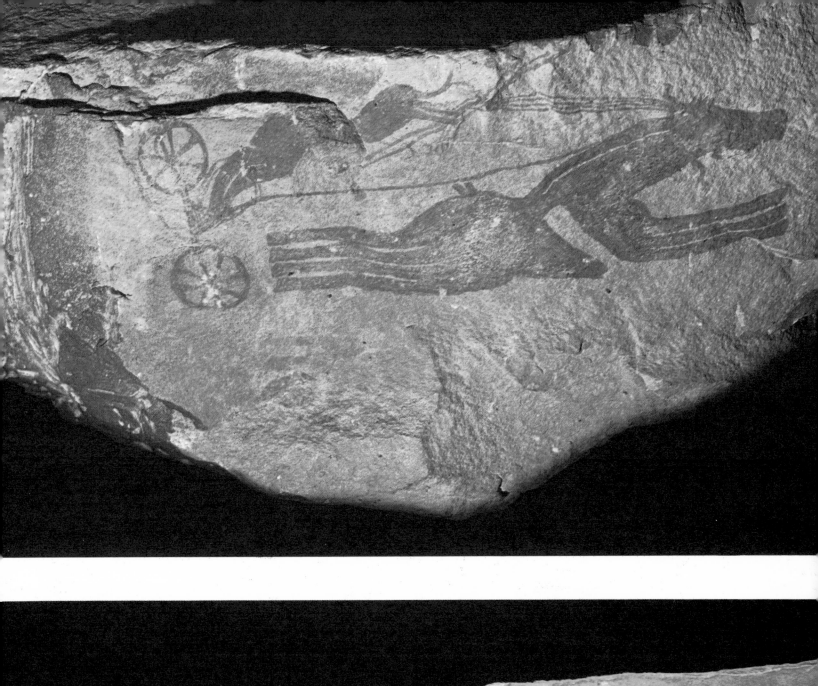

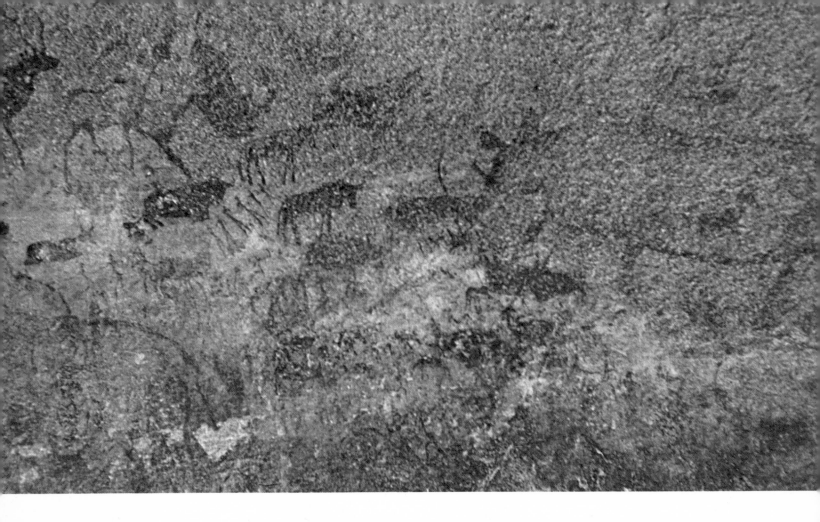

earlier, the metal-founders of Meroe on the Middle Nile had built a major handicraft industry in iron, and must have sent their products far and wide. Bronze and iron objects will certainly have crossed the desert lands to the grassland countries south of the Sahara before this time: the cart and chariot merchants will have carried them there, a means of communication which no doubt explains the occasional find of Pharaonic Egyptian metal objects south of the Sahara. But the actual setting up of iron-extractive and forging industries south of the Sahara seems not to have occurred until soon after 300 BC. At this point, however, the existence of an iron-using industry over a fairly wide area of the confluence region of the Niger and Benue rivers, in north-central Nigeria, is revealed by some very neat archaeological evidence.

This earliest known iron-using polity in western Africa has been named the Nok Culture after the village where its artifacts, mainly figures in terra cotta, were first recovered by modern tin-mining excavation during the 1930s. These figures are remarkable for their great artistic qualities, combining as they do a rare sensitivity to human character and features with a sophistication of style that seems extraordinary for the times in which they were made. Historically, though, the Nok Culture has proved even more rewarding for its clear evidence of being transitional between a Stone Age food-collecting culture and one that cultivated food. Carbon-14 dating suggests that this polity ranged between 900 BC and AD 200. The first of these dates is certainly too early for the transition to the use of iron and perhaps also for the transition to growing food; and the iron-using transition may be placed, with some assurance, as being soon after 300 BC, perhaps by diffusion from the metal-traders of Meroe on the Middle Nile or the North African Berber states, though possibly, of course, by local invention.

Whether by the same process of diffusion or by local invention, and most probably by a combination of the two, the knowledge of how to get and use iron then moved with astonishing rapidity into southern Africa. This knowledge had certainly appeared among peoples of the central-southern plateau country, north and south of the Zambezi, by AD 200 or 300 and possibly before. Large areas of continental Africa now entered their Iron Age. This is the development, above all, that is closely associated with a comparatively rapid growth in population, and more especially with the expansion of the great family of Bantu-language peoples who now inhabit most of Africa south of the Sahara.

Opinions differ on the full explanation of this 'Bantu spread'. Linguistic experts have made some progress lately in the reconstruction of *Ur-Bantu*, the root Bantu language which may be compared, for India and Europe, with the root Indo-European language. It appears that some of the derivative Bantu languages must have come into existence, at least in primitive forms, at some time before the population explosion which followed the invention of iron weapons and tools. An initial process of Bantu diffusion, in other words, may have taken place during the last phase of hunting and food-collecting during the Late Stone Age; and this, of course, makes sense for conditions of hunting and food-collecting by relatively small populations spread across a vast sub-continent.

But although it seems possible that groups of people speaking languages deriving from 'original Bantu' had established themselves during the Late Stone Age in many territories, it appears certain that their numbers were very few. Two new factors enabled them to multiply and ramify. The first was the better command of environment provided by the use of iron. The second was the arrival of Indonesian sailors on the coasts of East Africa, bringing with them at least one new crop of high value. This was a better banana than any that Africa itself possessed. The Asian banana took root in Africa and spread rapidly inland, greatly improving the available food supply.

These were the Indonesians, coming by way of southern India, who colonized the large East African island of Madagascar during the early centuries of the Christian era. The use of iron had reached Indonesia after 300 BC, no doubt with much the same expansive effect on population as in Africa; and the departure of many emigrants may perhaps be fixed at the beginning of the process of Hindu rule in the second century AD. Quickly absorbed along the mainland coast, where they have left some traces of their presence in the shape of out-rigger canoes and other equipment, they established themselves firmly in Madagascar and formed the initial stock from which the Malagasy people of today are mainly drawn. One modern view even thinks it possible, judging by the movement of non-African food crops, that they may also have sailed round the Cape of Good Hope and reached the coast of West Africa.

By about AD 800, with these events, the population picture had greatly changed. The whole of continental

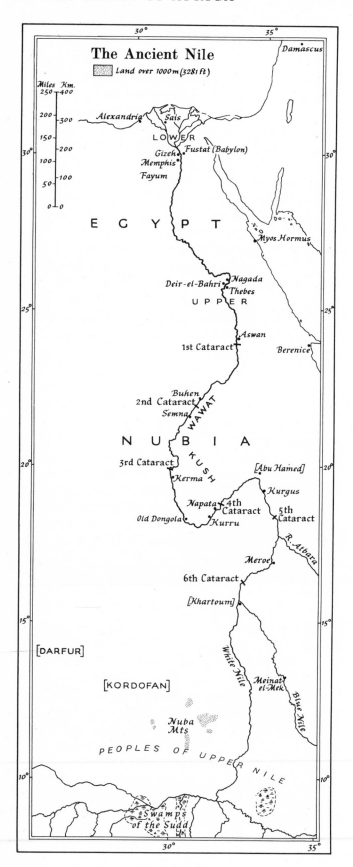

The Ancient Nile

Land over 1000 m (3281 ft)

Miles Km.

Alexandria · Sais
LOWER
Gizeh · Fustat (Babylon)
Memphis
Fayum

E G Y P T

Myos Hormus

Deir-el-Bahri · Nagada
Thebes
U P P E R

Aswan

1st Cataract

Berenice

Buhen
2nd Cataract
Semna

W A W A T

N U B I A

3rd Cataract
·Kerma
[Abu Hamed]

·Kurgus

Napata · 4th Cataract
Old Dongola · ·Kurru
5th Cataract

R. Atbara

Meroë

6th Cataract

[Khartoum]

[DARFUR]

[KORDOFAN]

White Nile

Meinat el-Mek

Blue Nile

Nuba Mts

P E O P L E S   O F   U P P E R   N I L E

Swamps of the Sudd

Damascus

Africa had entered a thriving Iron Age but for a few regions in the centre and the south, where Bushmen and their like continued a Middle Stone Age kind of life, hunting and gathering their food, painting and engraving on rock as the Iron Age Bantu-language peoples seldom or never did: a way of life that has continued, little altered even to this day, in remote segments of the Kalahari and among some of the pygmies of the Congo forestland. Everywhere else populations had greatly multiplied, developed their iron-using and farming technology, worked out their characteristic religions, embarked on new forms of social and political organization ranging from powerful states like ancient Ghana to intricate systems of tribal democracy among a wide range of different peoples, and laid foundations for the growth of their civilization into recent times. From this Early Iron Age until the colonial period of the nineteenth century, the course of continental Africa's development remains with few exceptions steady and continuous. Unbroken by any major outside intervention through ten centuries and more, highly various in form, repeatedly successful in its settlement and mastery of a difficult and sometimes harsh environment, this development offers a remarkably special but also remarkably unified chapter in the history of mankind.

In telling the story of these centuries it is to some extent necessary to regard the Sahara desert as a line of division. For while it is true that the Sahara was never a complete barrier in historical times, but rather a much-used zone of inter-communication, the fact remains that the peoples to the north of it – already differentiated from their fellow-Africans during Middle Stone Age times – none the less developed separately from the peoples to the south of it; and, to the extent that they developed separately, they developed differently. There was always much traffic between the two. Many migrants and many influences passed back and forth, especially during medieval times. Yet from the outset of the Neolithic in the Nile Valley and the north there was already a marked separation, and this increased with time. While the peoples of the north developed as part of the whole Nile-Near Eastern-Mediterranean complex of cultures, those to the south were left in gathering isolation to problems and solutions of their own. Before returning to the fortunes of the continental Iron Age, this is accordingly the place to consider what happened to peoples who lived on the northern side of the great desert.

A dwindling river of the Western Sudan: dry bed of the
Hadejia near Kano in northern Nigeria

2 Ancient Glories

Origins of Ancient Egypt, its growth and achievement – Links of Pharaonic Egyptians with neighbouring peoples – Emergence and history of the kingdoms of Kush on the Middle Nile, Napata and Meroe; and of Axum in Ethiopia – The old civilization of the Berbers – Punic and Roman North Africa and early links with West Africa

Gift of the Nile

In nothing more than in the way they conserved their history did the ancient Egyptians better reveal their masterful grip on the categories of space and time; not even in their mathematics, their monumental architecture, their making of calendars, or their elaborate machinery of government and collection of wealth. Herodotus thought them 'the best historians of any nation of which I have had experience', pointing out that at Memphis they had given him a written record of the names of no fewer than 'three hundred and thirty monarchs who succeeded Min . . . the first king of Egypt'. And about a hundred years after that, true to the habit of thinking big and thinking long, Manetho established the framework of thirty-one dynasties that still serves us, if with some additions and amendments, more than two thousand years later.

Yet Egypt, until lately, has figured little in the thought of scholars who have studied African history, and this in spite of the fact that Egyptian records already provide a host of dates that are useful to early African history. This attitude of leaving ancient Egypt out of the history of Africa has been generally defended, if at all, by reference to the racial hierarchies of nineteenth-century thought. The Egyptians of the Pharaonic Age were not Negroes, it was argued, and therefore they were not Africans; and so their civilization, no matter how firmly and enduringly planted on the soil of Africa, may be left outside the African context. This view has little to be said for it. If it now seems perfectly clear that the vast majority of pre-dynastic Egyptians

were of continental African stock, and even of central-west African origins, there is likewise serious dispute among the authorities as to whether the hypothetical 'dynastic race' associated with the foundation of Pharaonic Egypt had come from outside Africa. These early populations undoubtedly included the descendants of incoming migrants from the Near East. But to argue from this that the vast majority of the inhabitants of old Egypt, not being Negro, were therefore not African is as little tenable as to argue the same about the Berbers and the Ethiopians, whom nobody has yet proposed should be struck from the list of African peoples. The old racial categories of 'white' and 'black' can indeed make little sense in this or perhaps any other connexion. Thus the Berbers have been often referred to as a 'white race', yet it is 'quite impossible', in Capot-Rey's most expert view, 'to speak of a Berber race. Either one means, in using this term, a language spoken with much the same grammar and vocabulary from the Mediterranean to the Niger, or one means a moral and material civilization.' Whatever their pigmentation or physical appearance, the Egyptians of Pharaonic times may be safely assigned to African history.

Yet their part in African history was just as certainly a special one. And this special nature of Egyptian civilization, of the 'gift of the Nile' as Herodotus called it, detached itself from the general African context as early as the fifth millennium BC. Then it was that farming peoples of the Lower Nile and the delta evolved out of their obscurity, and, across a few brief centuries, built an urban civilization which had all the essential characteristics and acquirements of Egypt's later glory. Just how this was done remains to be discovered, and perhaps will never be known; yet the more one learns of this 'pre-dynastic Egypt' the more wonderfully impressive its achievements must appear. Almost overnight, as it were, primitive farmers seem to acquire the arts of writing, calendar calculation, obsessively ambitious building in stone, and the capacity to accumulate wealth in such a way as to yield, at any rate for ruling groups and governing families, a civilization of unprecedented comfort and sophistication.

The change in fact took several hundred years; yet the suddenness of all this growth and lavish diversity has suggested a crucial political intrusion into the Nile Valley, which may have been associated with the arrival of new rulers from elsewhere, presumably from the urban civilizations of Mesopotamia. Some of the old traditions, as well as some of the artistic and archaeological evidence, have been argued in support of this. 'It would seem probable', in Emery's view, 'that the principal cause [of the change] was the incursion of a new people into the Nile Valley, who brought with them the foundation of what, for want of a better designation, we may call Pharaonic civilization.' The late Gordon Childe was among those who have thought otherwise. He agreed that 'new ethnic elements from outside the valley' may have helped towards the unification of Egypt after 3400 BC, but 'they certainly did not introduce ready-made a culture superior to the native pre-dynastic.' Probably there were stimuli from the Near East, but 'there can be no question of civilization being introduced into backward Egypt from precocious Sumer', its Near Eastern contemporary. 'On the contrary . . . Egyptian civilization appears richer than contemporary Early Dynastic Sumerian.'

No doubt the truth lies somewhere between the two extremes of thought on this point; and, as Childe implied, the change derived really from a crucial climax of development peculiar to the Nile peoples – rapidly expanding their agriculture, their use of metals, and their accumulations of surplus food and other wealth – so that new rulers merely took advantage of a revolution which was already taking place and was now ripe for consummation. African history suggests many examples of the closely interwoven process of conditions-ripe-for-change and the fortunate arrival of immigrating groups who knew how to profit from the fact. Where such examples lie near to our own times, and can be studied in some detail, they generally indicate that the immigrating influence was of secondary

importance; and one may well think this of pre-dynastic Egypt as well. For even if those legendary 'Followers of Horus' had really come hot-foot from the courts and pavements of Mesopotamia, bearing news of new fashions and inventions, they could never have revolutionized Egypt unless most Egyptians were already prepared for the change. Even after the change, moreover, dynastic Egypt copied little or nothing from foreign contemporaries, but continued to evolve new ideas and fashions of its own.

The change was certainly dramatic. Two states emerged in Egypt, one along the Nile and the other in the delta, both being the product of wealth-accumulation from skilful using of the river's annual floods. These two states were never quite to lose their separate identities. But after about 3200 BC they were brought together under a king who wore the double crown; and from henceforth for three thousand years the hieroglyphic titles of the ruler of Egypt included not only the Horus falcon-figure of pre-dynastic times, but also the dual sign of the cobra of Lower Egypt and the vulture of Upper Egypt. Like those of the two states or great provinces on which it rested, this newly united country drew its governing power and revenue from the control of water supply, from taxation of landowners and peasants, and from other forms of tribute, including military service. It took over and reshaped the administrative services of the two pre-dynastic states, and developed a large corps of clerks and tax-gatherers, commanders and governors, artists and technicians. It brought a new peace and security to the peasants of the Nile, although the price they paid was not a small one.

Ancient Egypt's three main scripts: *Hieroglyphic* (dating from before 3000 BC); *Hieratic*, a priestly 'short-hand' evolved soon afterwards; and *Demotic*, a much faster cursive developed shortly before 600 BC

Opposite: The Great Sphinx at Gizeh, a colossal rock statue of the Fourth Dynasty (*c.* 2620–2480 BC)

Funerary temple of Queen Hatshepsut (1490–1468 BC) at
Deir-el-Bahri

'I am told you have abandoned writing and taken to sport, set your face to working in the fields and turned your back on letters', wrote a clerk of high dynastic times, chiding a colleague who had given up the stylus. 'But do you not remember the condition of the farmer who is faced with paying his harvest-tax when the snake has carried off half the corn and the hippopotamus has eaten the rest? Then the mice abound, the locusts come, the cattle devour, the sparrows bring disaster; and what remains on the threshing floor is taken by thieves . . . And now the clerk lands on the river bank to collect the tax. With him are guards with staves and Nubians with rods of palm, and they say, "Hand over the corn", though there is none. And the farmer is beaten, bound and ducked in the well . . .' White-collar jobs, then as in other times and places, seemed the safest way to a quiet life.

Yet the benefits of strong central government made Egypt flourish. Aside from the stupendous evidence of temples, pyramids and tomb furniture, all bearing witness to a hitherto unknown success in accumulating wealth and using labour-power, there is the scarcely less impressive fact of duration. After the great breakthrough into unification, complete by 3200 BC, there follow many centuries of brilliant development and growth. But there is no radical change. Its direction firmly set along the path chosen at the outset, Egyptian civilization continues unswervingly until the end. The 'gift of the Nile' enjoyed a wonderful strength and continuity, and used these advantages to marvellous effect; yet the framework was so strong and successful that it discouraged experiment. Egyptian history has rested on the counterpoint of these two opposing factors: steady growth, but also a certain stagnation.

The impact of this grand and long-enduring civilization on the rest of Africa was powerful at several points. By the Fourth Dynasty (c. 2620–2480 BC) its rulers were sending quite large maritime expeditions down the Red Sea as well as pioneering traders into the fertile lands of the south and west. For the Sixth Dynasty, beginning c. 2340 BC, there are several well-attested expeditions far to the south-west through country that was still green and watered, including one that 'went down with three hundred asses laden with incense, ebony, grain, ivory (and other goods)' and must have travelled far toward the fringes of the Congo forest. On the long western frontier with the Berber communities of the Sahara and Libya there must likewise have been many exchanges, though the records apparently say nothing

of far western travels; just as there were certainly many wars of defence against Libyan raiders and would-be settlers.

So far, such travels and expeditions were little more than exchanges within the Saharan-Sudanese community of peoples. After the end of the third millennium, however, Egypt began to exercise a directly military and political power over her southern and to a lesser extent her western neighbours. First of all, around 2200 BC, there came a time of confusion and reorganization which Egyptologists, extrapolating from Manetho's neat dynastic lines, have called 'the First Intermediate Period'. Asians raided the flourishing towns of the delta, and there were revolutionary upheavals among Egyptians themselves. 'The bowman is ready, the wrongdoer is everywhere', runs a nostalgic text of this period. 'A man goes out to plough carrying his shield . . . Men sit in the bushes until the benighted traveller passes by, and plunder his load. Thieves grow rich . . . He who had nothing is now a man of wealth, while the poor man is full of joy. Every town says: let us suppress the powerful among us . . . The children of princes are dashed against the walls.' But when all this Jacobin upheaval is over, with the beginning of the Eleventh Dynasty in 2130 BC, the great system takes over once more; and Egypt is again ruled by a single strong power dispensing law and order throughout the Upper and Lower Kingdoms.

Only now there is a significant difference. Power has shifted three hundred miles upstream from Memphis to Thebes. The Pharaohs turn their attention to the southern country beyond the cataracts, the land of Nubia and the source of gold, and send victorious expeditions both to raid the Nubians and subject them, as well as to fix their southern frontier and control all passage through it. They build huge forts and fill them with frontier guards. And during this Middle Kingdom – onwards from about 2130 for three and a half centuries – Egyptian civilization makes its first deep impress on the farming peoples of the various lands of Nubia, of Wawat and Irthet and Kush and the like, that lie beyond the second cataract. Then comes a Second Intermediate Period which terminates with the incursion of Asian conquerors who make great use of horse-drawn chariots, a technique that now spreads rapidly westward through the still habitable Sahara; but these Hyksos rulers fail to hold their conquests.

Once more the great system absorbs disaster and comes out intact. The Hyksos interlude, one of much tumult and upheaval, is followed by a powerful dynasty, the Eighteenth, whose rulers include some of the most majestic names in Egyptian history. It is rather as though the whole intricate system had required a thorough bureaucratic shake-up, every now and then, in order to recover its ambition and efficiency. The recovery now was even more imposing than under the pharaohs of the Eleventh and Twelfth Dynasties who had followed the First Intermediate Period of confusion. Egyptian armies pressed far southward, and the greater part of Nubia became an Egyptian colony. Tutmosis I of this New Kingdom, which lasted from about 1580 until 1050 BC, completed the work of his predecessor Amenophis and brought all the country of Nubia between the second and fourth cataracts within Egyptian control. He and others sent new naval expeditions down the Red Sea, fought off Libyans in the west and Asians in the east, and established an empire that was larger and more influential on its neighbours than ever before.

This New Kingdom radiates power and influence for nearly five centuries, but is far gone in political decline by 1000 BC. The system continues as before, just as do the irrigation conditions which have given it birth, but Egypt passes from one stiff crisis to another; and it is from now that the factor of stagnation becomes fatal to recovery. As before, a long period of centralized rule through a highly stratified bureaucracy, military and civil, is followed by revolt and invasion. Libyan princes seize power in parts of Egypt, and we have Manetho's Twenty-second Dynasty, beginning with Shoshenk I in 945. These Libyan princes rule for about two centuries, often with success, until their power in turn fritters itself away. While Lower Egypt has been ruled by a rather shadowy 'four kings of Tanis', making the Twenty-third Dynasty, and one or two still more shadowy kings of the Twenty-fourth Dynasty, a new power has gathered above the cataracts. Upper Egypt and then Lower Egypt are invaded by the rulers of the Nubians, the Kushites, who have often lived under more or less direct Egyptian rule, but have never lost their separate identity, ever since the conquests of Amenophis and Tutmosis in the sixteenth century BC. Kashta begins this Kushite conquest at some time in the first half of the eighth century. Piankhy (751-730) and his brother Shabako (716-695) complete it. Kush becomes a world power.

Deeply imbued with the ideas and beliefs of Egyptian civilization, these early Kushites might have held Egypt

for much longer than a hundred years if they had been left alone. But they were not left alone. In the 660s the Assyrians came south into the delta with iron-shod armies that drove their bronze-armed enemies before them. They fought the Kushites and set up against them a ruler of the delta city of Sais. The Kushite pharaoh Taharqa (689-664) felt the full weight of these Assyrian blows, and his successor Tanuatamun (664-656) was the last of the Kushite rulers of Egypt. The Saite kings took over after Assyrian and Kushite withdrawal, and stayed in power until 525. Then the Persians under Cambyses followed where the Assyrians had led but, unlike the Assyrians, pressed home their victories and conquered most of Egypt. In 332 they in turn were driven out by the Greeks under Alexander of Macedon, and the long period of Greek rule under a line of Ptolemaic rulers began. Then came the Romans, and after the Romans more confusion, and after this confusion the Muslim conquest and reorganization of the seventh century AD.

Pharaonic Egypt disappeared utterly from sight, its rich tombs rifled of their precious furniture, many of its monuments engulfed in sand, even its language surviving to some degree only among a small minority of Egyptian people; and would not be drawn into the light again for another thousand years and more. Yet the achievements and inheritance of this grand civilization had fed and given vigour in countless ways to the onward movement of other civilizations in many lands.

The Blameless Ethiopians

The ancient Egyptians thought it obvious that they themselves were the only true Men, but were ready to admit the existence of three lesser branches of the species, Asians, Nubians and Libyans. The ancient Greeks, taking a barbarian view of the matter, gave precedence of dignity and worth not to the Egyptians, in spite of the manifest superiority of Egyptian civilization over anything else they knew in that particular line, but to all those peoples who lived, lost in mystery, in 'Africa beyond Egypt'. These Africans they called Ethiopians – rather as later Europeans would indiscriminately call them Negroes – and it was to the land of the 'blameless Ethiopians' that Homer's gods repaired once a year to feast for twelve days.

Of these peoples beyond Egypt the Greeks in fact knew little or nothing, then or later, and even the valiant Herodotus failed to visit them. 'The furthest

Opposite top: Wall-painting from the tomb of Haremhad (1335-1308? BC) at Thebes, showing Nubians in procession
Bottom: Relief from Deir-el-Bahri celebrating the expedition sent by Queen Hatshepsut southward to the land of Punt, and showing a Puntite hut and (right) incense trees

Enthronement stela from Jebel Barkal
celebrating the accession of King
Aspelta (593–568 BC) to the throne of
Kush

Bronze mirror, eight inches long, from
Semna on the frontiers between Upper Egypt
and the Nubian lands (New Kingdom,
1575–c. 1000 BC)

Above: The Kushite viceroy at Thebes,
Prince Mentuemhat (died *c.* 650 BC),
from a temple at Karnak
Left: Statue of Narwa, Kushite
administrator at Thebes during the reign
of Amenartis, sister of the Kushite
Pharaoh Shabako (716–695 BC)

inhabited country towards the south-west', he observed in about 450 BC after visiting southern Egypt, 'is Ethiopia.' By this he meant Kush in Nubia and lands immediately to the south of Kush. 'Here gold is found in great abundance, and huge elephants, and ebony, and all sorts of trees growing wild. The men, too, are the tallest in the world, the best-looking, and the longest-lived.' Considering that Herodotus had to rely on travellers' tales during a period when relations between Kush and Egypt were anything but good, this is no bad description of the land and peoples of the Middle and Upper Nile. For there was much gold in these lands and many elephants, as we know from other evidence; while even to this day there are peoples dwelling along the Middle and Upper Nile, who, if not particularly long-lived, are unusually handsome and tall of stature. Yet apart from a few reports of this kind, the Greek writers have nothing to say about the lands beyond Egypt, a fact which helps to explain why European scholarship of later times, so often closely tied to the writings of Classical Greece, also has nothing to say on this interesting subject. Only the last fifty years have brought any real advance in the study of Kush.

Two great centres of metal-using civilization emerged among the blameless Ethiopians, and both are now recognized as having been of high importance for subsequent history. The first, whether in order of time or weight of influence, was that of Kush in Nubia; while the second, parent of modern Ethiopia, was that of Axum in the mountains along the south-western side of the Red Sea.

The origins of Kush lie in the remote settlement of early farming peoples along the Middle Nile above the first and second cataract, riverain peoples whose cultures were closely akin to those of the early pre-dynastic Egyptians, but were modified from time to time with the arrival of Saharans who moved in during and after the third millennium BC. Still probing for closer definition, archaeologists have as yet to be content with merely alphabetical or site labels for them. The more northerly of these peoples came under strong Egyptian influence during the Middle Kingdom after 2000 BC. Amenophis I (1991–1962) began this conquest by securing Wawat, northernmost province of old Nubia (as the Egyptians called it, though the Nubians of later times had yet to appear); and it is from about this time that southern Nubia begins to be called Kush in the Egyptian records. Sesostris continued the conquest. His armies 'passed beyond Kush and reached the end of

the earth', or perhaps as far as the third cataract or some way beyond, but secured no permanent hold there. During the Hyksos invasion of the Second Intermediate Period (c. 1750–1575), when the whole of Nubia regained its independence, a new state emerged in the Kerma region, immediately south of the third cataract; and it is partly in this Kerma state – evidently a very important and advanced early civilization of inner Africa, but of which little is securely known – that the ancestral origins of the later Kushite system may perhaps be traced.

With the end of the Hyksos interregnum and the rise of the New Kingdom in Egypt, expeditions were renewed towards the south as well as in other directions; and the vanguards of the great conquering Pharaoh Tutmosis I, who pushed far southward through Kush and established his frontiers at Kurgus between the fourth and fifth cataracts, may even have gone as far as the region of modern Khartoum. From 1500 until about 800 BC the greater part of Nubia, composed of the two great tribute-paying provinces of Wawat and Kush, lay under close Egyptian supervision and at times under direct Egyptian rule.

Yet its peoples remained distinct from the Egyptians. They went on living by their own ideas and customs. Even the highly Egyptianized pharaohs of the Twenty-fifth (Kushite) Dynasty lie in their tombs, at Kurru near the fourth cataract, in a posture used traditionally by their Nubian forebears but not by the Egyptians whose gods these Kushite rulers had none the less largely accepted. Although strongly marked and shaped by Egyptian culture, early Kushite civilization cannot properly be considered as a mere emanation of Egypt or even as a second-class copy. It was peculiar to itself even in early times, though much more so in later growth after 500 BC.

The two main phases of Kushite development are associated with successive capitals at Napata, near the fourth cataract, and at Meroe some two hundred miles further south. The first of these phases began with the obscure rise of Kushite political power, based largely on the control of the sources of Nubian gold, after the New Kingdom of the Pharaohs had begun to disintegrate in the eleventh century BC. While Libyan princes ruled from Thebes, the capital of Upper Egypt, chiefs in Kush could safely raise their heads in Nubia. They were perhaps further encouraged in this, during the late tenth and ninth centuries, by their local priests of the god Amun and of other gods associated both with

Opposite: Built near the Nile along a ridge that once looked down upon the great city of Meroe, these pyramids are the tombs of most of the rulers of Meroitic Kush

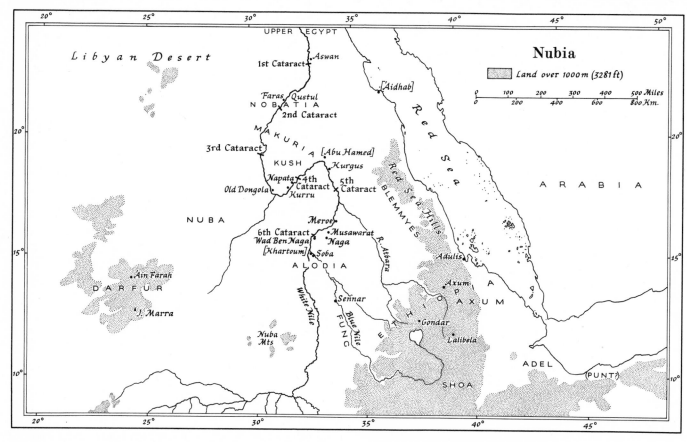

Upper Egypt and Nubia. Their power grew. Early in the eighth century, as we have seen, the chiefs of Kush were strong enough to begin the invasion of Egypt itself.

These Kushite pharaohs ruled Upper Egypt for a century, and the whole of Egypt for more than fifty years; yet the impact of all this on their homeland seems to have been remote and even insignificant. Their own peoples continued to live as they had lived before. The kings and soldiers had gone down into Egypt, conquered and held it until the coming of the Assyrians, and then returned again. Though the Kushite court at Napata, at least after the death of Piankhy (730 BC), became heavily Egyptianized in its rites and manners, in its architecture and use of Egyptian hieroglyphics, the Napatan empire must be regarded, Adams tells us, as 'from first to last a Nubian culture and a Nubian population which for a brief time' – from about 730 until the death of Aspelta (568 BC) – 'took upon itself an artificial veneer of pharaonic tradition.' So far as most Nubians were concerned, the whole Egyptian enterprise might have been little more than a raid on the big scale; exciting and adventurous but yielding no important change. Yet something new had in fact occurred; and this was of the first importance. In their

furious delta battles of the 660s, the Assyrians had fought with weapons of a new kind, weapons of tempered iron instead of bronze and stone. However little noticed at the time, a new age in Africa had begun.

Content with their bronze, the Egyptians had ignored the spreading use of iron in nearby Asia. They had known iron for many centuries, but had made little effort to reduce its rarity or to master the skills of getting and working it. Prized as curiosities, iron weapons had formed no significant part of Egyptian military equipment. A fine dagger with an iron blade was buried with Tutankamun, who died in 1339 BC, yet not for another thousand years did iron tools and weapons become common among the Egyptians. Here again one may observe how the pace of technological change, once set in motion, grows by rapid progression. For while it required at least a thousand years for the highly evolved and in many ways matchless civilization of Egypt to pass from regarding iron as a curious rarity to accepting iron technology as a necessary part of daily life, it needed less than half that time for the knowledge and practice of iron winning and working to emerge across Africa as far west as the Atlantic, and as far south as the grassland plains beyond the Congo basin.

Pierced now by the railway from Khartoum to Wadi Halfa, these famous iron-working slag heaps of Meroe bear witness to the eminence of Meroitic Kush as an early centre of the African Iron Age two thousand years ago

Overleaf left: The great enclosure at Musawarat as-Safra is in some ways the most imposing of all the ruins of Meroitic Kush. Dating from the last centuries BC, it was a place of royal prestige and power
Right top: With the rise of the Meroitic Empire the Kushites raised the worship of their own gods above those of Egypt. Prominent was the lion-god Apedemak, seen here at Naga
Bottom: Frieze from Musawarat as-Safra. Elephants were of ceremonial and military importance in Meroitic Kush, and the Meroites were skilled in training them

The effects of iron-working upon Kushite civilization, basically a riverain farming culture, can as yet be gauged only by inference. About a hundred years after their retirement from Egypt, a new centre of Kushite civilization emerged at one of their southern cities, Méroe, lying about one hundred miles north of Khartoum, although not for another two centuries would Napata lose its old importance. Gradually, however, the weight of political and economic interest shifted southward. Detectable reasons for this include the continuing desiccation of the Napatan region and its consequent shortage of timber and pasture. No doubt the very destructive Persian raid on Napata, in 591, may have had something to do with the move. There is also the suggestive fact that the region of Meroe, unlike that of Napata, has large deposits of good iron-bearing ore; and this was a period in which the demand for iron was spreading rapidly. Within some three hundred years of the southward move, the metalworkers of Meroe had in fact turned their city into one of the greatest iron-founding centres of the ancient world.

Whatever the precise reasons for the southward move may have been, they were accompanied by a growing anti-Egyptian reaction among the Kushites of the towns. Meroitic civilization – what Adams has called 'the Meroitic Renaissance' – became far more self-consciously and deliberately Kushite than its Napatan predecessor had ever been, and revealed 'a whole series of developments and accomplishments which are by no means prefigured in the late Napatan era, and which are symptomatic of a marked return of cultural vigour'. Its gods and rituals were primarily those of Meroe, not Egypt. While good Egyptian hieroglyphs continued to be used in temple inscriptions, the Kushites now began writing their own language in an alphabetic script which has yet to be deciphered. The fine painting of pottery reached a new excellence, and the styles used were purely Kushite. Meroe became very much a civilization in its own right; and this civilization was one of great depth and range of culture.

The history of Meroitic Kush covers at least six centuries of energetic and often quite distinctive development in many fields, especially those of town and temple building, metal manufacture, and the elaboration of international trade with countries as remote as India and even China. Here on the Middle Nile there gradually unfolded, from about 350 BC onwards, a far-reaching process of indigenous expansion whose influence on the lands of inner Africa, notably in the spread

of iron technology, was undoubtedly of great importance. From Meroitic Kush the caravan trails went eastward to the ports of the Red Sea, northward to Greek-ruled and then Roman-ruled Egypt and the Mediterranean, and southward up the Atbara into the lands of Ethiopia. But the caravan trails also went westward and south-westward; though archaeological evidence east of Lake Chad has yet to produce anything earlier than Christian Nubian potsherds.

Like some other geographically remote civilizations of antiquity, Kush was forgotten by a later world. There is a stray reference in the Book of Kings to the Pharaoh Taharqa (fifth of the Kushite Dynasty), and another in the Acts of the Apostles to an envoy of the Queen of the Ethiopians (that is, of the Kushites of Meroe) who was converted by one of Christ's apostles on the road that 'goeth down from Jerusalem to Gaza'. But indiscriminate use of the Greek term 'Ethiopian', together with a general indifference to the historical claims of Africa, tended to sink the Kushites deep within a sea of scholarly indifference. Even when the

Alphabetical script invented by the Meroites in about the third century BC

Opposite top: Green glazed steatite scarab with a human face from Kerma in Nubia. It is mounted in gold and its back is covered with ten rows of small flies (Period of Middle Kingdom. Length: 1 in.)
Bottom: Painted pot with cover from Kerma (Middle Kingdom. Height: 4¼ in.)

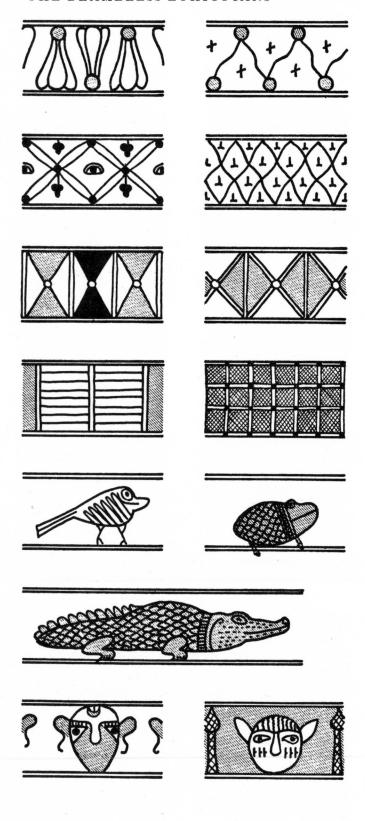

Designs from Meroitic painted pottery

nineteenth century brought a new interest in ancient civilizations, the early travellers and excavators were understandably dazzled by their brilliant discoveries in Egypt; and Kush was generally regarded, in so far as it was thought about at all, as no more interesting than a provincial poor relation.

The last fifty years, but above all the last dozen years, have wrought a change in this. Much remains to be understood about the Kushites of Meroe and their highly specific civilization, but enough is already clear to frame a picture of extraordinary diversity, creative skill, and technological success. They combined a stubborn attachment to their own traditions with a speculative and syncretic approach to new ideas and fashions that may be characteristic of all great trading cultures. Their temples and palaces owed a great deal to Egyptian examples, but none the less had styles and ornaments which were purely Meroitic. Much of their religion, like their language, their alphabetical script, and the best of their pottery, was all their own. Yet they had always welcomed innovation, and they continued to do so. As time went by, and the Ptolemaic Greek rulers of Egypt were displaced by the Romans, and trade across the Indian Ocean grew with greater skills in using the monsoon winds, the Kushites of Meroe and its sister-cities borrowed repeatedly from their neighbours and trading partners. One or two of their later buildings remind one of Syrian Palmyra. Not a few of their copper vessels seem to reflect Chinese styles. There is a Greek air about some of their art, while their four-armed lion-god Apedemak would almost look at home in an Indian temple. Yet the total effect remains powerfully distinctive and specific.

The high period of this civilization lay in the five centuries after the reign of Nastasen, whose period appears to have initiated or at any rate crystallized that profound cultural reaction against Egyptian ways and customs which led to many of the best achievements of Meroitic art and thought. Nastasen's exact dates are still contested, but he certainly ruled for about twenty years in the first half of the fourth century BC. Then it was, or perhaps under Arnekhamani (c. 235–218 BC) who built the great Lion Temple at Musawarat as-Safra, that the priests and traders of Meroitic Kush began to use their own cursive script, and pottery was painted with great beauty. By this time, too, Meroitic iron-using manufacture was getting into its stride, while Meroitic political and military power reached far to the south and west, eastward to the Red Sea, and

48

Opposite top: Black stone stela from Meroe, showing a ram-headed god and a queen of Meroitic Kush; with Meroitic script (Height: 7 in.)
Bottom: Detail of right-hand side of stela

Symbols of the power of the god Amun, these stone rams still guard the fallen temples of Naga, one of the principal urban centres of Meroitic Kush

Opposite top: As in many other parts of Africa, before and since, the python – seen here in a majestic engraving on the 'lion temple' at Naga – was a symbol of spiritual power in Meroitic Kush

Bottom: Facsimile of an inscribed votive tablet of red slate from a temple at Meroe, showing the lion-god Apedemak and a king in a long robe with a helmet-crown and sceptre. Inscriptions in Meroitic (Height: 6½ in.)

northward beyond Napata to the region of the first and second cataracts. By 100 BC Meroitic Kush had become a large and powerful empire, endowed with the means of far-ranging trade and the benefits of a self-confident and capacious native culture; and these benefits it continued to enjoy until the fourth century AD, when disaster overtook the Meroites from which they were never able to recover.

The second outstanding civilization of the lands 'beyond Egypt' took its rise at about the same time as Meroitic Kush, though little or nothing was known of its origins until systematic archaeological investigation began in 1952. Here again there was the same remote interweaving of a local culture, that of the people of north-eastern Ethiopia, with commercial, religious and political ideas from elsewhere, in this case from old Arabian civilizations across the Red Sea. In later times this distant process was nicely symbolized by Ethiopian adaptation of the biblical story of the Queen of Sheba's visit to King Solomon. That lady of Sabaea in southern Arabia went up to Jerusalem at some time in the tenth century BC 'with a very great company, and camels that bare spices, and gold in abundance, and precious stones', and afterwards came home again in good heart. She also came home with a son by King Solomon, according to the Ethiopian legend; and this son was Menelik, founder of the dynastic line of the Lions of Judah that still rules over Ethiopia. The little difficulty caused by a gap in time of many centuries between the dates of Solomon's reign and the rise of the kings of Axum, forerunners to those of Ethiopia, naturally failed to worry the story-tellers of long ago.

Yet the legend conceals a core of truth. It is now known that a strong trading polity was established along the coast and in the hinterland of north-eastern Ethiopia by the fifth century BC, and that this polity owed much to southern Arabia. Its altars were engraved in the boldly beautiful script of southern Arabia, and the language used was from the same source. Its gods were likewise from across the water. Yet even in the fifth century this culture had an originality of its own, as many objects recovered in the 1950s clearly show; and this local originality increased as time went by. After the fourth century BC, Ethiopian-Sabaean culture entered a transitional period during which the main outside influence ceased to be south Arabian and became Greek: now it was, for example, that the ocean trade between Ptolemaic Egypt and the lands of India and the Far East made extensive use of the north

Ethiopian port of Adulis. Ethiopia's early trading links with Kush and Egypt were multiplied by many contacts with the ports of the Indian Ocean and beyond. Adulis became a centre of world trade, and the Ethiopian capital of Axum, in the hills behind Adulis, felt the influence of all this. Writing of the later years of the first century BC, Strabo could note that no fewer than one hundred and twenty ships were known to have sailed from the Egyptian port of Myos Hormus on business connected with the Indian Ocean trade, while a Greek-Egyptian sailor's guide of the great period of Axumite expansion describes Adulis as a vital link in the long chain of ports which lay between the central coast of East Africa and the Red Sea.

This great period began soon after AD 50 when Axum became the seat of a new line of kings. By now the cultural break with Arabia was complete, and Ethiopian civilization was as distinct from its early Sabaean relatives as was Meroitic Kush from Napata or Egypt. Its gods, like Almaqah the moon-god, might still be the old gods of Arabia, but altar and other inscriptions were now in Greek or in Ge'ez, language of the Axumites and parent of modern Ethiopian. Zoscales, reputedly the first of these new kings, was followed by other powerful monarchs who raised in Axum those towering

This fragment of an inscription from an altar near Axum shows the Sabaean form of script used by the Ethiopians early in their history

Opposite left: Gold cylinder sheath of King Aspelta of Kush (593–568 BC) from Nuri near Napata (Height: 3¼ in.)
Right top: Cover for a vessel, a fine example of Meroitic graphite pottery
Bottom: Silver libation bowl, found in the tomb of Netaklabah-Amon (538–519 BC) at Nuri. Inscriptions in Egyptian hieroglyphs (Napatan Kush. Height: 8¼ in.)

stelae – usually though misleadingly called obelisks – which overtopped all other standing stones in this land of megalithic profusion, and whose sole tall survivor is still the admiration of the world. Some of the names of these kings are known from their fine gold and silver coins and from other sources, but no sure dates are available until the fourth century AD with King Ezana; and even Ezana's dates have lately been questioned by scholars who believe they really lay in the fifth century.

It was Ezana, at all events, who completed the downfall of Meroe. After centuries of trading intercourse between Meroe and Ethiopia, the two had grown far apart. During the early part of the fourth century, if not before, new peoples came filtering into the settled lands of Kush. A famous inscription of Ezana's calls them the Black Noba and the Red Noba; they were in any case the last of all those many peoples who had moved out of the dry lands of the Saharan west and found the comfort of the Nile Valley to their taste. These Noba or Nubians seem to have settled down alongside the urban Kushites without much trouble, although here the records are entirely lacking. But with Ethiopia they were repeatedly at war. Ezana's inscription tells self-righteously how he was provoked by the Noba, time and again, until he decided to make an end of their presumption. Gathering his armies, Ezana marched down the Atbara, the ancient road to Meroe, and defeated the Noba 'at the ford of Kemalke', pursuing them thereafter for three and twenty days. This brought his armies into the heartland of Meroitic Kush where they proceeded to ravage not only the 'towns of straw' of the Noba, but also the 'towns of masonry' of the Kushites; from all of which it seems that the Kushites and the Noba were at this time well allied to one another. Whether this invasion and ruin of Meroe and its sister-cities occurred in about 325, as many have thought, or a century later as some scholars now suggest, this is the last glimpse we gain of ancient Kush. Its cities never recover. Its rulers vanish from the scene.

But the history of Axum took a new turn. Ezana, or perhaps his predecessor, accepted Christianity as one of the state religions – Ezana's coins show both pagan and Christian symbols – and from this time onward the separation from its neighbours of Axumite civilization, merging later into the Amharic civilization of medieval Ethiopia, became ever more marked. While the Ethiopians developed their own strong Christianity, their neighbours remained pagan or accepted Islam, and wars of commercial or political rivalry became

religious wars as well. Out of this cultural isolation in north-eastern Africa the Ethiopians were to fashion unique traditions of religious custom and of art.

It would be valuable to know how far these advanced Iron Age civilizations of Kush and Axum were linked with other African peoples to their west and south. Little can as yet be said about this. The Meroites certainly traded far westward, and possibly it was in this way that the Chad-Niger peoples first learned the art of making sculpture in metal by the lost-wax process. (This involves the coating of a clay model with wax, and then the displacement of the wax by molten metal. The wax, being thus melted, is 'lost'.) It would be no surprise to find that West Africans sojourned in Kush, or Kushites in West Africa; and further excavation in the cities of Kush, as well as decipherment of Meroitic inscriptions, may yet make it possible to write this closed chapter in trans-African relations.

Southward movement from Kush was impeded by the nature of the Upper Nile country, and especially by the enormous swamps of the Sudd. If Kushites travelled to the land of modern Uganda and saw the Mountains of the Moon, or Ugandans to Kush, the records are silent on the fact. Yet this was probably the route by which the ancient world of the Mediterranean heard a little of the truth of inner Africa; and here again the Meroitic records, when at last they are properly examined and understood, may throw some useful light. Further eastward, the Axumites undoubtedly travelled far into the continent, whether for trade or plunder, and perhaps it was from Ethiopia that the developing Iron Age cultures of East Africa, at least after about AD 700, adopted such techniques as that of hillside farming by the use of stone terraces and water channels. A better understanding of these matters may even show that the important copper-producing centre of the Katanga in the eighth and ninth centuries may have enjoyed some distant link, through intermediaries, not only with copper buyers along the East Coast but also among the urban peoples of the north. The present state of the question suggests in any case that all these regions – whether in north-eastern, western or central Africa – were at least indirectly linked together over a long period in the past. In this, as in so much else, a certain underlying unity of ancient African cultures seems once more affirmed. And what was true in this respect of Kush and Axum, of the blameless Ethiopians, was likewise true of their neighbours in the west and north-west, the Berbers of the Sahara and the lands of the

Opposite: No aspect of Meroitic art was more distinguished for its brilliance and originality than the painted pottery. This marked a high point in a civilization which was superficially eclectic, but essentially and profoundly African. The illustration shows a light-coloured painted pot from Faras (Height: 7¼ in.)

Trading with many peoples near and far, the Kushites of the Meroitic Empire imported foreign goods and possibly foreign fashions. This bronze bowl from Gammai (Halfa) has a distinctly Chinese shape (Height: 2¾ in.)

Meroitic pottery cup from Buhen with upright lotus flower decoration (Height: 3½ in.)

Meroitic vessel of burnished black pottery from Meinat-el-Mek (Height: 3¾ in.)

Opposite: This bronze head of Dionysus was found in the pyramid tomb at Meroe of Prince Arikan-Kharer, son of King Natakamani (*c.* 12 BC–AD 12). Late Hellenistic in style, it was probably made about 150 BC, and is one of a number of Greek objects found in Meroitic royal tombs. Meroitic Kush and Ptolemaic Egypt often enjoyed good trading relations (Height: 4¾ in.)

Maghreb, modern Tunisia, Algeria and Morocco. They, too, developed a notable civilization which had many links with the cultures of their African neighbours.

Early North Africa

Not far west of Algiers there stands a monumental and majestic tomb of circular design; a great mound piled firmly on the ridge of the coastal hills, and visible from far away. The guidebooks call it the Tomb of the Christian Woman; but there is really nothing Christian about this strongly columned dome of masonry with its single internal corridor winding inward to a solitary chamber. It dates in fact from the pre-Christian period, and is the greatest of many thousand Berber tombs scattered along the length and breadth of north-western Africa. Its architectural origins lie neither in Europe nor in the Middle East. They belong to the distant centuries of Berber emergence.

Between those origins and the Berber king who was buried in the Tomb of the Christian Woman – probably the Bocchus who ruled in the western Maghreb during the second century BC – there reaches the long and often mysterious development of a civilization which owed much to the ancient peoples of the fertile Sahara, something to the Bronze Age cultures of south-western Europe, especially Spain, and a great deal to its own unfolding growth.

Here in north-western Africa there occurred a highly successful synthesis of cultures of Saharan origin together with native cultures deriving from Mediterranean forebears. By the middle of the second millennium BC these emergent Berber peoples – peoples, that is, who may be grouped together by their common use of the Berber language or its variants – had become an important part of the whole North African scene. They dominated the smiling Mediterranean coastland and its inland hills, while their poor relations sojourned throughout the Sahara from the shores of the Atlantic to the borders of the valley of the Nile. They were famous far beyond their own countries for the speed and beauty of their horses; and it was from them, according to Herodotus (in matters of this kind more often right than wrong), that the Greeks first learned the skill of harnessing four horses to a chariot.

Something of the inner and abiding strength of this old Berber civilization may be glimpsed by measuring the tales of Herodotus against the findings of modern research. Writing in the fifth century BC, the 'father of

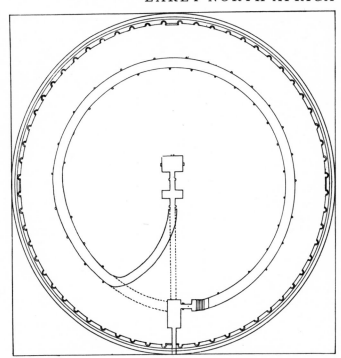

Plan of the winding tomb-corridor inside the '*Tombeau de la Chrétienne*'. An earlier straight passage is reconstructed by the dotted lines: see plate on p. 69

history' described how a people called the Auses, who lived in the southern part of modern Tunisia, 'hold an annual festival in honour of Athene, at which the girls divide themselves into two groups and fight each other with stones and sticks; they say this rite has come down to them from time immemorial, and by its performance they pay honour to their native deity, which is the same as our Greek Athene.' For a long time this was dismissed as Herodotian embroidery or pure invention. Yet anthropologists have lately shown that a ceremony of this kind really did exist in southern Libya, and even continued until it was suppressed a few years ago by the modernizing government of the new kingdom of Libya. In this most venerable ceremony it was the custom up to about 1960, very much as Herodotus explained, for the young girls of Ghat and El Barkat in the Fezzan, and perhaps elsewhere as well, to gather for a 'feast of salt' in their best clothes and wearing all the jewellery they could lay their hands on. Got up like this, they paraded in military style with flags and musicians, each being armed with a stick or whip, and celebrated the salt harvest with a mock battle. Even if they did not know it, they were acting in a play that was at least two and a half thousand years old.

While it was only with Herodotus that the Berbers enter written history, they had long had a script of their

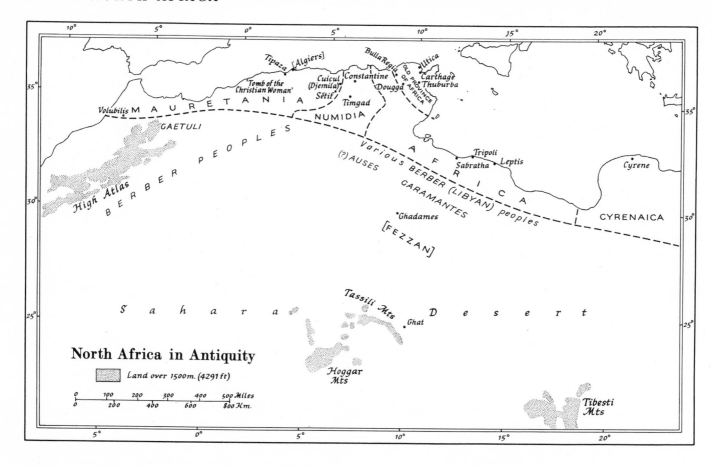

own, ancestral to the *tifinagh* still used by the Tuareg Berbers of the Sahara, though it is also true that inscriptions in Old Berber have as yet yielded very little of historical value. Herodotus in the fifth century had many different names for their branches or tribes: Garamantes, Nasamonians, Machyles, Auses, Mauretanians and others, corresponding to cultural or political divisions which had come into existence in much earlier times. These ancient divisions are faithfully reflected today by the still existing divisions of North Africa, with distinctive peoples of Berber origin (if later mixed with incoming Arabs) occupying Morocco, Algeria, Tunisia, the Fezzan and Libya; for it appears that the Berbers were never united, except perhaps in very early years, into a single group or even into a single confederation of peoples. Onwards from the first millennium BC they occasionally combined against foreign enemies or rivals, but never sank their differences for more than brief periods.

Although they appear in written history only in the fifth century BC, they were already a vital part of the African side of the whole Mediterranean trading circuit of antiquity. By the middle of the second millennium BC

they were in touch, and sometimes in military alliance, with those 'peoples of the sea' who helped to ravage Egypt. So much is clear from the Egyptian records; but aside from these there are several strands of evidence for their contact with Mycenean Crete and Greece, not least a magnificent 'flying gallop' rock-painting from the Tassili n'Ajjer mountains. Even in that early time they were quite possibly crossing the Sahara, somewhat less wild and hostile in its nature than it soon became, with caravans of horse-drawn chariots and horsemen.

With the coming of the Phoenicians to the western Mediterranean, the Berbers were drawn fully into the commerce of the ancient world. The process was of course a gradual one. Phoenicia's earliest settlements along the Berber shore were intended as little more than staging-posts which could securely link the Phoenician trading colonies in Spain, great exporters of tin and copper, with their homeland ports at the eastern end of the Mediterranean. But these energetic businessmen took root in their little colonies. Their North African entrepôts grew into trading states in their own right. Carthage, the greatest of them all, has a traditional founding date at the end of the ninth century BC;

Opposite: The origins of the Axumite kingdom of ancient Ethiopia, dating from the first century AD, are still wrapped in some mystery. New light was thrown on them by discoveries in the early 1950s. Among these was a 31½ in. high statuette in limestone of a sitting woman found at Haulti, about eight miles from Axum, of which the head is shown here, and which dates from the fifth century BC

Above: An early Ethiopian altar from Melazo, near Axum,
dedicated to the moon-god Almaqah (Fifth century BC)
Opposite: This remarkable 18½ in. high limestone statuette
from Hawile-Assaraw, near Axum, is another pointer to the
early Ethiopian culture which developed in the fifth and
fourth centuries BC and was a parent of the Axumite
civilization of the first century AD and later. The Sabaean
inscription seems to be a prayer for childbirth, but the
plinth may not have belonged originally to the statue

but as a city rather than a staging-post for Spain it probably dates only from the seventh. Within another hundred years, however, Carthage had become a city of the first importance, its trading strength being drawn no longer from Spain but from the African interior. By the fourth century many Phoenician ports had sprung into being along the North African littoral, ports such as Leptis and Sabratha, whose principal *raison d'être* was not to act as intermediaries in the west-east Mediterranean trade, but as intermediaries in the trade between the African interior and the rest of the ancient world. They bought gold, ivory, and other African goods from Berber neighbours, who in turn had carried these things across the Sahara from West Africa, linking North and West Africa in the same way as their descendants were to do, though with still greater success, after the Muslim conquests of more than a thousand years later.

These trading Berbers were never much influenced by Phoenician city life. United in their several kingdoms of the Maghreb, Fezzan, and Libya, they allied themselves with Carthage and its sister-cities, or quarrelled with them according to the shifting fortunes of the day. The most famous of the kings of Numidia – roughly, western Tunisia and eastern Algeria – even led a Berber army as an ally of Carthage against the Romans in Spain. This outstanding man, Massinissa, afterwards warred with Carthage as well as sending several contingents of his cavalry, and one of elephants and riders, to fight in Roman wars against Philip of Macedon. Carthage responded by siding with Massinissa's most powerful Berber rival, Syphax, king of the Mauretanians of Morocco.

In 146 BC the long struggle between Rome and Carthage ended with the ruin of the latter. The Carthaginian 'home territory' in eastern Tunisia became a Roman province. For the Berbers, this was merely exchanging one probable enemy for another. As with the Phoenicians, they were ready to trade with the Romans provided that it paid, or even fight for them, but they were unwilling to give up their independence. In the end the Roman Republic was able to master Numidia and turn it into a client state, yet only with great difficulty; while further west, in Morocco, Roman order never became secure. Only with the rise of the Roman Empire and its highly organized military power did Tunisia and Algeria, and to a lesser extent Morocco, come under strong Roman influence. Then through four remarkable centuries there was peace and

great prosperity. Many cities were founded. Many of them flourished. Many Berbers of the coastland became city dwellers and citizens of Rome.

This was much more than mere Romanization. Those who visit Carthage today may well receive from its almost entirely Roman ruins the impression that Rome completely supplanted Phoenician or Phoenician-Berber civilization. The impression is misleading. Little was destroyed by the legions of the Roman Republic except Carthage itself, the capital of African Phoenicia. Elsewhere the cities remained much as they had been before. Then with the growing power and prestige of Rome there came a long and highly successful synthesis. Roman government and Roman settlement gradually reshaped North African civilization without fundamentally changing it. Along these fertile coastlands, rich in grain and cattle, Phoenician-Berber cities acquired Roman habits, gods and customs – and, what was perhaps most important of all, Roman markets – while continuing to stand on the cultural soil of their old pre-Roman traditions. New Roman colonies, staffed and defended by Rome's veterans of foreign wars, grew into cities that were among the finest in the world; but they were Roman with a big difference, and the difference was African.

Leptis, for example, had come into existence as a junction for the Saharan-Mediterranean trade during the fifth century BC. From the first it was heavily influenced by its large dependence on Berber contacts with the interior. On these it thrived, and the treasury at Carthage looked to Leptis for a substantial annual contribution to the costs of the capital and empire. But the Libyan Berbers also looked to Leptis for a living. During the upheavals of the Roman conquest, they even tried to capture it. And when Rome acquired a Leptian emperor in the person of Septimius Severus, Berber links were further strengthened by the positioning of a permanent Roman garrison at Ghadames in the heart of Garamantian Berber country. This garrison was designed to guard the trade-route south into the Fezzan, but it strikingly confirmed the dependence of the coastal cities on their hinterland.

There followed years of growth and great expansion. The North African coastlands became a land of milk and honey, 'a country that was nothing but one shaded grove', as an Arab writer would later picture it, 'one unending series of villages'. Many of the tremendous ruins of this Romanized civilization of North Africa are still there to tell the tale. One can follow their fortunes

Opposite top: The great stela at Axum
Bottom: Stela at Axum with an inscription in Greek of King Ezana (Fourth century AD)

almost year by year. Cuicul, or Djemila by its Arabic name, is a good example. In AD 96 or 97 the emperor Nerva ordered veterans to set up a colony in a fine steep-sided valley bottom that could guard the mountain road between Sétif and Constantine. These veterans called their settlement by its Berber name, married local girls, and greatly prospered. Within fifty years their modest huts had given way to large houses, and soon these were so crowded within the walls that their new theatre, another evidence of civic pride, had to be built a hundred and fifty yards beyond their outer rampart. In AD 161 they added a superb arch between the rampart and the theatre. In 183 they built a comfortable bathing establishment two hundred yards beyond their south gate. The line of the old rampart now became lost within a vast aggregation of suburban dwellings. Many more large public buildings were added during the thriving Severan period of the third century AD: a forum, fountains, public lavatories, new temples and meeting halls. By now the population was around ten thousand strong. It was a population, we may be sure, that was well pleased to be Roman in its citizenship, but was anything but Roman in its origins or its everyday language.

With the rise of these grand and comfortable cities, Timgad and Leptis, Tipaza and Dougga, Cuicul, Thuburba and many others, the trans-Saharan trade passed into a new phase of growth and orderly organization. No doubt it was in this period, after the second century AD, that the earliest trading states beyond the Sahara began to take shape in response to steadily strengthening commercial demand from the north. The trade grew for several reasons. The cities of the north had become ports of entry to the almost inexhaustible markets of the Roman empire. Widening use of the camel went hand-in-hand with security along the trade routes, at any rate within Roman borders, and with the opening of new wells and the conservation of old ones. Beyond the *limes*, moreover, Roman power interested itself in keeping the peace along these routes. There were even two or three Roman expeditions far into the desert country towards the Sudan beyond it, though none of these seems to have gone further than the Tibesti and Hoggar mountains of the eastern and central Sahara. Generally one has the impression, if from scanty factual evidence, of a well-ordered system of trade through many Berber intermediaries who were in regular and frequent contact with those Africans of the Western Sudan who dealt in gold and ivory, and

who would soon form West Africa's earliest known political units.

Not all went smoothly. The massive ruins of Cuicul, lying within their bastion of tall Algerian hills, may once again be called in evidence. After the death of the emperor Severus Alexander in AD 235 there came a temporary weakening of Roman power, and poor harvests, and revolts; but the city recovered in about 280 and enjoyed another period of civic comfort in the fourth century. Now its public buildings included many Christian churches, and Cuicul became a place of pilgrimage. With a local end to the Donatist schism in 411, the bishop of Cuicul, Cresconius, built an imposing basilica with five naves; and the pilgrim traffic grew apace.

This newly Christian civilization was sorely threatened by the Vandal invasions from western Europe in the fifth century, but the end came slowly. Cuicul, for instance, continued to be a Christian city of importance, sending a bishop to Constantinople in 553, until it was finally destroyed, violently and mysteriously, at the end of the sixth or early in the seventh century, probably by the revolt and ravaging of nearby subject peoples. In breaking up the Roman system, however, the Vandals opened the way for more than the destruction of cities like Cuicul. Lacking any firm base, and unable to engraft themselves into the urban culture of Roman North Africa and thereby carry on the empire, or at least a part of it, these ambitious raiders signalled the close of an epoch, the end of Antiquity. With their breaking of the gates, there came a final interruption in all that long process of growth which had coupled the Berber Bronze Age of the second millennium BC to Phoenician enterprise and Roman organization.

What came now would be singularly different. In 641 the followers of the Prophet Muhamad seized Babylon in Egypt, capital of that Byzantine province. A year later they had Alexandria; in 647 Tripoli; in 670 most of Tunisia. Everywhere they marched they were triumphant. After a hundred and fifty years of ruin and upheaval they offered a new hope of peace to men long wearied of the dangers of the times; and Islam conquered here, as it would elsewhere, as much by its revolutionary message of unity and brotherhood as by the vigour of its military arm. Within another hundred years or little more, the Trans-Saharan trade was once more on the path of large expansion. The history of northern and much of western Africa had entered a new stage.

Overleaf left: Numidian Berber tomb about 70 ft high at Dougga (Tunisia). It dates from the second century BC and was built by Punic craftsmen
Right: The so-called '*Tombeau de la Chrétienne*', about 115 ft high and greatest of all the Berber tomb monuments. It was almost certainly that of a king who reigned in the second or first century BC, the most likely being Bocchus II, king of Mauretania

Above: Three masks, between 6 and 7½ in. high, from a Punic necropolis in Carthage of the seventh or sixth century BC

Above right: Fragment of a stela dedicated to the cult of Baal Saturnus and Tanit Caelestis, dating from the second century AD. The Greek inscription shows Hellenist influence

Right: A Tophet (Phoenician graveyard) at Salammbo, the Phoenician port of Carthage

3 The Factors of Growth

Development and diversity of community life in ancient times south of the Sahara – Growth and importance of trading centres – Further evolution of Iron Age political systems – History of some of the largest of these systems in western and central-southern Africa up to the sixteenth century – The Christian kingdoms of Nubia and Ethiopia – Rise and early consequences of Islam

African Solutions

If all he could hope to explain was how one barbarian succeeded another, Voltaire tartly observed to an intending historian of the Turks, where could be the advantage to mankind? The point should be well taken by an intending historian of the Africans. There is little difficulty, as it happens, in setting forth a list of kings or regnal dates for quite a number of African states and empires; and of kings, moreover, who were no more barbarian in the sense of being violent, irrational, or vowed to blind destruction than most of their contemporaries in Asia or Europe. The notion that African life before the colonial period was 'blank, uninteresting, brutal barbarism' – to offer the definition of a professor of Colonial History, Egerton, at the University of Oxford half a century ago – is thoroughly exploded now. But any 'scissors and paste' approach to African history, relying centrally on lists of kings, battles and 'big events', would go badly wrong from the start. For it would miss more than half the story. It would suggest, for example, that those African peoples who developed forms of centralized self-rule and empire were the only ones worthy of attention, leaving aside as insignificant those many other peoples who did not.

This kind of approach would miss not only the great diversity of African social and political experience, but also, and even more, the underlying unities and similarities which give to all of them, practically without exception, their profound inner coherence and inter-relationship. This political and social unity-in-diversity may be reasonably compared with the African lin-guistic scene: more than a thousand distinctive languages, according to the present view, have flowed from four or five root tongues, *Ursprachen*, of unknown but certainly venerable age. And on the political and social scene a correspondingly great diversification has likewise fissured from unities which first took shape in distant Stone Age times. Especially within the last two thousand years, the historical period since the beginning of the African Iron Age, this diversification has supported, and to some extent continues to support, an extremely wide and complex range of political and moral authority, so that there is scarcely a single case where one people governs its behaviour by the same rules and precepts as those of any of its neighbours. Now the reasons for this seeming confusion of system and belief deserve some brief examination as a prelude to our narrative. They make it possible to place many of these types and sizes of system and authority within a meaningful if summary perspective which helps to explain their origins and nature.

If people recognizably like ourselves began to multiply in Africa about 35,000 years ago, as the anthropologists now assure us was probably the case, they were far from numerous. They multiplied, then or thereabouts; but slowly. By the final period of the Makalian wet phase after 2500 BC, when the Sahara began to draw a wilderness of desert between continental Africa and the rest of mankind, scattered groups of hunters and food-gatherers had long since appeared in all the main regions of the continent; yet even by this comparatively late period they were still few in numbers. At the outset of the Iron Age, two thousand years ago, the peopling of Africa in anything like its

Opposite: Ruins of a Roman temple at Tipaza, west of Algiers

later density and universal presence had only just begun.

The central problems which had to be solved by these early Africans were thus of two kinds. In the first place they had to master an often very hostile environment to at least the point where they could support their own settlement and multiplication: in other words, they had to improve their economic understanding and organization, they had to invent new tools and discover new techniques. Secondly, they had to elaborate socio-cultural superstructures of thought and belief such as would enable them to establish and support the self-confident identity not only of numerically large groups of people, but also of many separately distinct societies. Their simple economies could seldom allow them to multiply and stay *in situ*: some of them had to be constantly moving and spreading their numbers. What happened, time and again, was that a given group would divide and hive off a lesser group, and this lesser group would march off into new territory, for a long time into territory possessing few or no people of its own; and there they would settle and begin a new life, work out new rules of law and order, redefine their morals and beliefs, and then again, as multiplication continued, themselves divide and hive off still other groups who would repeat the process.

Now the principal ways in which this interplay of environment and social relationships worked to establish Africa's patterns of belief and behaviour were much the same, fundamentally, as the experience of other peoples in other continents who were faced with much the same problems. A main starting-point was the 'extended family', a more or less close-knit group of relatives comprising several pairs of grandparents, or possibly great-grandparents, with all their living descendants except those who had married out of the group into another but comparable group. Such groups would be larger or smaller according to the nature of the country in which they lived: larger in fruitful country, smaller in country that was dry or poor in game. As soon as a group grew markedly above its optimum size, some of its members would have to withdraw and move elsewhere. In withdrawing, however, they were posed not only with the problem of finding another place where they could live in peace, or at any rate support themselves; they also had to solve the problem of authority within their breakaway group. Putting this another way, they had to cement their new and isolated identity. They had to

explain to themselves who they were, what they had become; and they had to do it in such a way as to enable their coherence to survive in the face of many dangers and exertions. Their systems of behaviour – their systems of religion, if you will – had to be both mandatory and explanatory.

Something like this process, greatly simplified in these few words, went on over wide regions of Africa through a very long period of Stone Age and early Iron Age multiplication, spread, and development of community life. Out of it there came a large number of political and social systems based on the structures of lineage and family kinship. Each of these systems supported, and was in turn supported by, its own adherent forms of religion and ritual. These forms were applied to the consecration of accepted custom and authority, and to all those situations where decisive change in custom and authority was found desirable or necessary. That is why African religions, far from being 'the whimperings of frightened children', have ideally displayed or have been intended to display a completely rounded explanation of life. Their essential *raison d'être* has been to provide the individual with his firm place in society, furnish him with evidence of his own identity, and generally equip him with beliefs appropriate to the acceptance of his social condition and survival within his environment.

In doing this, no doubt, the religions of Africa have performed the same kind of social and political work as other religions in other lands, but they have none the less been characteristic of Africa and nowhere else. To grasp even a little of their moral and emotive force, valid for so many peoples over so many years in so many different and testing situations, one must at least to some extent envision the varied manner of their teaching and acceptance – whether by the rehearsal and catharsis of rhythm in the movement of dancing or the power in the patterned playing of drums, whether by sanction in the shape of masks and figures carved in wood and ivory or forged in metal, or by the persuasion of belief conserved in shrines and gods and ancestors, magic and enchantment. All this has been a work of long sophistication and creative practice. Nothing shows it better than the splendid arts with which these religions are organically and inseparably linked. Like the religions of Africa, the arts of Africa are not the crude imaginings of primitive men. On the contrary, they are the embodiment and statement of old and intricate speculations and traditions about the nature

Opposite top: The ruins of Roman Carthage
Bottom left: Inscription in Libyan on a fragment of sandstone (Height: 29¼ in.)
Right: Man sacrificing a bull in front of a temple; from a stela, just over 6 ft high, dating from the second century AD and decorated in a Hellenist style

Ruins of the Roman city of Dougga in Tunisia: (*above left*) one of the temples; (*below left*) a street through the city; and (*opposite*) the theatre

of the world and man's possible place in the world. They are the literature, the holy books, the poetry of African belief.

All this, too, has belonged to the underlying structure of every kind of political development in Africa. Immensely varied though they became as time went by, it was the vertical divisions of African society, divisions framed by lineage and kinship loyalties and fixed by ritual and religion, that governed and impelled the machinery of diverse growth within a given environment. These divisions operated at different levels and in different ways; but they were universally present. Some of them promoted social organizations which have remained relatively simple even into modern times, such as those of the Bushman hunters of the Kalahari or the pygmies of the Congo forest. Others ramified and reconstructed themselves into large political organizations which we call states and empires. But all derived from the same root patterns. It is possible for the sake of convenience to classify African societies into a number of general types, distinguishing those with much government from those with little, those with centralized forms of rule from those whose cohering authority has been dispersed among heads of clans or extended families. Yet the distinction remains at best an artificial one. There is no true division to be made between African 'states with kings or central governments' and African 'societies without kings or chiefs'. Each of them derives from one form or another of what latter-day sociologists call the 'jural community', recently defined by Middleton as 'the widest grouping within which there are a moral obligation and a means ultimately to settle disputes peaceably'.

It is the elaboration, of course, which makes the stuff of history; it is there that the drama lies. The 'blank, uninteresting, brutal barbarism' which was all that Professor Egerton could see in pre-colonial Africa, fifty years ago, gives way on better understanding to a major chapter in the survival of mankind and the growth of civilization. For the elaboration has been various and vigorous in every geographical region of the continent. In West Africa, for example, the last fifteen hundred years have seen the growth of large and long-lived systems of central rule involving great hierarchies of privilege and government, intricate systems of justice, regular recruitment into a wide range of professional services, civil or military, including a sometimes numerous and literate bureaucracy. Other West Africans, at the same time, have continued to live under

rules so simple as to raise the question of whether the rules may be said to constitute government at all. A people like the Tallensi of northern Ghana have never desired institutions which could be called central government, nor persons appointed to political authority, nor use of writing or written records. Yet it would be absurd to suppose that the Tallensi or others like them, peoples who have generally remained on the margins of political change and movement in Iron Age Africa, have been in some way less gifted or intelligent than their state-forming neighbours. Their mode of individual and collective social life, with its niceties of check and balance, its strength and flexibility, its bare simplicities of form combined with tolerance for stress and error, allows no place for any such idea.

It would be agreeable to follow this line of thought; but the result could be nothing like a compact history of Africa. What we have rather to do is to try to select those political forms, changes and departures which best reveal and illustrate the growing complexity and onward shift of socio-political organization and its corresponding action on the general scene. In the case of Africa, where the writing of history has so far made no beaten paths, any such selection is bound to be something of a personal choice: in what follows, however, I have tried to keep a balanced view of the significant and less significant. Yet it may be useful, before going any further, to say a little more about the variety of Africa's historical development.

Much of this variety can be traced to fairly obvious environmental differences. The peoples of the Sudanese grasslands have developed differently from their near-neighbours of the tropical forest for reasons that are not difficult to isolate; just as it is easy enough to envisage why the peoples of the East African uplands, excellent country for grazing cattle, should have followed a different path of growth from those of the Congo river basin and its densely tangled woodlands. But not all the reasons for variety are obvious, at any rate when considered from a distance. If the plough developed in the north as early as the fourth millennium BC, it was nonetheless banished from large areas of the rest of the continent by the tsetse fly, a pest which appears to have been present in Africa since the earliest times of human habitation, and has certainly been present since the earliest times of animal domestication. If some peoples developed an imposing socio-political organization on the basis of mining for minerals and trading in minerals, other peoples had no such opportunity. If the concept

Opposite: Ruins of the Roman city of Thuburba Majus, Tunisia

of divine kingship proved helpful to some societies, it was evidently useless to others.

Ideas and things received and adapted by Africans from other continents have also played their part, and often not a small one. Here again some peoples were well placed to profit from external influences, or to suffer from them, while others were not. In the Western Sudan, time and again, the steady demands of the trans-Saharan trade drew enterprising and ambitious rulers into an effort to enclose large areas of trade and production within single systems of power and revenue. Famous markets appeared at the cross-roads of commercial exchange. Peoples who lived along or near such trading routes were often impelled, whether as rulers or ruled, into new forms of political organization. Islam, arriving in the ninth century and greatly expanding in the eleventh and twelfth, brought its own solutions to the new problems of power.

Sea-merchants mooring on the coast offered another kind of stimulus. City-states grew and flourished in the swampland of the Niger delta where only fisher-villages had lived before. Other city-states, still older, and more successful, came into being along the coral seaboard of eastern Africa, and were raised to brilliant life and commerce by connexion with the traders of the Indian Ocean on the one hand, and with the producers of inland Africa on the other. Southern Bantu-speaking peoples opened tens of thousands of mineral workings, whether for gold or copper or other metals, in response to manufacturing demand from far across the eastern seas: and they too, while doing this, likewise changed their forms of political organization.

Some peoples accumulated wealth, at least in the hands of their kings, chiefs and governors, while for others the concept of accumulation remained impossible and undesired. The great lords of the Western Sudan grew famous far outside Africa for their stores of gold, their lavish gifts, their dazzling regalia and ceremonial display. When the most powerful of the emperors of Mali passed through Cairo on pilgrimage to Mecca in the fourteenth century, he ruined the price of the Egyptian gold-based dinar for several years by his presents and payments of unminted gold to courtiers and merchants. A sixteenth-century emperor of Kanem-Bornu was even said to have equipped his cavalry with golden bits and his hunting dogs with golden chains.

Of those for whom accumulation was impossible, or simply wrong, the Dinka farmers of the Upper Nile provide a good example. They live in a country which might well have baffled any attempt at settled habitation. North of them lies the grim and thirsty land of Kordofan; southward is the trackless wasteland of the swamps of the early Nile. Their own country is a plain of grass and woodland that is drowned for part of every year by floods from rain and river, and where permanent homesteads and gardens are possible only on slips and stretches of higher ground that seem to float upon the sky-reflecting waters all around. Most of Dinkaland has no minerals or none that can be reached, little timber, and practically no stone. 'Apart from imported metal and beads', writes Lienhardt about this extraordinary people, 'there is nothing of importance in Dinka material culture which outlasts a single lifetime. The labours of one generation hence do not lighten, or make a foundation for, those of the next, which must again fashion by the same simple technological processes, and from the same limited variety of raw materials, a cultural environment which seems unchanging and, until the extensive foreign contacts of modern times, was unchangeable.'

Such apparently primitive peoples were regarded by Europeans who went to Africa a hundred years ago, and later, as the more or less tormented victims of savage ignorance and hopeless superstitition. They were often thought of as children who had somehow failed to grow up, whether from lack of cranial capacity or some other supposed physiological defect; and they were accordingly approached as being proper subjects for control by others who knew better. What we now understand about the Dinka should dispel any lingering notions of this sort. For it may easily be seen that a people living in nudity on the brink of starvation once a year, manufacturing nothing that endures and accumulating for inheritance only a few cattle and a few tools or ornaments, are not necessarily a people who have failed significantly to evolve. On the contrary, it becomes obvious upon reflection that the very stability of Dinka life can only be the outcome of successful adaptation to a stubbornly hostile environment, and that any less careful or ingenious a compromise must have rapidly destroyed them. To dismiss this kind of achievement as belonging merely to the 'unrewarding gyrations of barbarous tribes in picturesque but irrelevant corners of the globe', as a successor of Egerton's at Oxford has lately urged us, may well appear a curiously provincial impoverishment of the proper study of mankind.

Above: Part of a mosaic pavement depicting fishing in a large lake full of many kinds of fish: on the banks an African hut, together with fragments of Classical architecture. From a Roman villa at El Alia (Second century AD)

Right: Mosaic from a double tomb found in the ruins of a martyr's chapel at Tabarka, west of Thabraca, Tunisia. Above is a scribe, and below a woman, Victoria Elias (?), in an attitude of prayer. On either side of her is a dove. Below on her left is a lighted candle, and on her right are two Numidian chickens (Fourth or fifth century AD. $94\frac{1}{2} \times 31\frac{1}{2}$ in.)

Overleaf left: The interior and a pavement mosaic from two of the underground villas at Bulla Regia, Tunisia

Right: Villa at Utica, Tunisia, the only Roman villa still standing on African soil

These few remarks by way of prelude to modern African history – to the history, let us say, of the last twelve centuries – indicate that the record is far richer than any brief survey can possibly encompass. With that word of warning, we may now begin to detach the purposive movement of African history by concentrating on a few main themes and sections in the story. This movement can best be apprehended, at the present stage of historical knowledge, by looking at certain ways in which Iron Age societies grew and changed; at the transformation of early political organizations into states and systems of increasing size and complexity of government; and at the forms in which trade and production for trade took shape in the foundation of cities, in the forging of communications, and in many efforts at meeting the expansion of demand for African goods both inside and outside the continent. We shall also look at the manner in which vertical divisions in society – lineage and kinship systems – became progressively influenced and overlaid by horizontal divisions, by caste and class systems; and, last but not least, at the way in which major influences from outside Africa made their own specific contributions to the changing scene.

In this way, I hope, due value may be given not only to a number of leading elements in the movement of African history, but also to the great diversity of culture which occurs from one end of the record to the other. A little repetition may be unavoidable here and there, as well as an occasional leaping back and forth across the years; but these should do no more than clarify the movement of events. We begin with the years up to about AD 1500, taking the eighth or ninth century as a general starting-point.

Trading Cities

With the emergence of new and stable systems of Muslim law and order in the Near East and North Africa, the arteries of economic growth became healthy again. In the Mediterranean, as in all the seas surrounding Arabia, the carrying-trade of antiquity recovered and was steadily enlarged. Responding to their new opportunities, as well as to the challenge of their new unity and faith in themselves, Muslim merchants pushed their ships and enterprise far across the seas. They established themselves in little trading settlements along the coasts of India, Ceylon, Malaysia, and down the eastern coast of Africa, and in the ports of

southern China. They multiplied the old Phoenician links between southern Spain, soon to be the seat of much prosperity and intellectual achievement under a succession of Muslim dynasties, and the harbours of the southern and eastern Mediterranean as far as Alexandria and beyond. They reopened large channels of inter-continental communication.

What was true of the seas of water was also true of the ocean of sand. With camel transport a widely-used routine, Berber traders became ever more numerous along the trans-Saharan trails. Old wells were dug out again; new wells were driven. There came to be used in the Saharan oases the same technique of underground water-channels, *foggara*, as in the oases of the Central Asian desert of Chinese Turkestan, one piece of evidence among many of the constant interchange of ideas throughout the world of Islam. If the Berber middlemen of Phoenician times had mainly used two trails across the Sahara – westward from Morocco through Mauretania and southward from the Fezzan of the Garamantes to the Middle Niger and Lake Chad – their successors of early Muslim times were soon using many more. This wide world of Islam, reaching by many intermediaries from Spain and Morocco in the west to China in the east, now steadily expanded the demand for the goods of West Africa and especially for gold and ivory.

Meanwhile the same demand for ivory and gold, as well as for some lesser commodities like tortoiseshell, made itself felt through eastern and south-eastern Africa from the ports and cities of the Indian Ocean seaboard. Hindu brides bedecked themselves with the carved ivory of Kenya and Tanganyika. Chinese officials went to court in palanquins veneered and decorated with the same material. 'That is where the ivory goes,' complained al-Mas'udi in the middle of the tenth century 'and were it not for this demand, there would be plenty of ivory in our Muslim countries.' Even the smelted iron of East Africa acquired an international reputation. Collecting reports of Africa in twelfth-century Sicily, al-Idrisi was informed that the best steel came from India, but that India had its best iron from south-east Africa. This East African iron, he wrote, was supplied 'to all the lands of India . . . [and] at a good price . . . [because it is] most superior in quality and most malleable . . .' Slaves from Africa also went that way; judging by the documents, however, these were very few when compared with the oversea slave trade of much later times.

Opposite: The East African coast became part of a wide international trading community at least two thousand years ago. Red Sea traders from Egypt and Arabia visited ports at the Indian Ocean outlets of Tanganyikan rivers such as this

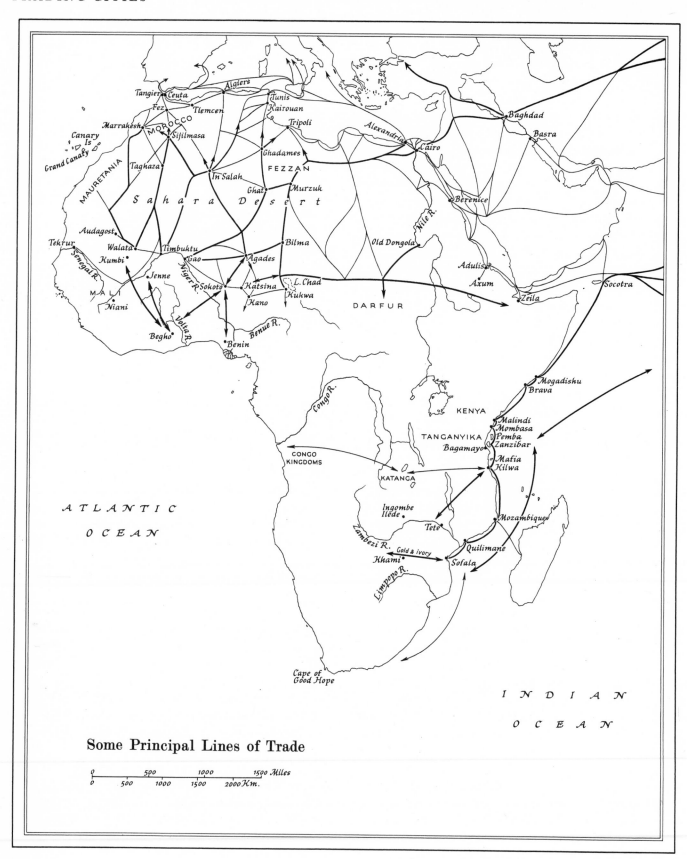

Some Principal Lines of Trade

0 ___ 500 ___ 1000 ___ 1500 Miles
0 ___ 500 ___ 1000 ___ 1500 ___ 2000 Km.

Opposite: *Mihrab* in carved coral of the principal mosque of Songo Mnara – Songo of the tower or minaret – on the island of that name five miles south of Kilwa Island. The style indicates a fourteenth-century date

This large octagonal bathing pool, unique in East Africa, was brought to light during Chittick's excavations in 1961 at the great Kilwa palace of Husuni Kubwa, which is believed to date from the late thirteenth or early fourteenth century

The Great Mosque at Kilwa, founded in the thirteenth century and much extended in the fifteenth

This Kilwa mosque is peculiar in its combining of the characteristic East Coast pillar-tomb feature with a place of worship. It appears to date from the first half of the fifteenth century

The castle on Kilwa Island was built originally in 1505 by the Portuguese, who abandoned it after a few years. Most of its visible remains date from the Omani Arab reconstruction of about 1800

Two large regions of old Africa were thus involved in the recovery and expansion of the carrying-trade in medieval times. There arose two correspondingly large and long-enduring networks of commerce that penetrated far into the continent; between North and West Africa, and, in somewhat lesser degree, between the East Coast and the mineral-rich plateau lands of the central-southern interior. Both of these trading networks were major features of the African scene by the tenth century. Even before this, moreover, they had given rise to the expansion of old markets and the founding of new ones. These early market-centres and their later rise to wealth and influence form a continuous aspect of development after about AD 800. They greatly help to shape the course of political change in West and East Africa. Their history illustrates both the capacity of Iron Age response to new trading opportunities, and the way in which this response was itself linked to the elaboration of new political systems.

Later in medieval times the reputation of some of these cities became world-wide and clothed in distant glamour. Long after he had travelled through East African Kilwa in 1331, the Moroccan scholar Ibn Batuta could still remember it as 'one of the most beautiful and best constructed towns in the world'; and he, by that time, had seen the cities of India, China, and his own Moorish countries. Writing for an Italian audience early in the sixteenth century, Leo Africanus described Timbuktu as a city of learning and letters where the king, besides disposing of an army of three thousand cavalry and 'countless infantry', supported from his treasury 'many magistrates, learned doctors and men of religion'. 'Here in Timbuktu', he noted, 'there is a big market for manuscript books from the Berber countries, and more profit is made from the sale of books than from any other merchandise.'

These travellers were not exaggerating the comparative comfort of fourteenth-century Kilwa or the bookish leanings of medieval Timbuktu. Yet the beginnings were certainly more humble. So far as the western regions are concerned, they appeared after the Muslim conquest and cultural unification of North Africa; but new growth was necessarily slow. The desert was little more hospitable then than now, perhaps the only real difference for travellers being in the greater number of usable wells; and the distances were as vast as ever. Camels were better than horses, yet no faster on their feet; given the continuing desiccation of the Sahara, they were probably even slower.

A good notion of the difficulties which had to be faced by Saharan travellers may be had from Ibn Batuta's celebrated description of his own crossing of the desert. Though made in 1352, when the trans-Saharan trade was nearing the peak of its activity, it was certainly valid for much earlier times. Ibn Batuta took the main western route from Sijilmasa, then the flourishing 'northern terminal' of the Moroccan-Mauretanian trails to and from the Western Sudan. Nowadays Sijilmasa is no more than a ruin of interest to archaeologists. But in Ibn Batuta's day it stood at the crossroads of the far western trade. Long used in antiquity, Sijilmasa had grown into a large and agreeable town whose abundant dates, in Ibn Batuta's view, were even better than the fabled dates of Basra, while 'the kind called *irar* has no equal in the world'.

At Sijilmasa, preparing to cross the desert, Ibn Batuta bought camels and a four months' supply of forage. Travelling with a company of Sijilmasa merchants, Berbers like himself, he reached the salt-making centre of Taghaza after twenty-five days of journeying through the northern fringes of the desert. He found it 'an unattractive village with the curious feature that its houses and mosques are built of blocks of salt, roofed with camel skins', an observation of no small interest in helping one to grasp the antiquity of the trans-Saharan trade. Nearly eighteen centuries earlier, Herodotus had described a place near the Pillars of Hercules where 'the houses are all built of salt blocks'; and Herodotus was certainly relying on the information of travellers who had passed that way.

Here at Taghaza, the real hazards had only just begun. After observing that the business done at Taghaza, a main point of salt supply both for northern and western Africa, amounted to 'an enormous figure in terms of hundredweights of gold dust', Ibn Batuta and his companions embarked on the nightmare journey across the true desert that lies beyond. They laid in water supplies for a first stage of waterless travel covering a journey of ten nights, movement by day being generally avoided because of the heat, but were lucky enough to light upon rain pools where 'we quenched our thirst and washed our clothes'. Encouraged by this, 'we used to go ahead of the caravan and whenever we found a place suitable for pasturage we would graze our beasts'. They continued doing this until one of their party went astray and was lost. 'After that,' says Ibn Batuta, 'I neither went ahead nor lagged behind.' Two months after leaving Sijilmasa they safely

Opposite top: The thriving cities of the medieval East Coast imported much Chinese ware. This superb flask recovered from the ruins of Husuni Kubwa palace is of the Yüan Dynasty, *c.* AD 1300, and is powder-blue in colour
Bottom: Tomb at Kunduchi, a settlement going back at least to the sixteenth century, fifteen miles to the north of Dar es-Salaam. This tomb probably dates from the eighteenth century

reached the first main 'southern terminal' of the western route in those years, the oasis town of Walata; and with that their troubles were over. Once arrived in Walata, then a thriving market-centre for the trade of the Western Sudan but nowadays exceedingly obscure, Ibn Batuta found a comfortable welcome before embarking on his passage across the Sudanese grasslands to the settled lands of Mali which lay beyond.

We can date the medieval expansion of this West African trade from early in the ninth century. Growing first by Muslim demand in North Africa and the Near East, it increased steadily as the cities of southern Europe embarked on their own expansion after the twelfth century. West African gold now became a staple export to Europe; and without it there would have been

Founded in the thirteenth century, the oasis city of Walata still has houses that are finely decorated. The drawing shows an ornamental panel in the inner court of a leading man's house

no general use of gold as a medium of exchange in high medieval times. Monarchs as far away as England struck their coins in the precious metal of West Africa. Even as late as 1832, plundering the treasury of the conquered Dey of Algiers, the French came upon a store of no less than 15,500 lbs of gold, nearly all of which must have come across the Sahara. There is a large sense in which the prosperity of the states and cities of the Western Sudan was founded on the export of gold, and supported by it through many centuries.

Some of the early market-centres are known only by report or by a few bare mounds on the surface of the arid grassland. Audagost, famous at least from the tenth century, remains a puzzle for the archaeologists, but lies probably beneath the much later town of Tegdaoust. Kumbi, largest of all the early cities of the Western Sudan, with a population of perhaps as many as 15–20,000 in the eleventh century, is nothing more than a mark on the map of the Kaarta region, two hundred miles into the southern fringe of the desert from the modern city of Bamako, capital of the Republic of Mali. Walata remains, remote and humble; so does Timbuktu, though in little better case. Gao and Jenne are still respectable towns, even if their old importance is long since gone. Yet in medieval times these and other cities were a vivid and dynamic part of West African life. They lay at the heart and centre of great events and changes. Through long years their merchants and soldiers faced and conquered the daunting misery of the trans-Saharan trails, linking many West African peoples to the onward drive of Mediterranean prosperity and power, and helping to evolve a civilization which has continued into our own day.

If one large link in this wide system connected North Africa with the plains of the Sudan – taking this Arabic term to mean all the grasslands between the Atlantic and the Nile – another link connected the peoples of the Sudan with the producers of gold and other goods in the near-forest and forest lands to the south. Here, indeed, the system was often independent of North African demand. From the fourteenth century, if not earlier, towns like Niani on the Upper Niger, then the capital of the Mali empire, looked south for trade even more than they looked north. They it was, and others like them, that organized the import of southern gold and other goods; while markets still further south, markets inside the forestland, came into being so as to organize the export of their produce, and

Opposite: A pillar-tomb at Kunduchi, characteristic of the East Coast. The tomb dates probably from the eighteenth century, while an embedded blue and white Chinese plate, showing an 'eternity' pattern, certainly does

Decorated doorway of a clay-built house at Kano in northern Nigeria

Door of the principal mosque of Mopti on the Upper Niger

buy what was needed in return. Thus it came about that Begho grew into a central market near the gold-producing country of modern Ghana, and one that was of quickly growing importance from about 1400 onwards. Similar pressures of trade and production may have helped the Nigerian city of Benin to emerge as a centre of exchange between the forestland and the plains of the north. Benin grew into a powerful city in the fifteenth century, its prosperity being partly based on the exchange of locally manufactured cotton goods for south-Saharan copper and Sudanese horses. By about 1400 or even earlier, accordingly, one should think of the whole of West Africa as being intricately traced with trading trails and market centres, an economic fact of great importance for understanding the political history of this region, and one to which we shall return.

Much the same type of long-range trading system forms an essential part of the groundwork of development in eastern Africa and its central-southern hinterland. Its links, too, are somewhat similar, though this East African trade never reached the vast complexity and value of its contemporary in the west. What the Phoenician-Berber connexion had achieved in north-western Africa, however, the traders and mariners of Greek-ruled Egypt, southern Arabia, East Africa and India largely repeated in the last centuries before the Christian era. By then the steady winds of the western half of the Indian ocean, blowing back and forth between West India and East Africa in regular seasonal variation, were being used by sailors who had learned how to trim their sails from peoples further to the east, and mainly from the Chinese. Writing in about AD 100, or soon after, a Greek-Egyptian captain of one of the Red Sea ports, probably Berenice, explained in a mariner's guide how the trade of Egypt was linked with that of Arabia and India, by way of such ports as Adulis in the Horn of Africa, as well as with that of the East African coast as far south as Rhapta. Exactly where Rhapta was remains to be discovered; its general location, in any case, was the coast of Tanganyika or one of the Tanganyikan off-shore islands.

This trade was conducted mainly by the merchants of southern Arabian cities, although Axum also had a hand in it. These merchants sent agents down the coasts of Somalia, Kenya and Tanganyika, men who settled there, learned the local languages, and married local girls. They bought cinnamon, tortoiseshell, ivory, rhinoceros horn, a little palm-oil and a few slaves, selling in exchange Arabian-made iron spearheads and axes, glass, and some wine and wheat; and transacted all this for transport in Arabian vessels whose visits down the coast seem to have been fairly regular and frequent. As yet, however, this eastern trade was still on a small scale. Among the coin finds of the East African seaboard only twenty-five of the Ptolemaic period (third to first centuries BC) are so far known, as well as three Parthian coins (first to second century AD), nine Roman and two Sassanian (third century AD). Although more early coins may yet be found, this paucity suggests that East Africa was still outside any major trading circuit.

In the ninth and tenth centuries there came a change that is comparable with the commercial expansion in the west, and for much the same reasons. Islam had now given a sense of unity, at least against their non-Muslim rivals if seldom among themselves, to all those Arab trading interests and enterprises which had spread along the coastal countries of the Indian Ocean. Many of these countries meanwhile began to flourish in a new way, forming among themselves a wide community of commerce and production. At the same time the Arab sailors whose exploits were afterwards embroidered in the *Thousand and One Nights*, Sindbad and his like, took their new faith far down the African coast. They converted some of the coastal peoples, or at any rate some of the coastal rulers. They established themselves in settlements that were wealthier, stronger, more ambitious than before, intermarrying with local women as their predecessors had done. They drew these ports and settlements into the community of the Indian Ocean trade, and thereby laid the foundations for a distinctively East African variant of Islamic civilization. By the tenth century Kilwa had become a market of importance, as had some of its sister-ports as far south as Sofala and Quilimane in modern Mozambique, building its wealth and power on its trading connexions with the ivory and gold producers of the interior.

By the thirteenth century Kilwa and Zanzibar, and probably Mogadishu on the Somali coast, had acquired mints of their own; their kings struck copper coins in fair quantity, usefully inscribing their names but not, unhappily, their dates. The whole long seaboard was now linked together by a string of thriving ports and city-states, Mogadishu, Brava, Malindi, Mombasa, Pemba, Zanzibar, Kisimani Mafia and Kilwa being among the most prominent. Islamic in their faith, strongly conscious of their membership in the Muslim world, the peoples of these ports and city-states were none the less African, being of various origins in the north and Swahili in the centre and south. They traded with all the peripheral countries of the Indian Ocean, exporting metals, ivory, tortoiseshell, a few slaves, and buying cottons and luxury goods from as far afield as China. Some 240 Chinese coins, for example, are so far known from East African hoards and scattered finds, ranging from those of the T'ang emperors (618–906) to much later times, though mostly of the Sung period (960–1279). Yet more revealing for the Far Eastern trade is the amount of porcelain that was landed on these shores. This was imported from China (as also from the Persian Gulf states) in such quantities over so many years that any casual visitor may pick up many fragments in a few hours' wandering along the gleaming sands of the Tanganyika coast or its neighbouring islands. These wares range from cheap kitchen types to fine examples that were often used for the embellishment of private houses, mosques, or the characteristic pillar tombs of the East African coast; and they have greatly helped to establish a broad chronology of sites which cover a time-span of several centuries.

The Portuguese who ravaged and largely ruined these flourishing Swahili cities have made some slight historical amends by recording what they looked like at the end of the fifteenth century, zenith of medieval civilization along this coast. Sailing up from the Cape of Good Hope in 1498, Vasco da Gama and his crews were astonished and relieved at Quilimane in southern Mozambique to find that they had swum once more into a zone of trade and frequent ocean voyaging. They had news of ships still bigger than theirs, and pressed on up the coast. At Malindi, in modern Kenya, they borrowed a pilot who was familiar with the route to India. Other Portuguese followed where da Gama had led. Kilwa, they found, was a town 'with many fair houses of stone and mortar, very well arranged in streets . . . with doors of wood, well carved with excellent joinery'; and the archaeological excavation of Kilwa, undertaken in the 1960s, has fully confirmed this description. Mombasa was likewise a 'very fair place with lofty stone and mortar houses, well aligned in streets after the fashion of Kilwa'.

The fate of these cities will be told later. Here it is important to note that their importance lay not only in themselves, but also in their stimulus upon the peoples of the interior. Just like the trans-Saharan trade, the Indian Ocean trade was reproduced between the coast and the inland country by another and internal trading system which came to have a life and meaning of its own. Many traces of this internal system may be found in the archaeological records of Central Africa for as far back as the eighth or ninth centuries AD: conus seashells from the East African coast, beads from India and perhaps beyond, fragments of Sung and Ming porcelain at some of the big stone-built sites of the plateauland between the Zambezi and the Limpopo, even an early Dutch gin bottle at Khami near Bulawayo. But mainly the import trade was in cotton goods, and these of course have perished. Every year, recorded a foreign trade commissioner of one of the cities of southern China in 1226, the north-west Indian kingdom of Gujerat and the ports along the Arabian shore despatched their ships to East Africa with cargoes of cloth for sale. Much of this cloth must have found its way far inland, being paid for in ivory and tortoiseshell but above all, at least in the heyday of this trade during the two or three centuries before 1500, in gold and copper from countless mine workings. All this trade was accompanied in the interior, just as it was along the coast, by far-reaching political changes.

Iron Age Departures

The earliest political systems south of the Sahara that are recognizable as modern states began to appear in the ninth or tenth century, although in some cases their origins were considerably older. They were modern states, that is, in the sense of having at least in embryonic form an institution of central government, some kind of primitive civil service, an executive arm composed of an available military force (though of vassal levies, not professional soldiers), and more or less regular sources of revenue (though paid in kind, not cash). Their emergence and growth were intimately related to their skills in making and using iron tools and weapons, whether for farming, hunting, mining, or subduing their neighbours; to their general development of a social stratification dividing rulers from ruled; and to their grasp of the new trading opportunities which had opened with the Muslim commercial unification of all the lands to the north and north-east.

Their beginnings rise from those little-known transitional cultures which carried Africa into an early Iron

Opposite: Gate of the Great Mosque at Gedi, a ruined city dating from about AD 1100 and lying eight miles south of modern Malindi on the Kenya coast. This mosque was probably begun about 1450. The city itself was finally abandoned around 1650

Age two thousand years ago: from the Nok Culture, for example, in the Niger-Benue region of West Africa; from a comparable development, as yet vaguely identified by the archaeologists, along the line of plateau southward from the East African Rift Valley; and from other early cultures that were transitional to farming and the use of metals, mainly iron. These transitional cultures embodied and developed many characteristics and customs reshaped from their Stone Age inheritance, whether in the forms of kinship loyalty, religion, or social organization; and they lie at the root of nearly all subsequent political and social growth.

Most of the evidence is archaeological. Yet much is clear in general outline, if not in any reliable detail, from the early writers of Muslim North Africa and Arabia. Having sailed down the East African seaboard in about 917 on the 'stormy seas of the Zanj' – of the Africans – al-Mas'udi could write of the existence of a large state or empire, ruled by a king 'who commands all the other kings of that country' and situated far down the coast, adding details which make it clear that this was the work of a Bantu-speaking people. They had cattle but no horses, mules, or camels; they were well provided with cereals and fruit, especially bananas and coconut palms; and they enjoyed the right to depose their rulers if these should seriously abuse their power. This 'empire of the Zanj' was clearly a successor-culture to early Iron Age political departures in the south-eastern region, and is perhaps to be identified with an early phase of the mining civilization of the Monomotapan empire of five centuries later.

There are no documentary references to the Nok Culture (transitional from Stone to Iron Age between about 300 BC and AD 200), nor to any other transitional culture in West Africa; but the oral traditions of ancient Ghana, written down in Timbuktu long afterward, speak of many kings before the beginning of the Muslim Era (AD 622), while al-Fazari in about 800 could already call Ghana 'the land of gold'. By this time, clearly, Ghana was a state of some importance in the Western Sudan. So was the future empire of Kanem-Bornu, lying eastward of Ghana round the shores of Lake Chad. Some of the famous market cities of the Western Sudan, Audagost, Gao, perhaps Timbuktu, likewise have their rise in about 800 or soon after. If we are to believe Ibn Khaldun, who wrote much later, the Middle Niger city of Gao was certainly in existence by the later part of the ninth century: he refers to it as the birthplace of a Kharidjite dignitary, Abu bin Kaidad;

while the first Muslim ruler of Gao, converted early in the eleventh century, is remembered by tradition as the fifteenth of his line.

All these, like the south-eastern 'empire of the Zanj' reported by al-Mas'udi, were manifestly the product of Early Iron Age growth. Having opened their way to cultivation, stock-raising and mining, Africans had spread across the vast and thinly peopled lands of the interior, multiplied in numbers, evolved new ways of mastering nature, and embarked upon barter-trade with their neighbours and even with foreign countries. Already their situation was in one respect crucially different from that of their Stone Age forebears. These, who had survived by hunting game and gathering food, had lived by an economy of the merest subsistence, neither producing nor being able to produce any surplus above their very modest needs. But Iron Age farmers increasingly faced a new situation. They could produce a surplus, even though this was minimal at first, such as gradually enabled them to settle longer in a chosen place and engage in barter with their neighbours. With the appearance of surplus and its derivative changes there came new political demands; and these the diffuse tribal rule of Stone Age times was no longer adequate to meet. Modern politics, the politics of class differentiation, took their embryonic rise. Stone Age simplicity gave way to Iron Age development. Vertical divisions of lineage and kinship authority began to be matched by horizontal divisions, by the emergence of castes of craftsmen, traders, warriors, labourers and kings, but also by the splitting of society into peoples who were rulers and peoples who were ruled. The questions of who should govern whom, and how, became the stuff of conquest, change and revolution. Although the old vertical divisions of lineage and family remained important, they were no longer the only arbiters of everyday authority, nor even the most important of them.

Such crucial points as these come repeatedly from the archaeological record. In 1960, for example, the Water Department of the Northern Rhodesian (now the Zambian) Government set about excavating the site of a proposed pumping station on the hill of Ingombe Ilede not far north of the Middle Zambezi. In so doing, they came upon a number of gold-decorated skeletons and uncovered one of the most important early Iron Age sites ever to be found in central-southern Africa. Comparing these 'golden burials' with those of simple but contemporary burials found nearby, the

Opposite: View of the trading city of Jenne, on the Niger some 1500 miles from the sea, seen from the roof of the Great Mosque

archaeologists Fagan and Chaplin, who examined this site between 1960 and 1963, have pointed to 'considerable social stratification'; and Ingombe Ilede, we may note from the several Carbon-14 dates so far secured for it, flourished between AD 700 and 900. Other Iron Age sites to the south of the Zambezi, and even to the south of the Limpopo, help to support these conclusions.

This Iron Age revolution was slow but irreversible. It brought profound changes. North of the Sahara, at least, many must have despaired. How was anyone to control the explosive potentialities of this new metal whose use was so much greater and wider than copper or bronze, and whose spread seemed impossible to halt? Where was the end to be if every man could own his own spear or sword? Bronze-clad kings and chiefs had monopolized their rare equipment. But the monopoly of iron weapons, once the techniques of manufacture became widely known, was utterly beyond their reach. Like the nuclear powers of our own day, they might desperately wish to keep the new knowledge to themselves; the task was beyond them. It is little wonder that Herodotus should have written, as of a perfectly obvious fact, that 'the discovery of iron was a bad thing for mankind'. Under the impact of this rapid multiplication of iron equipment, one great empire after another crashed and foundered. Not until AD 700 or 800 did a new but still very partial stability become possible.

South of the Sahara conditions were different. Here the use of iron was crucial for enabling Stone Age peoples to move into a fully agricultural economy, to penetrate their dense forests, to live in settled and larger communities, and to complete the peopling of their continent. Here the use of iron cannot have seemed 'a bad thing for mankind', or not at least to a majority of people. Yet as time went by, and the process of expansion continued on its way, there arose an increasing need to solve new political and social problems associated with this gradual transformation of community life, and to establish larger and more effective systems of law and order such as could absorb and exploit the impact of new materials, new techniques, and new types of social relationship. Many solutions were found. Though nearly all of them were variants on the same essential pattern of Iron Age diversification and growth, they differed much in their detail and their development. It is their changing record, above all, which forms the history of continental Africa between 800 and 1600.

Ghana and Kanem-Bornu

The origins of ancient Ghana lay among West African peoples, mainly Soninke of the Mande-speaking group, who lived at a crossroads of trade between the oasis peoples of the Sahara and the gold and ivory producers of the grassland and forest country to the south. This crossroads, a wide area of pastoral plains situated to the north of the Upper Niger and Senegal rivers, is the now remote region of the Sahel. Its markets were important because they were vital relay-points for trade along the Mauretanian-Moroccan routes across the desert to North Africa. Most famous among them, at least up to the twelfth or thirteenth centuries, were Audagost and Kumbi, cities which have long since vanished from the map.

Surviving traditions suggest an initial coalescence of the old Ghanaian state in the fifth or sixth century AD. But it is quite clear that some form of state organization must have existed much earlier than this, for it was from these Sahel markets that the Berbers of antiquity will have carried gold and other West African goods to Sabratha, Leptis and other sister-cities of the Mediterranean seaboard. Though trade along these routes was probably much depressed during the Vandal upheavals of the sixth and seventh centuries, it picked up again with the establishment of Muslim power in the north. After 800 there seems to have been a fairly rapid expansion. By 1067 the Andalusian writer al-Bakri knew of Ghana as a large and powerful empire.

North African demand for gold and ivory was one side of the picture. West African demand for salt was the other. Then as now salt was indispensable to the comforts of life. But salt was a rare commodity beyond the Sahara. Much of it came from deposits like Taghaza far into or across the desert. Even during the middle of the twentieth century, when factory-made salt had become a commonplace, annual caravans to the Bilma oasis, north of Lake Chad, have continued to carry several hundred tons of salt southward into Nigeria and the Cameroons, employing great caravans of several thousand camels at a time. The salt trade was no less important than the gold trade, and was probably much older. So far as the westerly regions of West Africa were concerned, the salt trade likewise found good relay-stations in the old markets of the Sahel.

This meant that ancient Ghana, approaching maturity in the Western Sudan at about the same time as the

Opposite: Tropical forest in the Niger delta

Above: Terracotta 'Nok' head found at Wamba, Plateau Province, northern Nigeria
Opposite: Terracotta head of the Nok Culture with a fragment of an arm holding an object on the crown of the head. Found near Jemaa, northern Nigeria, in 1963
Right: Terracotta head found at Nok in 1962

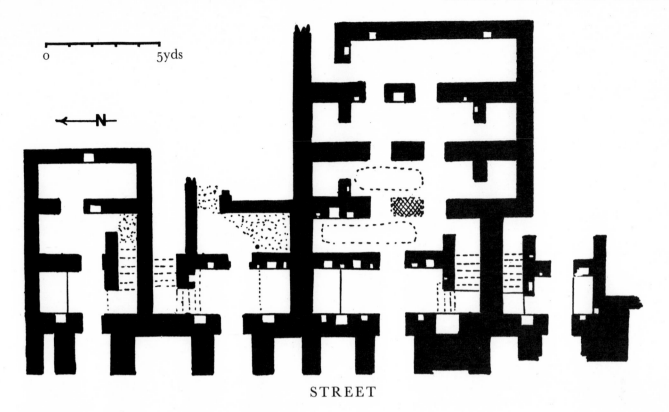

0   5yds

← N →

STREET

Group of houses excavated in 1950 at Kumbi Saleh. Note the narrow rooms, staircases and thick walls giving on to the street

Franks were organizing their empire in Western Europe, could draw strength and revenue from the movement of two precious minerals: gold from the south and salt from the north. Other commodities were of course added as the years went by: copper and cotton goods, fine tools and swords from Arabian workshops and afterwards from Italy and Germany, horses from Barbary and Egypt, ivory and kola nuts and household slaves from the south; but the staples of the trade, in earlier times and later, were always salt and gold. These were the prize of political success. These were the means by which the new states and empires could support their soldiers, their governors, craftsmen, courtiers, singers of songs. And the power of these empires became legendary as the years flowed by: writing in the twelfth century at the court of the Norman King Roger II of Sicily, al-Idrisi described how the lords of Ghana would often feed thousands at a time, spreading banquets more lavish than any man had ever seen before.

Thanks to al-Bakri, who wrote in the eleventh century, we can even penetrate a little way into the system of revenue collection that made it possible for these lords of Ghana to promote and buttress their power and patronage. Dominating all the relay-stations of the western trade routes south of the Sahara, they applied two kinds of taxes: one on production, the other on the import-export trade. 'All pieces of gold that are found in this empire', notes al-Bakri, who had excellent sources of information from traders and travellers, and who used these sources with outstanding care and caution, 'belong to the king of Ghana, but he leaves to his people the gold-dust that everyone knows. Without this precaution gold would become so plentiful that it would practically lose its value.'

One may doubt the truth of this last statement: the trans-Saharan demand for gold was so capacious, then and later, that no obtainable amount could have much depressed its value in exchange. But the fact remains that the king of Ghana, at any rate in al-Bakri's time, took care to follow the same course of action as the diamond corporations of a later age: he monopolized the worthwhile pieces so as to control the market. On the import-export trade, moreover, he applied a regular

Opposite: Bandiagara hills south of the middle Niger: tomb cave of 'Tellem' people, lying between the much later Dogon villages of Sanga and Ireli. Carbon-14 tests on material obtained here by the Dutch expedition of 1965 have suggested that 'Tellem' culture was early Iron Age, perhaps contemporary with the (Nigerian) Nok Culture

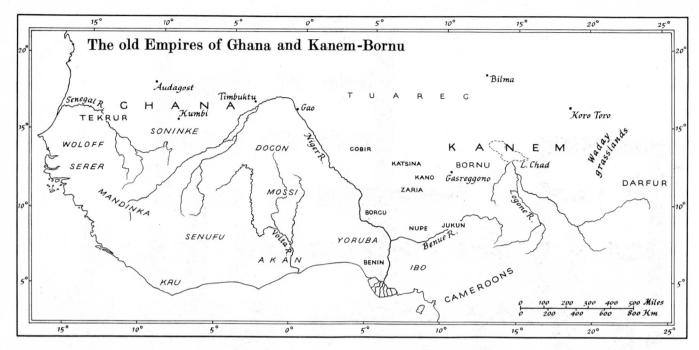

The old Empires of Ghana and Kanem-Bornu

scale of duties, being apparently strong enough to ensure that these could be collected at every market of importance. He took through his agents a certain weight of gold or its equivalent value as import duty on 'every donkey-load of salt that enters the country', and twice as much again on 'every donkey-load of salt that goes out'. A load of copper, coming from the north, had to pay a duty of five *mitcals* (though a distressingly uncertain entity, the *mitcal* in somewhat later times was often the equivalent of about one-eighth of an ounce of gold), while every load of merchandise had to pay as much as ten *mitcals*. These details are of course far from precise. If donkeys were used in the Western Sudan, camels were the only regular means of desert transport; and we have no idea how a camel-load was broken down into donkey-loads for purposes of taxation. But the main system firmly emerges. Ghana was a state and empire based on a grouping of peoples whose Soninke overlord had the titles of *ghana*, 'war chief', and also of *kaya maghan*, 'master of the gold', and whose primary interest lay in controlling a large but crucial area of trade in several staples. At least to some extent its revenues were expressed in gold; and with these the king supported his court and lavish ceremonial, rewarded his vassal chiefs and lesser kings, handed round the gifts and gave the 'free dinners' on a massive scale such as custom looked for from a mighty ruler.

Endowed with strong ritual powers necessary to this new post-Stone Age situation, the Soninke king (like other Iron Age rulers) was also in some sense 'divine'. He personified the spiritual being and welfare of his people conceived as a community of the ancestors, the living, and the yet unborn; but while this divinity made him powerful it also hedged him round with many limitations on the exercise of his power, which could seldom become despotic. In other words, with the growth of Iron Age patterns of social reorganization and central rule a new hierarchy of gods came to be modelled on a new hierarchy of rulers, although, of course, appearances made it seem that the kings were an emanation of the gods and not the other way round.

Grown famous by its wealth, Ghana attracted rivals and invaders. For three centuries after the Muslim conquest of the north, the Berbers of the western Sahara had been content with peaceful trade. Early in the eleventh century they embarked on their own path of conquest. These obscure peasants of the far west, inheritors of the Berber Bronze Age of remote antiquity, became fired with the hope of a new and better life. Gathering amid their pastures of the Mauretanian plains, infused with conquering ambitions by Islamic leaders of devotion and austerity, they rode out to pillage the rich and comfortable. Some of them went northward and eventually took possession of Moorish Spain, ruling from Seville through a dynasty which lasted from 1061 to 1147; others, still earlier, turned southward and invaded Ghana. Tradition has it that one of their leaders established himself and a few

Opposite: The village of Fassi in the Forécariah region of Guinea. The people of Fassi are Muslims of the Sussu group

followers on an island in the river Senegal, and lived there a monastic life of preparation for great deeds, after which they set forth to master the lands of the south and south-east. This at all events gave them their name among Muslims, the people of the monastery, al-Murabethin, whom our own histories call the Almoravids. They warred on Ghana in about 1052, seized Audagost a few years later, but were unable to capture its capital – almost certainly then at Kumbi, some 200 miles north of modern Bamako – until 1076. These were remembered as years of devastation. Ibn Khaldun wrote three centuries later that the Almoravids had 'spread their dominion over the Negroes, ravaged their lands and plundered their goods, submitting them to a poll tax and compelling many of them to become Muslims.'

Restless raiders, the Almoravid Berbers could not maintain their power. They withdrew or they scattered. But they had weakened the old Ghanaian system beyond recall. Others now reached for a share in the spoils of a time of confusion. In about 1230 a people from Tekrur (the northern-most part of modern Senegal) seized the last Ghanaian capital, and the empire came at last to a close, having endured as a principal factor in the onward movement of West African development for nearly half a millennium.

Chronologically, Ghana was accompanied by another imperial system in the easterly lands of the Western Sudan, that of Kanem-Bornu. The rise of this second system was less dramatic and perhaps a little later, less influential too, because Kanem had no neighbouring or native source of gold, the commodity above all else that North Africa expected from trade with West Africa. Yet the general importance of Kanem for the easterly regions of the Western Sudan was not much less than that of Ghana for the westerly regions. Moreover, Kanem endured until the other day: its ruling dynasty, the kings of the Sefuwa family, came to power at some time in the ninth century or not much later, but their last representative quit the throne of Bornu (lineal successor of the Kanem-Bornu empire) only in 1846.

The strength of Kanem, reaching east and north and west of Lake Chad, and some way to the south as well, rested on the same kind of trading foundations as that of Ghana. Northward lay valuable deposits of salt, notably at Bilma, and also of copper; southward were the sources of forest goods and the fine cotton stuffs of southern Nigeria. Between these two, centred in the lands of Kanem, were the relay-markets necessary not only for trade along the eastern trails across the Sahara, mainly to the Fezzan, Tunisia, Tripoli and onward to Egypt, but also for trade through the grasslands of Waday and the hills of Darfur to the cities of the Nile.

Having endured into very recent times, the ancient organization of Kanem (or more properly of Kanem-Bornu, since the centre of its power shifted in the course of time from Kanem east of Lake Chad to Bornu west of the Lake) has conserved useful traditions about its kings and their reigns. For the earliest times, they seem to point to the Kanembu people of the Chad region as being among the makers of a remarkable culture which flourished in settlements along the Logone river. This culture has generally been called 'Sao'. But the term is misleading if it suggests a distinctive people, for Sao evidently meant no more than 'heathen' to the Muslim converts who took over power in the eleventh century, and may be compared with the word 'kaffir' applied by Muslims to pagans of south-eastern Africa. Exactly who the makers of the Sao culture were is still in dispute: at all events they were excellent artists in metal and terracotta, and enjoyed an urban but non-literate civilization of some distinction. They form part of the background to the growth of Kanem.

Originating in a council of powerful family heads, the Sefuwa chiefs institutionalized their system of rule into an early form of central government during the ninth century. Late in the eleventh century their ruling monarch, Humé (c. 1085–97), accepted conversion to Islam for reasons we shall discuss at a later point; and from about this date one may reckon the emergence of the first Kanemi empire. It now disposed of a more or less systematic hierarchy of administrative power through governors and sub-governors, some of whose titles, such as *chiroma* and *galadima*, still survive in northern Nigeria.

Three main periods may be distinguished in Kanem history. There is the early period of formation when the Kanembu under their early chiefs were striving for leadership in the grassland country around Lake Chad. With the eleventh century conversion of the Sefuwa to Islam, there comes an increasing involvement in the trade of the region, together with a successful effort at establishing a single overall system of law and order throughout a wide region of trade and pasture. This is the period of the 'old empire' based on Kanem to the east of Lake Chad. It collapses in the fifteenth century with the rebellion of some of its subject peoples, notably the Bulala, and there follows a time of confusion while

Opposite: Nigeria: Terracotta head excavated from the former grove of Olokun Walode at Ife (Height: 5 in.)

107

sovereignties are violently contested. This terminates with the rise of a new empire whose main seat of power has shifted west of the Lake, and lies in the land of Bornu. In 1571, after many adventures, the greatest of all the kings or *mais* of Kanem-Bornu, Idris Alooma, at last comes into his rights and launches out upon a superb career of political achievement. He unites the whole grassland country from the borders of Darfur in the east, and perhaps Darfur itself, to the frontiers of Hausaland in the west; maintains diplomatic missions in Tripoli and Cairo; exchanges gifts with the Ottoman Sultan in Istanbul; and rules as the most successful West African monarch of his day.

West of Bornu the early states of Hausaland composed another segment of the general process of state-formation that had certainly begun to crystallize, throughout the grassland country, by the end of the first millennium AD. Here the traditions may not be far astray in assigning the origins of the early Hausa states to the eleventh or twelfth century, a period of much change and movement in this region of the Sudan which saw the political expansion of the Kanembu and their allies and possibly, as other traditions suggest, a south-ward migration out of this region of some of the ancestors of the Yoruba of western Nigeria. There is likewise some evidence for this period of small colonizing groups pushing westward from Hausaland into the lands south of the great bend of the Niger, groups that took the lead over local Gur-speaking folk and eventually built in the course of time the highly stable and enduring states of the Mossi of modern Upper Volta. By the thirteenth century, at all events, a number of Hausa settlements had appeared, each centred on its own strong walled village or *birni* and governed by its own council of notables and chiefs.

In later times Katsina took the lead over Gobir, Zaria, and the rest. After Katsina, Kano became the greatest of all the Hausa cities; and by the sixteenth century this seat of government, trade and Muslim scholarship was among the most important in West Africa. These Hausa states never formed more than a loose confederation of partners or rivals, sometimes on good terms with one another, at other times competing for a bigger share of the north-south trade which had so greatly helped their foundation and growth. Not until the early nineteenth century, with the Fulani conquest, did the greater part of Hausaland come within the boundaries of a single over-riding authority, that of the Sultan of Sokoto.

Mali and Songhay

With the collapse of Ghana there followed for the Western Sudan one of those times of confusion which the historians of Egypt have called 'intermediate periods', marking in this way both the end of one system of law and order and the prelude to another. In Egypt, as it happened, the end of the first and second 'intermediate periods' brought the rise, respectively, of the Middle and New Kingdoms, each of them being an advance upon its predecessor in terms of power and efficiency of organization. One may detect much the same kind of progression in the Western Sudan: Mali, which followed Ghana, grew more powerful and highly organized, while Songhay, which in a looser sense may be said to have followed Mali, likewise outdid Mali in administrative sophistication and political power.

Ghana split apart into a number of successor states, under new or established rulers, as previously subject peoples took advantage of the chaos of the times and made their bid for independence. Among these were the Mandinka of the little state of Kangaba on the banks of the Upper Niger. They it was who formed the core of a new empire which took its rise in the thirteenth century and remained effective over a wide region for nearly two centuries. Their initial success is explained by tradition as being due to the strength and skill of some of their early rulers, notably the renowned Sundiata Keita. But the conventional date of Mali's appearance on the scene is generally assigned to a great battle at Kirina, fought in about 1240, when Sundiata triumphed over his main enemy. This was Sumanguru, king of a people from Tekrur who had seized the capital of old Ghana and were themselves trying to build a new empire.

Though historically respectable, these explanations need to be viewed against the special and in some ways specially favourable circumstances of the Mandinka at that time. Their position was an unusual one in that many of them were intermediaries in the trade between the grasslands and coast to the south, producing a wide variety of goods from gold to dried seafish, and the big Sudanese markets to the north. At any rate from the fourteenth century, Mandinka traders organized in little companies or combines, and travelling far and wide, were active elements in the whole West African trade. They called themselves Dyula, a title and meaning which have survived to this day; cemented their internal unity by allegiance to Islam and the efficiency

Opposite: Terracotta head excavated in 1957 at Ita Yemoo, Ife (About two-thirds life size)
Overleaf: Two bronze heads found at Wunmonije, Ife, in 1938-9. Such heads may have been portraits of members of the Oni of Ife's court or of the Oni himself (about life size)

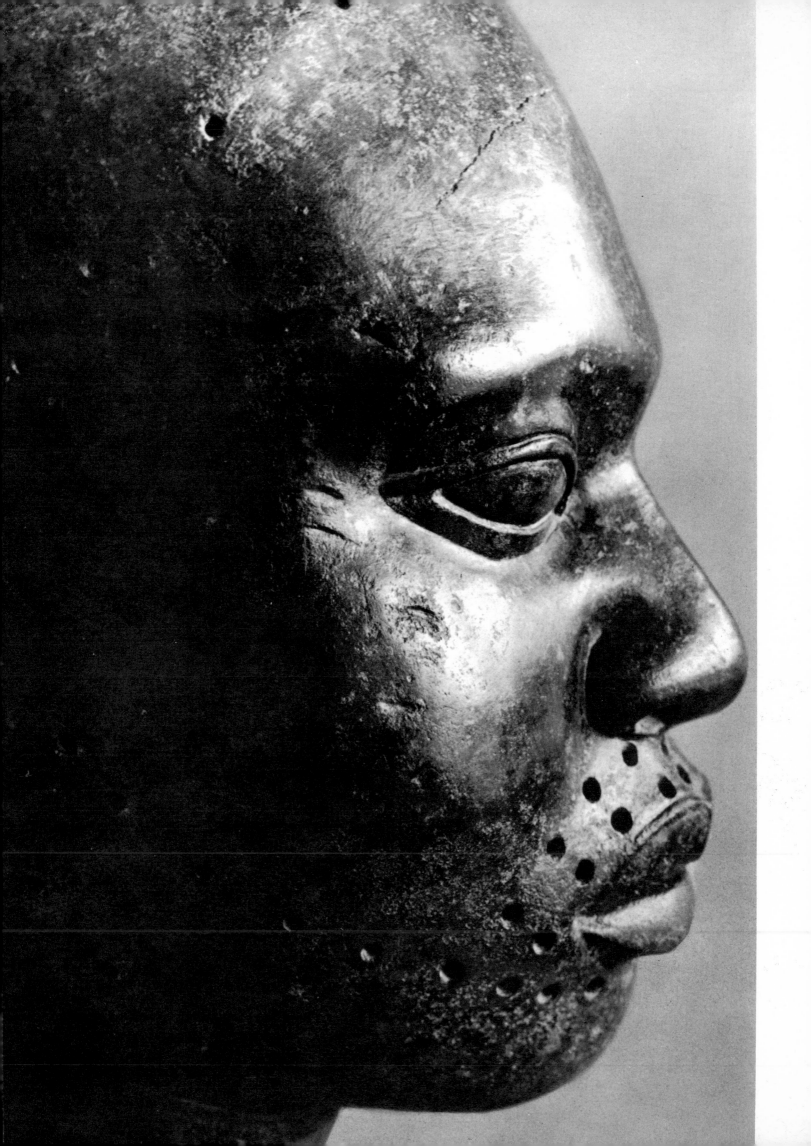

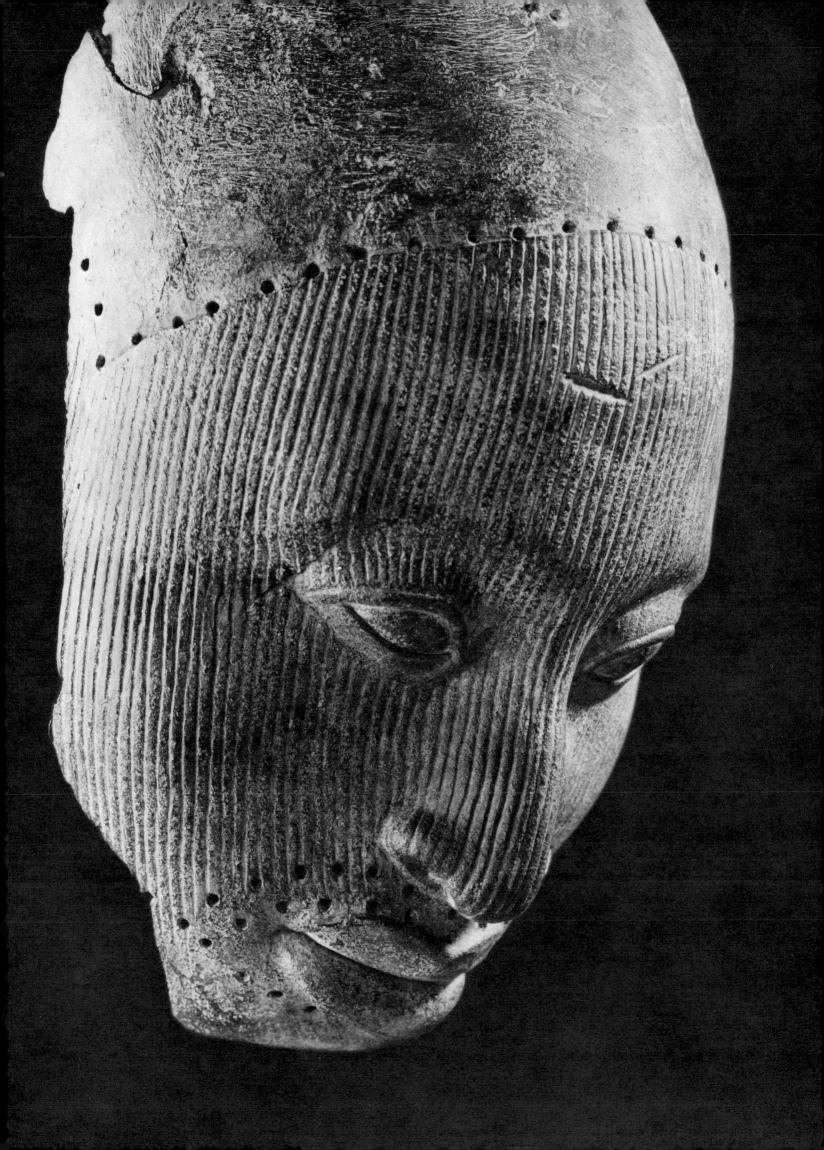

of their organization by recognition of a 'company chief' or Dyula-mansa; and became in time the founders of market-towns, cities, and even states. But their origins almost certainly go back to the early gold and other trade of Ghanaian times. They occupied a favourable middleman position, and they exploited it.

Together with this, the Mandinka may have had other circumstances in their favour. They and their immediate neighbours were among West Africa's most successful – and perhaps earliest – cultivators of the soil, producing rice and other foods in the rich hinterland of the Casamance and Gambia rivers. This strong agricultural base seems likely to have played an important part in their growth in numbers and their rise to power. Together with their trading skills and opportunities, the Mandinka occupied a country which had become rich. With the collapse of Ghana, their chance of large political power was opened. They grasped it with a sure hand.

Having defeated Sumanguru at the battle of Kirina – a clash so memorable that magical legends of what happened there still circulate in the villages of the Western Sudan – the vigorous Sundiata Keita ruled for about twenty-five years and died, according to Ibn Khaldun, who is our best source of information on the chronology of the Mali kings, in about 1260. He it was who transformed the little state of Kangaba into the core of an imperial system. Like other leaders of Sudanese states greatly involved in trade, Sundiata had accepted conversion to Islam, no doubt as a gesture of friendship to the Muslim loyalties of Kangaba's northern trading partners. Yet Sundiata, again like many leaders of this time and later, none the less owed much of his political success and authority to his powerful exploitation of traditional religion. Characteristically for rulers of his kind – the founders of large or wealthy states in the Sudan, but not the men who ruled these states in the time of their maturity – Sundiata is remembered not as a good Muslim but as a powerful man of magic and enchantment. One may usefully note a close parallel in this respect between Sundiata of Mali and the founding emperor of Songhay, the still more famous Sunni Ali of two centuries later.

Sundiata's successor, Mansa Uli, made the pilgrimage to Mecca (as some of his predecessors may also have done) and, like Mansa Qu and several other rulers next in line, worked at the consolidation of Sundiata's conquests. After Mansa Abu Bakr, who appears to have been a grandson of Sundiata, the throne was seized by a freed slave, Sakura, in about 1298. This usurper founded no dynasty but proved a capable ruler. 'Under his powerful government', according to Ibn Khaldun, who collected his information on the subject about seventy years later, 'the possessions of the people of Mali were expanded, and they overpowered the neighbouring nations. . . . Their authority became mighty. All the nations of the Sudan stood in awe of them, and the merchants of North Africa travelled to their country.' Mandinka achievements had become the biggest single political factor in the Western Sudan.

These achievements were now carried to their furthest point by the most famous of all the Mali emperors, Mansa Musa, who came to the throne in 1312 and died in 1337. Under Musa this empire reached from the shores of the Atlantic, west of Tekrur, to the borders of modern Nigeria, and from the margin of the tropical forests northward into the Sahara. Gathering information in Cairo a few years after Musa had made his lavish way through that city on pilgrimage to Mecca, al-Omari was told by a fellow-Egyptian who had lived for thirty-five years at Niani, the Mali capital, that 'the kingdom is square in shape, being four months [of travel] in length and at least as much in breadth': an exaggeration unless the travel was on foot, and yet not a large one even if it were by horse. Mali was now counted as one of the great empires of the Muslim world, and the maritime nations of southern Europe also began to recognize it as such. Composing his remarkable atlas of Africa in 1375, the Majorcan cartographer Cresques shows the lord of Mali seated in majesty upon his throne, holding an orb and sceptre, while the traders of all North Africa march sturdily toward his markets.

This central age of Mali was afterwards remembered as a golden age of prosperity and peace. Much of the grassland country west of Kanem-Bornu lay within the rule of a single overriding system of law and order, and the system was both strong and tolerant of local variation. Less than twenty years after Musa's death the globe-trotting Ibn Batuta, still restlessly wandering after nearly thirty years of eager observation up and down the Muslim world, found complete and general safety in the land. Its inhabitants, he considered, had 'a greater abhorrence of injustice than any other people', while their sultan showed no mercy to anyone who should be guilty of it. 'Neither the man who travels nor he who stays at home has anything to fear from robbers or men of violence.'

Opposite: Terracotta head from the Iwinrin grove at Ife

113

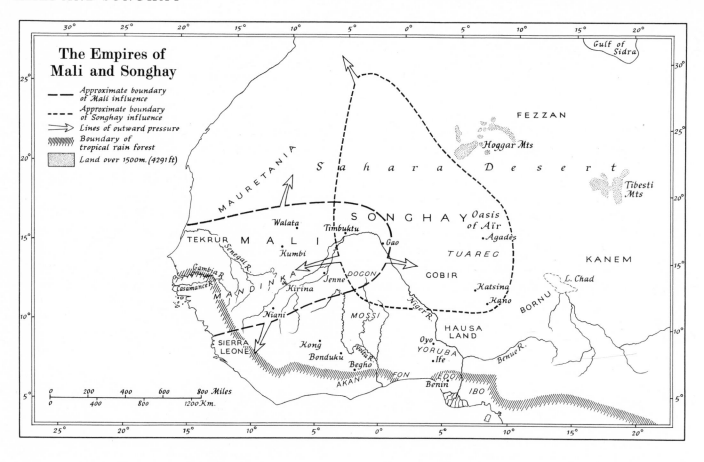

The Empires of Mali and Songhay

————— Approximate boundary of Mali influence
— — — Approximate boundary of Songhay influence
———▷ Lines of outward pressure
〰〰〰 Boundary of tropical rain forest
▨ Land over 1500m. (4291 ft)

This was also a period of commercial expansion, much of it the work of Dyula enterprise. These Dyula traders penetrated southward into the forest country, travelling the roads with their own armed escorts, establishing themselves at regular relay-stations, patiently linking one zone of production with another. In the course of time they accomplished for the western regions of West Africa what the Hausa and Yoruba traders achieved for the eastern regions; and the story of Dyula enterprise runs like a vivid thread through the records of West Africa from the early times of Mali to the present day.

Mansa Musa is remembered for much else besides military success and the growth of trade. He brought back an architect from Arabia and caused new mosques to be raised in Timbuktu and other cities. He presided over the introduction of building in brick where *pisé*, or pounded clay, had formerly prevailed. He patronized Muslim scholarship, making himself far more the exponent of proselytizing Islam than any of his predecessors. This was the time when Timbuktu and Jenne began their long career of scholarship and learning;

and from now onwards the reputation of their schools of theology and law spread far into Muslim Asia. Government became more methodical; administration began to become literate. Mansa Musa, al-Omari could note from first-hand witnesses, 'has secretaries and offices'. Yet government was still very much a personal affair: 'legal cases go up to the sovereign who examines them himself.' Only with the later rise of Songhay does imperial administration begin to operate by a regular delegation of authority to a civil service.

The next main landmark in the records of the Western Sudan was the growth of the trading city of Gao, downstream from Timbuktu on the Middle Niger, and its transformation into the seat of an empire which gradually eclipsed Mali. The Songhay today are a people numbering about three-quarters of a million farmers, fishermen, and traders who live along the banks of the Niger between the borders of Nigeria and the lake region west of Timbuktu. Their occupation of Gao, already an ancient trading centre because of its nearness to the southern terminal of one of the old Berber trans-Saharan trails of Carthaginian times,

Opposite: Guinea: head of a 'Pombo' funerary figure. These figures have been used by the Kissi for divination, but were probably not made by them. The whole figure, of grey soapstone, is 14 in. high

Two 'Pombo' funerary figures

seems to have occurred in the eighth or ninth century. There they formed a strong little city-state under a line of rulers who accepted Islam at the beginning of the eleventh century while conserving, in the manner of their kind and situation, their old faiths as well. Mansa Musa brought Gao within the Mali system, no doubt because of its profitable relationship with the trans-Saharan trade, and exacted tribute from its rulers. But Gao soon grew strong enough to make a bid for independence, and afterwards for empire, being favoured in this by the weakness of the Mali emperors who followed Mansa Musa. In 1375 the second of a new line of Songhay rulers in Gao, known as the Sunni or Shi dynasty, successfully refused to pay tribute to Mali, and in 1400 the Songhay cavalry, increasingly on the warpath, even made a raid on the city of Niani, capital of Mali.

In 1464, with the appearance of Sunni Ali, the Songhay embarked on the systematic conquest of their neighbours. Here again one may see how the power of local loyalties and religions became interwoven with the political and commercial ideas and enterprises of Muslim groups who dominated the market towns. Generally, the towns became Muslim, at any rate so far as their leading families were concerned, while the peasants of the countryside, caring little or nothing for trade but much for their own traditions, remained faithful to their old beliefs. Out of this dichotomy there repeatedly came a shuttling of power between town and countryside. The Songhay empire, like Mali and Kanem before it, emerged under a strong ruler who rested his power mainly on the peasants of the countryside. But he was followed, just as in Mali and Kanem, by other rulers whose mainstay increasingly became the men and merchants of the largely Muslim towns. This was a factor that goes far to explain the instability of these medieval empires. Their kings could prosper and pay their way so long as they could use the Islamic system of belief and government for the promotion both of central rule and long-range trade and credit. But this very reliance on the towns tended to alienate the peoples of the countryside. In times of crisis, the town-centred empires could quickly fall apart.

Sunni Ali was immensely successful. He drove off a varied host of eager raiders, among them the Mossi from the south and the Tuareg of the north, riveted his government on many peoples of the Middle Niger grasslands, brought Timbuktu under his firm control and, together with Timbuktu, controlled a vital seg-

ment of the whole commercial network of the central region of the Western Sudan. At the same time he devised new methods of administration; defined provinces to which he appointed governors; regulated his hierarchy of command through many long-term administrative appointments; created the beginnings of a professional army and even of a professional navy on the Niger; and presided over a large extension of the area of watered cultivation. Organizationally, the Songhay of Sunni Ali was already an advance on Mali, just as Mali had been in this respect an advance on Ghana.

Of this undoubtedly great man the records in Arabic have little good to say, while the sixteenth-century writers of Timbuktu describe him as a cruel tyrant. It is not difficult to see why. Although the evidence shows that he well understood the need to mollify his Muslim townsmen and tolerate their special loyalties, Sunni Ali remained much more a man of the countryside than a man of the towns, much more a potent force in Songhay traditional religion than a good Muslim. He repeatedly played a skilful game of balancing the often opposed ideas and interests of townsmen and peasant; but the townsmen were not yet strong enough to have the upper hand in the empire. Some of them undoubtedly tried. When the Tuareg of the north successfully took and held Timbuktu during Sunni Ali's time, the leading families of that city seem to have shown little energy in defending themselves. Probably they saw in the Tuareg a useful Muslim ally in promoting the independence of Timbuktu against Songhay overlordship. Sunni Ali, at any rate, believed that they had deliberately betrayed their formal loyalty to him in order to advance their own freedom of action. Retaking the city in one of his furious campaigns, he fell upon the qadis of Timbuktu with a ruthless hand, and was for long afterwards remembered there with horror and dismay.

For the same order of reasons, but in reverse, the records of Timbuktu have fulsome praise for Sunni Ali's outstanding successor, the Askia Muhamad Turé, who founded a new line of rulers – taking their title from a Songhay military rank – and largely switched from reliance on the peasants to reliance on the towns. This, as we have seen earlier, was the same kind of break with tradition which had occurred with Mansa Musa of Mali, and it was to have something of the same general consequences. So long as the towns of Songhay remained strong and prosperous, the empire survived and grew. Once they failed, Songhay collapsed even more rapidly than Mali had done.

Not content with commanding the wide region of the Middle Niger, Askia Muhamad thrust both east and west. He had returned from his pilgrimage in 1496 with authority to act as Caliph of Islam in the Western Sudan, and he now proceeded to play the part. He pushed an army as far west as Tekrur, submitting its non-Muslim rulers to his tribute and command (at least in theory, for they were far from Songhay); fought off the Middle Nile raiders once again, the Mossi and the Dogon and their like; and then ordered his generals eastward. These overran the western Hausa states, Gobir and Katsina, and were halted for a while only at the gates of Kano. Having taken Kano, and exacted regular tribute from this city through a tax-collecting governor established for the purpose, they turned north and marched across the plains to the great oasis of Aïr. There they attacked the Tuareg in their native stronghold, temporarily drove them out, and settled in Aïr a colony of Songhay settlers whose descendants may still be found here. Having done all this, Askia Muhamad had achieved a success comparable with that of Mansa Musa of Mali. Once again the greater part of the central regions of the grassland country were brought within a single overriding system of law and order.

In 1528, now more than eighty years old and growing blind, Askia Muhamad was deposed. He died a few years later, and was buried in a tomb at Gao which is still in a fair state of preservation. He was followed by a son who reverted to Sunni Ali's policy of basing himself mainly on the peasants of the countryside. But the towns were now stronger than before. This ruler was sharply and quickly removed from power. From henceforth until the end of the century it was to be the men of the towns who exercised predominant influence in the empire, although most of the Askias remained careful to placate their country folk by permitting the observance of traditional customs and ceremonials. Under Askia Dawud (1549–82) there was more expansion, and through nearly half a century the Songhay empire was little disturbed by internal upheavals or revolts. Then in 1591 came invasion from Morocco, disaster in battle, widespread rebellion of subject peoples, and irreversible collapse. With this the long and memorable era of medieval empire in the central and western regions of the West African grasslands drew at last to a close.

South of the Sudan

These few examples may serve to show how the subtle yet persistent pressures of Iron Age transformation carried many peoples of the Sudanese grasslands from simple systems of political organization to more complex systems, and how this ripening process continued over a long period more or less contemporary with the European Middle Ages and Renaissance. This is the period, taking shape roughly between AD 1000 and 1300, and displaying its full potential between AD 1300 and 1600, of what I shall call the Mature Iron Age in Africa.

Throughout this period, one may note in passing, there are several interesting parallels with Europe. Although Sudanese peoples never evolved systems based on the effective private ownership of land, such as in feudal Europe, they undoubtedly built systems based on taxation and tribute, on lord-and-vassal relations, on forms of slavery akin to European serfdom, that were not unlike some of the contemporary social structures of Europe. Here and there these African systems have been directly compared with European feudalism. But while this comparison can be useful as a stimulus to thought and argument, it will be misleading if made without serious reservation. These African societies never developed the autocracy of feudal rule that reposed on the alienation of land from those who used it. There occurred here no such crucial stratification of society.

Built on the collective ownership of land with market-cities playing no *dominant* part in their economy, these African states remained much more broadly democratic, at any rate in the representative and consultative senses of the word, than their contemporaries in Europe. Yet the parallel between the position of the towns in western Africa and western Europe remains interesting. For if it is true, to glance at another comparison, that the Western Sudan produced no parliamentary forms of a kind that were recognizably close to those of western Europe, it is also true that the question of political representation was always present, often arduously and urgently present, and was certainly among the knottiest of problems ever laid before the rulers of states such as Mali or Songhay. As between the men and merchants of the towns and the chiefs and spokesmen of the countryside there developed an increasingly acute rivalry for power in councils of state,

Opposite: Nigeria: two of the bronzes found at Igbo Ukwu, eastern Nigeria, in 1939. They may have been ceremonial wine-bowls, drinking cups and ornaments for a priest-king, and were cast by the lost-wax process. Dating tests by Carbon-14 methods suggest that they were made as early as the Ninth century

Bronze bowl cast by the 'lost-wax'
process, Igbo Ukwu

Mali: terracotta from Sarro in
the Segu region

at least from the time of Sundiata Keita in the thirteenth century. The triumph of the townsmen of feudal England in winning at that very time their first right of representation with the calling of Simon de Montfort's Parliament, in 1265, would have been well appreciated in the cities of the Western Sudan. With a deeper understanding of this long period there will be more parallels and comparisons of this kind.

The same processes of maturing Iron Age transformation were at work in the forest lands to the south of the Sudan as well as in the upland countries of central-southern Africa. Here too it is possible to speak of the gradual development of a Mature Iron Age between about AD 1000 and 1600. The transformation took effect in very different conditions, and its consequences were accordingly diverse, yet here too there were parallels with northern experience. This remains a subject of much complexity; but one possible method of tracing the crystallization of states in many African countries is to isolate those institutions which seem to have a common origin. Among these institutions there is that of divine kingship, or rule by a supreme chief whose powers are conceived as given by God and whose person is thought of as embodying divine sanctions for the welfare of his people. Such divine kingships became common to the emergence of many of the states of Africa south of the Sahara, often with attributes and customs that were remarkably close to each other.

This being so, it is tempting to suppose that such institutions of central government, of state government, were diffused southward from a northern source, at first into the tropical rain forests and afterwards into the plateau lands of central-southern Africa, by peoples who carried Iron Age ideas and habits into these distant countries. And it does indeed appear likely that some such process of diffusion took place. The general southward shift of Iron Age technology, traced by types of pottery and other archaeological evidence, together with the spread and multiplication of Bantu-speaking peoples through central into southern Africa during the first millennium AD, lends force to this view. Local traditions of southward movement add their meed of confirmation. In the case of West Africa, for example, it is reasonable to suppose that the political origins of many later and fully historical states were in being by the eleventh or twelfth centuries, if not earlier, and a number of local traditions can be interpreted as bringing these origins from the north, from the Western Sudan. Thus Akan traditions generally bring the ancestors of state-forming chiefs and groups from 'somewhere in the north'. These are the traditions which have enabled the nationalists of modern Ghana to link their state to the ancient Sudanese empire of Ghana far away in the north-west. Old Yoruba traditions likewise bring the state-forming ancestors of Oduduwa, their legendary founding hero, from far in the east (even, in some versions, from Arabia); and these may also be taken as possibly indicating a Sudanese origin. And when it is recalled that the rulers of the Akan and the rulers of the Yoruba shared some of the characteristics of Sudanese divine kingship, the diffusionist case looks remarkably complete, repeatedly buttressed as it is by other examples of the same kind.

Yet it will be unwise to push the case too far. Institutions of divine kingship are certainly first identifiable in Pharaonic Egypt. They may have passed from there to the Sudan and thence again onwards, with the development of Iron Age polities, into continental Africa further south and west. But little or nothing is known of the process. Meanwhile, to suppose a simple diffusion from Egypt of such notable characteristics of Iron Age society would be to risk adopting an extreme position comparable with the opposite view, popular until recent years, according to which the links between ancient Egypt and continental Africa were of no consequence at all.

There is a second reason for caution. Traditions of southward migration, no matter how common they may be (and they are very common), can seldom or never be taken as indicating the displacement of large numbers of people, or the mere substitution of one population or culture for another. Wherever they contain a core of truth, these traditions should rather be taken as pointing to the movement of small but strong groups who set forth in search of a new homeland. Finding it, they conquered or otherwise settled down with its indigenous people, acquired governing power through their superior techniques and organization, and thereby conserved their own traditions at the expense of the traditions of the peoples among whom they had settled. But this does not mean that one culture was automatically displaced by another. For the migrating groups would be without women, or with few women; arriving in their new home, they would take wives from their new but indigenous fellow countrymen, so that within a generation or two there would occur a profound intermingling of the two cultures, the immigrant and the indigenous. People A,

121

in other words, moved southward and settled down with People B, whether by conquest or agreement. But out of this combination, as People A and People B intermarried and intergrew, there would soon emerge a new people, People C. There thus occurred a frequent process of diversification; and this goes far to explain the great variety of cultural forms and systems which came into existence alongside each other.

We know little of this process, largely because it began to occur so very long ago. Just how long ago this really was is tentatively indicated by the modern study of African languages. Their time-scale appears to be immensely long. English and High German separated from their parent tongue some seventeen or eighteen centuries ago; yet it would seem that the languages spoken by the Yoruba of Oyo and their near-neighbours, the Edo of Benin, may have divided from *their* parent tongue almost twice as many years before the present. Even so, a few points seem clear enough. While People C in the above example will have inherited some of the new techniques of government and handicraft skill brought in by People A, they will have inherited a great deal more from People B, the indigenous stock. In the measure that People A took wives from People B, for example, People A's language will have disappeared, since it was the mothers who decided what the children spoke, not the fathers; and with the loss of its language, much of People A's culture will have gone as well.

Thus we may take it as certain that the vast majority of the inhabitants of fourteenth-century Ife, Benin or other early states of the forest country were descended from ancestors who had lived in those countries since remote Stone Age times. If they modified their culture with the arrival of migrants from the north, the migrants will have changed their own much more. So the resultant cultural patterns were neither exotic nor entirely local. On the contrary, they were the creative product of a marriage between local conditions and new social and political solutions whose origins may have lain elsewhere, but whose forms had become peculiar to the city-states of Bono, Ife, Benin and their like. Hence the southward diffusion of such institutions as divine kingship, if this did really happen, must be regarded as anything but a simple transfer of ideas and methods.

If one probes a little further into this intriguing problem as to why states emerged in this or that part of Africa, one is constantly faced with the need to isolate

and explain those crucial changes which called for a shift from older and much looser forms of community life to new and more structured forms. It was not the appearance of divine kings, after all, that led to the formation of states, but the formation of states that led to the appearance of divine kings. Expressing this another way, the need for more centrally organized forms of rule arose not merely or mainly from the habits of dominant groups who moved southward across Africa. Far more important, in fixing the change to new forms of organization, were local changes in social and economic need. Behind the divine kings, in short, lay the pressures of Iron Age transformation.

But what were these pressures? When trying to answer this question, one comes repeatedly across an apparently quite central factor: the growth of trade and production for trade. Here, of course, there is also need for caution. To reduce these intricate processes of transformation to the growth of trade and production for trade might be not much less of an over-simplification, perhaps, than to suppose that the transformation was the mere work of southward diffusion from Egypt and the Sudan. But there is no doubt that the factor of trade and production for trade, wherever it can be traced, is often illuminating and instructive.

If one applies this explanation to Bono, for example, the results are immediately helpful. One of the traditions of Bono has it that gold was discovered in the country during the founding reigns of Asaman and Ameyaa in about 1400, and that this discovery brought wealth and progress in its train. As so often, the traditions manifestly turn things upside down. They make the discovery of gold and the gold trade a product of the reigns of Asaman and Ameyaa, the founding rulers, whereas the truth is likely to have been just the reverse. Gold must have long been known in the Akan forestlands, and sporadically mined as well. These lands were already several hundred years into their Iron Age. But the rise of Bono followed the rise of Mali, and the rise of Mali had promoted a rapid expansion of southward trade through the Mandinka agents whose professional name was Dyula. With increasing demands for gold the peoples of the gold-producing country must have been faced with many new and difficult problems. Who was to mine the gold, for instance, and who was to trade in it, and how were they to be protected from competing neighbours? There came the need for tighter political organization, and the state of Bono was founded.

Opposite top: Ghana: funerary terracotta head from Kwahu. Placed on top of the grave, the figure represents the deceased or one of the mourners (Height: 8¼ in.)
Bottom: Nigeria: one of a group of carved stone figures of unknown age from the area of the Cross River in the Niger Delta

Terracotta funerary head from Borada, Buem, in the Volta region of Ghana (Height: 8½ in.)

Opposite: Asante: brass weights for gold, and two *kuduo*, or brass caskets, cast by the 'lost-wax' process and used as containers for valuables, especially gold dust, or for religious purposes. The lid of the lower one is of great interest, having a central sculpture of a woman, similar to those found on funerary pots known as *Abusua Kuruwa*, and reliefs of objects often depicted on gold-weights, such as foot-cuffs, an elephant-tail whisk, a blacksmith's bellows and an axe

Something of the same explanation seems applicable to many other early states. If the Yoruba states emerged from cultural cross-fertilization between Early Iron Age populations in Yorubaland and immigrant groups from the Western Sudan, possibly from the Chad region, it appears likewise true that this coincided with an extension of north-south trade through the rising power of Kanem-Bornu and the Hausa states in the north. Neighbouring Benin, to offer another example, is traditionally said to have drawn its political institutions from Ife and other Yoruba states. Yet these institutions took forms of their own that were native to the Edo-speaking people of Benin. And the resultant political structure of Benin was appropriate not only to this intermarriage of ideas but also to the needs of growing trade with the north, based quite largely on the exchange of Benin cotton goods and tropical products for Saharan copper. Trade and production for trade, and all the new social and economic problems and needs they brought in their train, appear once again as

a root cause for major changes in political organization, for the emergence of a Benin state.

This movement, two-way assimilation, and transformation of Early Iron Age structures into Mature Iron Age structures may be traced right through the continent as far as the Cape province of South Africa. By at least 1400 the evidence of far-reaching local adjustment to new techniques of farming, mining, trading and state-formation may be found throughout the Bantu-speaking areas of central and southern Africa, which means, by this time, throughout the greater part of this vast region. Entering their Iron Age some two thousand years ago, peoples of the central plateau (Zambia and Rhodesia today) had undoubtedly reached the point of socio-political reorganization, by the ninth century, where they were producing quite large quantities of minerals and exchanging them with their neighbours. The 1960–3 excavations at Ingombe Ilede, not far north of the Zambezi, prove as much. There, by all the signs, ninth-century chiefs were buried

Above: African methods of iron-working as shown in an old missionary account

Opposite: Asante brass weights for weighing gold. One (*top left*) represents an executioner (Height: 3¼ in.), another (*top right*) two men eating from one bowl (Height: 2¼ in.) and another (*bottom*) is in the form of a chief's stool (Height: 1¼ in.); others (*centre*) are of a geometrical design (Average dimensions: 1 × 1½ in.)

127

with impressive quantities of ornaments made in gold, some of which may have been imported from south of the Zambezi, where most of the gold workings lay. Not long afterwards, far away on the East Coast, ports like Sofala and Kilwa were growing strong by the purchase of central African ivory and gold in exchange for Indian, Arabian and even Chinese goods. Reacting in turn from the consequences of this trade, the gold-producers also changed their socio-political institutions.

The archaeology of the large stone structures at Zimbabwe, not far north of the Limpopo in modern Rhodesia, offers another demonstration of this process. This shows that the earliest settlement there was of an iron-using people, not yet building in stone, whose appearance dates from the second or third century AD. In about 1100, with trade and production for trade beginning to exercise their influence on the stratification of society, there came a clear cultural change, and the first stone structures were erected. Already, as the archaeological records indicate, there were groups who ruled and other groups or peoples who were ruled. Thus the miners seem to have been socially and culturally distinct from the people for whom the many stone structures were built. A state based on divine kingship had come into existence. Later again, after 1400, with the East Coast now at its zenith, this early state was transformed into a much larger group of states, the empire of the Monomotapa. And with this the same dynamic was clearly at work as with Mali and Songhay in the Western Sudan. Like their western contemporaries, what the lords of the Monomotapa desired was to impose a single system of rule and revenue across a wide region of revenue and trade.

One should add at this point another word of caution. Although changes in social relations linked to the development of trade and production for trade do often help to explain the growth of new political structures in the period between AD 1000 and 1600, they are by no means everywhere satisfactory. Several states of some importance emerged in fifteenth-century Uganda, as we shall see. But excavation of their sites has yet to reveal much evidence of trade, while here and there, as notably at the great Iron Age site of Bigo, there is so far no sign at all. Nor, to offer a West African example, does it seem that trading factors played any significant part in the foundation of the Mossi states. In explaining such political phenomena as these, one is forced back on the evidence of cultural diffusion by immigrant groups who brought state-forming ideas and techniques with them, and on general suppositions about the likely effects of introducing these ideas and techniques.

In any case it will have been true that the pressures of Iron Age change acquired a dynamic of their own, and that this dynamic could and did operate even where there were no precious metals to mine and trade in, or where the peoples concerned lay far outside the circuit of any large system of exchange. For it was these pressures of Iron Age growth, after all, which had carried central-southern Africa into its Early Iron Age at a time when trade or production for trade still lay in the future, and when the problems were the clearing of forest, the tilling of land, and settlement defence by the superior strength of iron tools and weapons over those of wood and stone.

Summing up, then, Iron Age transformation of most African communities south of the Sahara – and south of the Sudan – had matured by about 1400 to a point consistent with great internal development of the potentialities inherent within themselves: inherent, that is, within metal-using cultures based on subsistence farming, on the collective ownership of land, and on a certain amount of production for exchange. These Mature Iron Age cultures possessed an underlying unity of content because they were the outcome of the same social factors operating within comparable conditions and in solution of comparable problems; but they were highly various in form. Before looking at their history, even in outline, we must however catch up with some contrasting developments elsewhere.

The Christian Epic

By 1400 there were peoples in north-eastern Africa who had long experienced a very different cultural history from their southern or even their northern neighbours. They owed little in their ideological framework to the traditional religions of Africa and even less to Islam, but much to a devout and penetrating Christianity. Many of the outward forms of their political systems, as well as their religious concepts, customs and sense of separate identity, had by this time been Christian for nearly a thousand years.

At some time in the fourth century a philosopher of Christian Tyre, one Meropius, was travelling at the southern end of the Red Sea with the aim of improving his mind as well as those of two young relatives, Aedesius and Frumentius. Unhappily for Meropius, the Roman ship in which they were voyaging put into

Opposite: Egypt: Coptic limestone statue of the god Nilos (Third century)

an Ethiopian port at a time when the Axumites, who were now the major power at the southern end of the Red Sea, considered themselves in dispute with the Romans. Their local people boarded the Roman ship and forthwith massacred the crew, and Meropius as well. But Aedesius and Frumentius, being examples to all good children, were not found idling on board ship: on the contrary, they were preparing their lessons under the shade of a nearby tree, and were accordingly spared for service to the Axumite king, Ella Amida, the father of the Ezana who would afterwards invade Kush. Pleased with these worthy young men, Ella Amida showed them his favour. Aedesius became his cup bearer and Frumentius his secretary. And it was to be through Frumentius, afterwards raised in Alexandria to be first Bishop of Axum, that Christianity became a state religion of the Axumite kingdom, and afterwards the only religion of the Amharic Ethiopians.

We see this clearly with Ezana, Ella Amida's successor, for Ezana's coins bear the symbols of Christianity as well as those of traditional Axumite religion. Unfortunately there are as yet no certain dates for Ezana's reign. His invasion of Kush and destruction of Meroe and its sister-cities, well attested by a fine but not dated inscription, has been generally attributed to about 325, which would place the arrival of Meropius at the beginning of that century. Recently, however, it has been suggested that Ezana's conversion really fell a good deal later, perhaps in about 420, and his invasion of Kush a little after that. The point is important because the difference of a century in the destruction of Meroe must weigh heavily on any proper evaluation of the impact of Meroitic Kush upon its western and south-western neighbours. In this immediate connexion, however, we need note only that Ezana's invasion of Kush, whether in the fourth or fifth century, did not bring Christianity to the Middle Nile. The epic of Christian Nubia sprang not from Axum but from Egypt.

After Ezana's invasion, the cities of Kush appear to have passed into the hands of the Red and Black Noba upon whom Ezana had chiefly warred. Like other nomads, they took to city life and liked it: they mingled with the urban Kushites and a new culture arose from this union. Politically, the old Kushite empire fell back into its ancient provincial divisions. These were the Kush of northern Nubia, of the villages and towns south of Aswan; the Kush of middle Nubia, of the old Napatan kingdom near the fourth cataract; and the

Kush of southern Nubia, of Meroe itself. Into all these, though the details still escape us, neighbouring peoples infiltrated and gradually settled, including the Nuba of the western desert and the Blemmye of the eastern desert, these being perhaps the Black and Red Noba of Ezana's famous inscription. Prudently avoiding premature identification, archaeologists have gathered the peoples of this immediately post-Kushite culture under the safely anonymous name of X-Group.

From about the fifth century the X-Group people acquired a taste for settled life as well as the opportunity of indulging it, took over many Kushite customs and beliefs, and intermarried with Kushite townsfolk. By the sixth century they had somewhat reconstructed their three small states – northern, middle and southern – whose culture was in quite a large degree the continuation of Kush at a lower level of civilization. While the X-Group people conserved a characteristically Kushite interest in foreign goods, especially of the luxury sort, together with a nice mingling of Kushite and nomad art styles, funeral procedures and the like, they failed to recreate the literacy of the Meroitic age.

This development occurred only with the conversion of the Nubian states, whose monks at first wrote in Greek and then in Old Nubian, an achievement lessened for a later world by the lamentable loss of most of their writings. Yet a good deal is known of the conversion, while excavations in 1961-4 have had wonderfully fruitful results at Faras in the discovery, among other things, of an eleventh-century list of no fewer than twenty-seven bishops of that place, many splendid frescoes, and a fine cathedral. Like much subsequent Christian endeavour in Africa, the conversion owed more than a little to acute rivalry between two branches of the Church: not between Roman Catholics and Protestants, as in later days, but between Monophysites and Melkites, the one being under the patronage of the Emperor Justinian and the other under that of the Empress Theodora. Two missions set out from Alexandria in about 542 but the Monophysites, thanks to influence at court, managed to get the Melkites held back by the Roman governor of Upper Egypt. Their man Julian was the first to pass beyond the cataracts and arrive in Nobatia, the northernmost of the three kingdoms established on Kushite foundations by the urbanized X-Group.

Julian spent two years in Nobatia, suffering greatly from the heat like other visitors then and since, and being obliged, according to a contemporary account, to

Opposite top left: Part of a Coptic funerary stela made from limestone (Fourth century)
Top right: Detail from a third-century Coptic relief, showing a Saint holding the Cross
Bottom: Detail from a fourth-century limestone frieze, with lion and acanthus-leaf decoration

take refuge during the day 'in caverns full of water, where he sat undressed and girt only in a linen garment such as the people of the country wear'. By about 580, thanks to the labour of Julian and other missionaries, all three Nubian kingdoms had accepted Coptic or Byzantine Christianity: Nobatia in the north with its capital at Qustul and then at Faras; Makuria in the middle, reaching along the Dongola region of the Nile with its capital at Old Dongola; and Alodia (or Alwa) in the south with its capital at Soba, another old Meroitic city which lay a few miles up the Blue Nile above the latter's junction with the White Nile at Khartoum. These Nubian kingdoms were generally at peace with one another, and a union was made between Nobatia and Makuria at some time before 710.

Having become Christian in the sixth century, the Nubians remained so for many centuries of often remarkable and brilliant development in their civilization. Just how great this was could not be clearly seen, and only then in outline, until the archaeological discoveries of the 1960s that followed on an international effort to excavate and understand a large number of sites above Aswan before the waters of the High Dam closed above them. As a result of this and previous archaeological work by many hands, Adams has been able to suggest a broad chronology of Christian Nubia from the sixth to thirteenth centuries, though emphasizing that only about a dozen of more than two hundred and fifty known Christian sites in Lower Nubia, not to mention many others in Upper Nubia, can as yet be dated on the basis of direct or documentary evidence. After a brief period transitional from X-Group culture, Christian Nubia became well established soon after 600, grew strong enough to dominate Upper Egypt by 745, and entered a long period of peace and prosperity, when church-building flourished and fine arts were practised, during the ninth and tenth centuries.

During all this time these remote kingdoms on the Middle Nile were cut off from the rest of the Christian world by the Muslim occupation of Egypt (640–2). Yet they were strong enough to resist Muslim encroachment and even to threaten Muslim positions in Egypt, making a treaty with the Caliph of Bagdad in 836 and occupying southern Egypt in 962. Not until 1173 did there come the first big Muslim raid by Saracen cavalry from the north. A startling panorama of the wealth and distinction of their religious life was revealed in 1961–4 by Polish excavations at Faras (old Pachoras) under the leadership of Michalowski.

Like many other international expeditions working at that time in the tremendously rich area above Aswan, now flooded for ever by the waters of Lake Nasser rising against the new High Dam, Michalowski and his colleagues were only in the nick of time. Yet by 1964, with the waters already closing in on them, they had uncovered an outstanding Christian complex of architecture and art. This included a great church or cathedral founded probably at the end of the seventh or beginning of the eighth century, and much extended and embellished in the late ninth and early tenth. Long engulfed in dry protecting sand, its walls still gleamed with more than a hundred painted murals, many of which were rescued for the museums of Khartoum and Warsaw. Its numerous inscriptions in Old Nubian, Coptic and Greek, including a list of twenty-seven bishops of Pachoras, have thrown a vivid light on the history of Nobatia. Another and slightly earlier indication of a different kind, yet likewise pointing to the strength of Christian Nubian culture, was the suggestion in 1958 that brick ruins at 'Ain Farah, seven

Part of a Christian text, in Old Nubian, written in a fine hand using the Coptic form of the Greek alphabet

Opposite: Coptic limestone relief of the third century representing the metamorphosis of Daphne into a laurel tree

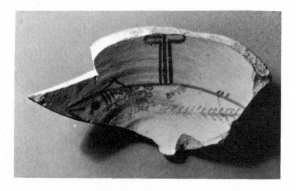

Above: Fragment of Christian Nubian ware found in the ruins of 'Ain Farah, Darfur

Right: 'Ain Farah, showing, in the foreground, the ruined building where the sherds illustrated were found, and a hilltop structure in the background. It has been suggested that these ruins were originally a Christian church and monastery, the farthest known outliers of Christian Nubian culture towards the west; this interpretation remains controversial

Opposite: Ethiopia: votive crown of Menelik II, similar to traditional crowns of the Emperors of Gondar, dedicated after his victory at Adowa (1896); from the treasure of the Cathedral of Our Lady of Sion at Axum

Above: Detail of a fine architectural carving from the Christian Nubian ruins at Faras, excavated in 1961-4 by Michalowski, and since covered by the waters of Lake Nasser

Right: Another of the pottery sherds found at 'Ain Farah

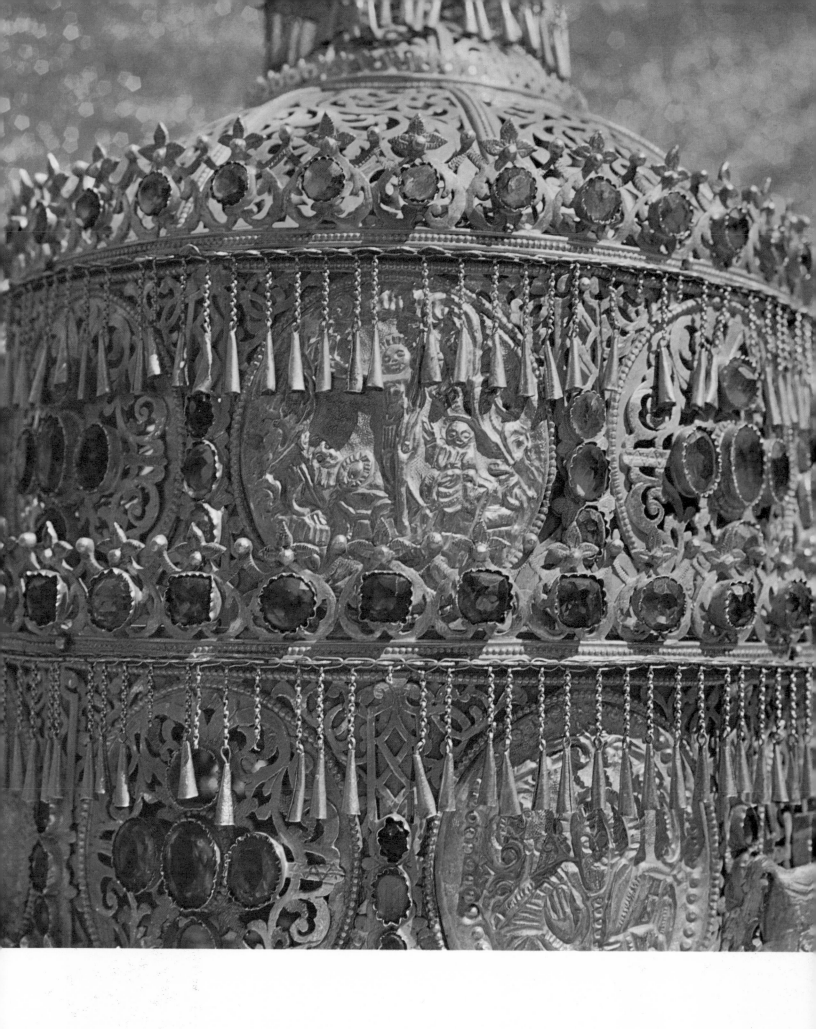

hundred miles from Faras in the hills of Darfur, were very possibly those of a Christian monastery, which may have remained in being until the fifteenth century.

Such remote monasteries as that of 'Ain Farah were the outliers of a rich urban culture. What travellers thought of these cities may be glimpsed in words reported by Maqrisi, telling the impressions of Ibn Selim al-Assuani after seeing Soba, capital of distant Alodia. 'Fine buildings, roomy houses, churches with much gold and with gardens lie in this city . . . The land is more fruitful and bigger than Makuria . . . They have much meat . . . good horses and camels. . . .'

By 1250, however, Nobatia in the north was far in decline, and in 1275 the Mamluk soldier-kings of Egypt established Muslim superiority there. Further south, in Makuria, Christianity persisted for a while longer, and for longer still in the southernmost kingdom of Alodia, overthrown by the Fung sultans of Muslim Sennar only in 1504. But from this time onward the inheritance of the Christian kings and monks of Nubia disappears rapidly from the inner lands of Africa where they had conserved it for so long. The engulfment was strangely complete, but not perhaps surprising. These monks and kings had stood for a valid and vigorous culture, that of the Nubians of the Middle Nile. Yet they were identified like the Kushites before them with the life and manners of their towns. Drawing a reasonable parallel with what happened in countries of West Africa where Muslims occupied that position, one may think that these Nubian Christians can seldom have been very sure about the loyalty of the peoples of the countryside, immersed as these must often have remained in the older beliefs of pre-Christian times. Underlying that dichotomy, too, there will have been something of the same conflict of interests as occurred in the Western Sudan. The support of monasteries, for example, implies the existence of secular labour: all round the base of the hill that supports the brick-built monastery of 'Ain Farah, in distant Darfur, there are the simple hut foundations of a numerous village population. When Muslim missionaries and invaders appeared on the scene they will surely have found willing listeners among the humble folk who laboured for the monks. And when the monks were gone, together with their literary habits and comparatively privileged way of life, their books destroyed or lost, their records ruined or consigned to the flames, there was indeed nothing left but a handful of broken pottery to suggest the Christian beginnings of this place.

The Nubian kingdoms vanished from the scene: un-honoured and unsung, or almost so, until the twentieth century. Yet Ethiopia survived both as an independent kingdom and a Christian culture, though not easily. Like Nobatia, Makuria and Alodia, it was cut off from the Mediterranean by the Muslim conquests of the seventh century. A hundred years later the Ethiopians had even lost their Red Sea ports to the soldiers of the caliph. But they still possessed good mountain country in which to rally and recuperate. They re-took their ports in the tenth century and became once more a maritime power, fought off their pagan neighbours of the inland country and eventually, though at a date that is far from certain, attained a new strength and stability. During these 'dark ages' their capital was moved from Axum to Lasta by the first of a new line of rulers called the Zagwe. There began the gradual transformation of the old Axumite empire into its Amharic successor. Famous churches were built in Lasta by King Lalibela, great hollowed monuments of solid rock of which the largest, the Church of the Redeemer of the World, is a hundred feet long and seventy-five feet wide, its interior divided into five cavernous aisles.

Overthrown in about 1270, the Zagwe dynasty was followed by another line of kings claiming descent from Solomon. In fact, however, the first of these Solomonic kings was Yekuno Amlac, prince of the inland Ethiopian province of Shoa; and it is from now onwards that a distinctively Amharic culture becomes dominant. The capital is shifted from Lasta in the centre to the less precipitous land of Shoa to the southward. There is a rebirth of learning and literature. Not only are Greek and Coptic religious works translated into Ge'ez, often embellished with fine illumination, but there is also a beginning of the writing of history. Biographies of local noblemen are made. Most striking of all, the *Kebra Nagast*, the Glory of the Kings, an often legendary history of the Solomonic rulers of Ethiopia, is composed in Ge'ez. More and more contemporary chronicles are put into writing by court scribes and monks. Prominent among the kings who preside over this energetic growth of a truly national culture and self-consciousness are Amda Sion (1314–44) and Zara Yaqob (1434–68), warriors and reformers who carry on the wars against Muslim raiders or neighbours with more than usual success, while ruling at home with an iron hand.

'In the reign of our king Zara Yaqob,' recalls a chronicle written soon after 1500, 'there was great

Opposite: Ethiopia: Icon covering a door in the church of Debra Berhan (Abbey of Light) at Gondar, built by Yasu the Great (1682–1706)

137

terror and great fear in all the people of Ethiopia, on account of the severity of his justice and of his authoritarian rule.' The people of the ancient city of Axum are described as welcoming the king 'with rejoicing'; and they did not go unrewarded. 'After arriving within the walls of Axum, the king had much gold brought to him, and this he scattered in carpets spread along his route as far as the city gate. The amount of gold was more than a hundred ounces. . . .' More information now becomes available because European travellers began visiting this distant Christian ally. The first such traveller was probably a Papal delegate entrusted with the task, an impossible one as it proved, of submitting the Ethiopian church to the authority of Rome rather than Alexandria; while an Italian painter, Niccolò Brancaleone, arrived a few years later and decorated many churches, getting into trouble at one point for painting the infant Jesus on Mary's left arm, considered less honourable in Africa than the right arm, but generally exercising an influence on the development of Ethiopian art.

These stray visitors were followed by others from Portugal, Pedro de Covilham in 1488, seeking Prester John, and several more soon afterwards. Of these the most useful to history was Fernão Alvares, who sojourned in Ethiopia between 1520 and 1526 and, as the chaplain of a Portuguese diplomatic expedition, wrote an invaluable description of what he saw and heard. In 1541 the fourth son of Vasco da Gama led a military expedition to the succour of an Ethiopian king then facing disaster at the hands of a strong Muslim invader from Adel, a state which neighboured Ethiopia on the east.

Having weathered so many years of danger and assault, Ethiopia came to rest on strong foundations. They were foundations of a special kind, once more emphasizing this mountain country's cultural separation from the life of its neighbours. They supported a structure of lord-and-vassal stratification which was far more rigid than elsewhere, and gave Ethiopia a remarkably 'feudal' social atmosphere and appearance. At the head of the state was an anointed king surrounded by a court of priests and officials and army commanders who were drawn from ruling families. Like feudal sovereigns, this monarch could seldom afford to remain for long in any one place. He had repeatedly to move his armed camp from one region to another, exacting fealty from nobles and governors, ensuring their payment of tribute and participation in military campaigns, while exiling rivals within his own family to the chilly eminence of hills with flat tops but very steep sides.

The result was a close-knit system of rights and duties into which every significant person in the state was bound. 'In this feudal country', wrote a French traveller of the nineteenth century whose words apply as well to earlier times, 'men are united by an infinity of ties which would count for nothing in Europe. They live together in a reciprocal dependence and solidarity which they value highly and consider a matter of pride, and which influences all they do.' This highly personal system of rule, matched to the needs of a sturdy people often fighting for their lives, proved strong enough to endure through all of Ethiopia's many times of trouble and invasion. It was essentially against this system that the Italian invaders of the 1930s were to strike their heads, and only in the wake of the Second World War would there be serious inroads into its all-pervading influence. What is perhaps most impressive about the long tale of Ethiopian history is precisely this resilient continuity of attitude and action since the remote times of Axum.

ሳን ጸይታን ሕግ ወለከ ተጸለውዎ ወእዘዙ ግ ቲ በሥርዓት ወእኴንዴ ዋ ወስረርፐ ወአጸሀት ዋ ለገበር ይእቲ መገስ ሉ ከመ እኔትሀክሂ

Ge'ez script from an Ethiopian manuscript

Opposite: An Ethiopian landscape near Axum

Church of St George, one of the churches at Lalibela
hewn from the living rock, a monument of the powerful
Zagwe dynasty of the twelfth and thirteenth centuries

One of the castles at Gondar, the Ethiopian capital built by
Emperor Basilides (1632–65)

In the Name of Allah

Of the headlong rush of Islam through North Africa and Spain the dates speak almost for themselves. They are dramatic dates; even, at first sight, impossibly so. On 16 July 622, four men travelling on two camels quit Mecca for another obscure Arabian town, Medina. Within as few as twenty-two years the movement of religious and political revolution thus set going by Muhamad had won the whole of Arabia and Syria, engulfed Egypt, seized the Byzantine fortress of Babylon at the southern apex of the delta of the Nile, captured Alexandria, and was everywhere preparing new departures.

Expeditions swept eastward and westward. In 670 'Uqba ibn Nafi established Muslim rule over most of Ifriqiya – Tunisia – and founded Kairouan, weaving with confident prophetic hands the fabric of an entirely new civilization, rejecting what displeased him, suppressing what offended him, and turning what still seemed valuable, such as the Roman pillars and capitals embodied in the Friday mosque of Kairouan, to Muslim use and purpose. By 683 Muslim pioneers had seen the ocean waves of the Atlantic. In 711 Tariq thrust his way into Spain across the straits and northward through the Spanish kingdom of the Visigoths. A year later Musa ibn Nusayr went further still. In 713 'Abd al-Azziz ibn Musa rode beyond the Tagus and harried into central Portugal at the head of battle-hardened troops. A year later again, 714, raiding Muslims were far into France and watering their horses in the Upper Rhône; and it was not until 732, in the decisive battle of Poitiers near the Loire, that Charles Martel at last turned back the flood of conquest and incursion, defeating 'Abd al-Rahman al-Ghafiq and opening, but under Muslim pressure and example, a new period of history in western Europe.

Yet the really impressive aspect of these and other advances over many hundreds of miles to west and east was not, after all, their speed. Raiding bands of highly trained cavalry could always burst through frontiers and city gates if their leaders were sufficiently determined, and this the early Muslim leaders almost always were. Far more remarkable were the political stability and economic recovery which followed in their wake. In Africa, Spain and Asia these victories laid the groundwork for a civilization that could and did unite men of religion, learning, and philosophy from the Mediterranean to Arabia, from the plains of the Western Sudan to the hills of China, and bore a light of tolerance and social progress through centuries when Europe, impoverished, provincialized, and almost illiterate, lay in distant battle and confusion.

But when one pauses to enquire how it could possibly come about that slender regiments of hard-riding Arabs or Berbers were capable of founding a civilization such as this, a number of interesting if as yet insufficiently explained phenomena need to be remembered. To begin with, the Muslim conquests came in the wake of long insecurity and turmoil. Two centuries earlier the barbarian riders of the north had shattered the great imperial systems which had governed Roman Africa, the Near East, and Western Europe since times long before. Yet these newcomers, Vandals and Goths, Franks and Visigoths, had failed either to engraft themselves into the Roman system and relaunch it under new management, or to build any other wide system of their own. In their attitudes and group behaviour they remained much what they had always been: men of clannish loyalty for whom the notions of a universal culture, a culture capable of embracing many peoples and glowing with the vision of a new society, long remained beyond their grasp. It was by intellectual and spiritual limitations such as these that they differed greatly from their Muslim rivals; and it was largely because of this kind of difference, one may think, that the Muslim cause triumphed where its enemies faltered and failed.

The difference goes back to the beginnings of Islam. Thus the 'Constitution of Medina', either an original document composed soon after the *Hijrah* or 'migration' from Mecca to Medina or a conflation of several early documents, lays it down that the Muslims 'are a single community distinct from other people'. But distinct, be it noted, by religious conviction and not by clan or national origin. This is a central point. For what Muslim generals could offer the peoples over whom they came to rule was not only subjection to a foreign victor but also the promise of membership in a new and broad community, the *umma* of Islam, within whose boundaries all men could be at least theoretically of equal dignity and worth. The promise, perhaps needless to say, was not always kept. For a long time there remained a powerfully exclusive sentiment among the victorious Arabs, and this the Caliphate encouraged by trying to keep the Arabs as a military class apart from their conquered peoples. Yet as soon as

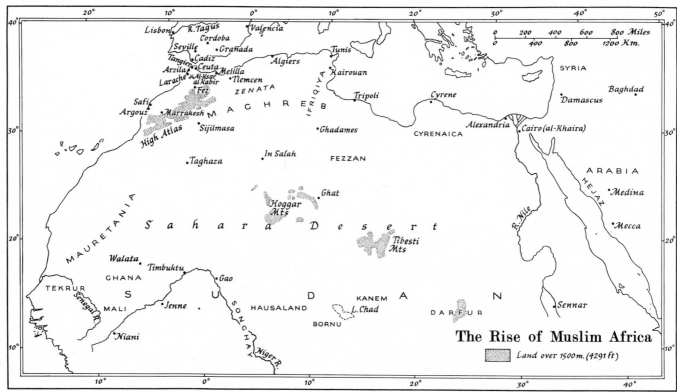

The Rise of Muslim Africa
Land over 1500m. (4291 ft)

conquered peoples became converted or acceptable within the *umma,* as many of them gradually did, Muslim rulers could appear not simply as conquerors but also as revolutionaries who could point the way to a better order of society.

Only along these lines can one probably hope to explain how the faith of their Arab conquerors could take root and flourish among peoples who owed nothing to the Arabs, knew little of the Arabs and seldom or never spoke Arabic, and who had often thought of the Arabs as their rivals or foes. Only from this approach, perhaps, can one begin to grasp the attraction of Islam for heterogeneous or harried populations which had long lacked a common focus or had never achieved one. Any parallel between Muslim imperialism and the European imperialism of later times would seriously miss the point. The latter remained – as, to some extent, the conquests of Rome had also remained – a foreign imposition, but the Muslim systems gradually acquired local garb and became the full possession of those they had enclosed.

Even the egalitarian message of Islam could have availed for little without the measure of reality that followed. But within a hundred years this civilization had established a community of ideas among a host of diverse populations. Out of this, of course, there flowed the political divisions of Islam. Having rooted in many soils, Islam flowered in many variants. Local loyalties soon thrust up through the surface of a system which, for all its ideological promises, could in fact do little or nothing to change the inner structure of the societies it affected. These local loyalties found local spokesmen. They argued their differences in terms of religious orthodoxy, but the real ground of difference was less theological or doctrinal than social or geographic. Such fissures became critical during the rule of the fourth caliph, 'Ali, in spite of the fact that 'Ali had married Fatima, the Prophet's daughter. A dissenting group emerged in Syria in 657 when Mu'awiya, governor of that country, became 'Ali's successful rival. From this there came an enduring schism between the Sunnis, who accepted Mu'awiya and his Ummayad successors, and the Shi'ites, who did not: yet all remained Muslim and continued, at least against the rest of the world, to assert their common identity. Another split with a basically social origin occurred when a group of nomads rejected 'Ali's claims and established the Kharidjite brotherhood, a puritanical movement of the oases and distant plains which denounced the easy-going tendencies of the towns and cities, and was to become of some importance in northern and western Africa.

Opposite: The minaret of the Friday Mosque of Kairouan, founded in 670
Overleaf: Modern Cairo seen from the site of ancient Fustat, where the earliest Byzantine settlement lay. Between the two may be seen the area where the earliest Islamic settlement was established. Beyond them are the later Citadel and the Muhamad Aly mosque

A hundred years later the fissuring process repeated itself, in the field of politics, when the centre of greatest Muslim power shifted from Damascus to Bagdad with the emergence of the Abbasid caliphate. Within another hundred years a political map of Islam shows the *umma*, the Islamic community considered in its widest sense, as divided among many local dynasties, the most ambitious of which were the Abbasids in the east and the Ummayads in North Africa and Spain. This east-west opposition deepened in the tenth century with the rise of the Fatimids, who drew their initial strength from the Berbers of central Algeria but soon, reaching out for power, pushed their rule far to the east. In 969 the Fatimid armies replaced Abbasid rule in Egypt, and then in Syria and Hejaz. In 973 the Fatimid caliph Al-Mu'izz shifted his capital from the Maghreb to Egypt, and established himself in a new city, al-Khaira, next door to old Fustat (itself the site of the Egyptian Babylon of Byzantine times); and Cairo began its long and often spectacular career.

The Fatimid caliphs ruled in Egypt for two centuries, but soon lost their North African and then their Syrian-Arabian lands. So far as the first of these were concerned, the Fatimids had forfeited Berber support in moving eastward. New Berber kingdoms appeared in Tunisia and Algeria, ruled by chieftains of the Sanhaja confederation. Looking for a means of removing these chieftains, the Fatimid caliph in Cairo worked an appalling revenge on the countries from which his ancestors had come. He urged a group of Beduin nomads under the leadership of the Bani Hilal to invade those fertile western lands. Disastrously, these trotted on their way in dust-trailing bands of hungry raiders, settled like locusts (as Ibn Khaldun was later to describe them) in the watered meadows and orchards of Ifriqiya, and began that profound if painful process of Arabization which was to submerge Berber culture in much of Tunisia and Algeria. Westward in Morocco, the Bani Hilal and their companions had little or no effect. Here the deepening of the *umma* into local variants had already taken another important turn with the rise of a southern Berber movement of a different sort. Unlike the Fatimid Berbers, who had gone eastward to the blessings of city life, the Almoravid Berbers of the Mauretanian grasslands were inspired by quite other ideas.

They were inspired by those profoundly moving though Utopian ideas of equality and justice set in being up and down the Muslim world by the Prophet and his immediate followers, but never afterwards entirely forgotten. Like other Muslim reformers before and since, the Almoravids sought to overcome the stratified and fissured nature of the society whose benefits they desired to possess; or this, at any rate, formed the idealist side of the preaching they followed. Like the others, they failed; and it is worth pausing for a moment to consider the reasons for their failure. This failure would repeat itself among other Africans in later times. Centuries afterwards, in the Western Sudan, the great reforming movement associated with the Fulani leader Uthman dan Fodio would draw its inspiration from an Utopian picture of the Abbasid Era of the tenth and eleventh centuries, seeing in it the prototype of that 'Rightly-Guided Caliphate' in which all Muslims had once enjoyed equality and justice. But the Almoravids, living in the very wake of the Abbasid era, knew better than this. For them the 'golden age' of Islam could not possibly lie in Abbasid times. Rather it lay during the earliest years when, in von Grunebaum's words, 'the ten years of the Prophet's rule in Medina and perhaps the thirty years following his death' were conceived as having formed 'an age in which human society had come as near perfection as could be hoped for . . .'

The golden age was an illusion. Islam possessed no ideological tool that was adequate to the levelling of a society embarked upon a course of deepening internal division between rich and poor, weak and strong. Even the first Caliph after the Prophet, 'Umar, who reigned between 634 and 644, had found himself obliged to recognize hierarchical differences among the faithful. These differences became sharper as Islam faced the wear and challenge of power. By the outset of the ninth century, as we are told by a somewhat later writer, Ibn al-Faqih, the Muslim societies of the Near East were divided into four classes: 'the ruler, whom merit has placed in the foremost rank; the vizier, distinguished by wisdom and domination; the high-placed ones, whom wealth has placed aloft; and the middle classes who are attached to the other three classes by their culture; while the rest of mankind is mere scum who know nothing but food and sleep.'

The scum no doubt objected; their opinions were no longer asked. What the Rightly-Guided Caliphate was really like, in those Abbasid times which formed an age of happiness for Muslim reformers nine centuries later, may be seen in an eleventh-century description of the great historian al-Biruni. Hierarchical distinctions had in fact reached an extreme of social prejudice and privilege. 'When the Abbasid rulers had decorated their assistants, friends and enemies indiscriminately with vain titles . . . the empire perished, for in this they went beyond all reasonable limits . . . [For after] the Caliphs had bestowed titles, there were other men who wanted the same titles and who knew how to carry their point by bribery. Thus it became necessary a second time to create a distinction between this [aspiring] class and those who were [already] attached to the court, so the Caliphs bestowed triple titles, adding besides the title *Shah-in-Shah*. In this way the matter became utterly opposed to common sense, and clumsy in the highest degree, so that he who mentions them gets tired [of reciting their titles] almost before he has begun, he who writes to them loses his time in writing, while he who addresses them runs the risk of missing the hour for prayer.'

Behind this towering structure of titled ranks there lay impoverishment for the mass of the people, for 'the scum who know nothing but food and sleep'. And it was this 'progressive impoverishment of the country', once more in von Grunebaum's words, that provided 'the mainspring of "revolutionary Shi'ism"', so that political and social conflicts were again fought out in religious terms. Here and elsewhere and at other times, established religion had become a bulwark of the rich and wealthy; and lesser people were not fooled. 'No, certainly I shall not pray to God as long as I am poor', wrote one of their spokesmen around AD 1000. 'For why should I pray? Am I mighty? Have I a palace, horses, rich clothes and golden belts? While I possess not a single inch of earth, it would be pure hypocrisy to pray.' Nine hundred years later, celebrating the virtues of the Abbasid era, Uthman dan Fodio and his companions would ignore the views of 'the scum' of those early times, their memory and their protests drowned in the torrent of the centuries. But the Almoravids were very close to the scene of Abbasid crisis, and it was essentially against this kind of crisis, though occurring in the westerly regions of Islam, that they carried their revolt.

Not the first or last of their kind, these lean and hardy countrymen looked out from barren pastures and saw the promise of a better life. Under their leader Ibn Yasin, a man of Sijilmasa, they identified their vision of relief from want and hunger with a reduction of their neighbours' comfort; and here again, like the earlier Muslim conquerors, they found a response from peasant peoples who laboured under the yoke of local lords and landowners. For they overran the fertile plains of Morocco within a few years and then, invited across the water by Andalusian Muslims facing Christian armies, within another twenty years brought all of Muslim Spain within their power.

Islam south of the Sahara was to owe nothing to Arab conquest but much to Berber influence. Except for the Almoravid raids and ravagings of the eleventh century, there was no movement of North African conquest until the Moroccan invasion of Songhay in 1591. Neither of these major incursions did anything to help the cause of Islam. On the contrary, both tended to undermine it. Yet Islam spread gradually and persistently in the Sudan westward of Lake Chad from the tenth century onwards, being partially barred from the Eastern Sudan only by distance or the Christian kingdoms of the Middle Nile.

This south-westward spread took shape in a slow extension of the Islamic community to include the settled populations of some of the leading cities and market centres. The pattern for this had almost certainly existed in times long before the Muslim era, since the trans-Saharan trading system of Phoenician and even pre-Phoenician times had no doubt planted little Berber communities in the markets of the south. But now the difference was that Islam could more effectively bind all these communities together, whether in the Western Sudan, among the oasis relay-stations of the desert country, or in North Africa. Increasingly, the trans-Saharan trade came to be conducted by Muslims of many ethnic origins, forming a vast and intricate network of exchange that brought wealth and power to the rulers of many African states, and fed the western world for centuries with goods of prime value.

To what extent did Islam find converts among the mass of West Africans? Here the picture is somewhat different from elsewhere. Briefly, one can distinguish four main periods in the history of Muslim influence. There is first of all a long period of slowly expanding trade through Muslim enterprise, accompanied by the gradual conversion of Sudanese traders by their Berber partners from the Sahara. Islam reaches the markets of the Western Sudan by at least the ninth century. But it makes little initial impact. The rulers of Ghana do not accept Islam as one of their state religions. Only at the beginning of the eleventh century are there a few such conversions, the earliest of any

Opposite: The tomb at Gao, on the Middle Niger, of the great Songhay emperor Askia Muhamad

Interior of the tomb of Askia Muhamad

The Great Mosque of Jenne at dusk

importance of which we know being that of the king of Gao, traditionally in 1010, followed by that of the king of Kanem-Bornu in 1086. These are tactical conversions, motivated as much by commercial convenience as by appreciation of the political and religious achievements and teachings of Islam. They do not touch the people of the countryside, while even the people of the towns whose rulers have accepted Islam regard this innovation with a doubtful eye, at the same time holding fast to their own traditional faiths in a duality of views that will continue. In its time and place, the same duality will apply to much of the African history of Christianity as well.

A second period begins with the thirteenth century. It follows a long confusion which includes the Almoravid invasions, the fall of Ghana, the rise and rivalry of the successor states of Ghana, and the emergence of Mali. But with Sundiata (c. 1235–60) the expansion of Islam begins to be enmeshed with the expansion of Mali. Under Mansa Musa (c. 1312–37) the correspondence is clear. Musa becomes caliph of 'the western parts'; and Islam now appears as the great religion of progressive government. It opens the way to a literate bureaucracy, to effective diplomatic links with distant powers, and to the inner reorganization of power and authority along lines which cut across the separatist loyalties of traditional religion. Out of all this modernizing trend there comes the foundation of solid schools of Islamic learning in Timbuktu, Niani, Jenne and elsewhere, schools that will flourish for three hundred years and will attract Muslim scholars from many countries and many trends of thought.

At the same time Islam remains the great religion of commerce. From Mali the Dyula traders push out along the trading trails. They are staunch promoters of Islam, the religion which has not only assured them of their livelihood through the traders of the Sahara, but has also given them an up-to-date and efficient set of commercial customs and credit procedures such as have not been available before. By 1400 and probably much earlier, strong little Muslim trading communities exist in most of the important market centres of West Africa right down to the coast itself. They still make few converts outside their own kind, but they form pressure-groups which grow into an influential component of West African life.

This long period of steady expansion continues, if with many ups and downs, until the Moroccan invasion of Songhay at the end of the sixteenth century. For reasons we shall look into at a further point, the whole trading network of northern and western Africa is now badly disrupted and partly ruined. There follows, in a third period, an anti-Muslim reaction which is also an anti-town reaction. The peoples of the countryside, true to the old faiths, raise their heads again and take the lead, among them many whom the town-based Islamic empires have thrust down into a servile condition. This continues until the eighteenth century when a fourth period opens with the revival of Islam by bold leaders and ambitious peoples, a revival which continues in one form or another until it is sharply checked by European colonial invasion.

Historically, then, the influence of Islam in West Africa must be considered, aside from its spiritual aspect, as having primary significance in two main fields: in the techniques of commerce, and in those of the government of cities, states and empires of growing power and importance. In both respects, moreover, Islam may be seen as having acted as an effective solvent of traditional society, repeatedly blurring the lines of ethnic separatism, displacing the old 'tribal' equalities with new hierarchical structures and servitudes, and generally, with an impact increasingly noticeable after the sixteenth century, deepening the horizontal stratification of West African society.

In all this, one may repeat, the Almoravid invasions were an eccentric interruption, not to be repeated for another five centuries. Perhaps that is the chief reason why the great Ummayad period in North Africa, the period of early Muslim development of this memorable trading system across the desert, is remembered with such honour and respect by the Muslim schoolmen of West Africa, and why, for example, the mufti of Bobo-Dyulasso, who was born as late as 1897, should have noted the downfall of the Ummayads as marking the end of something like a golden age. Yet the trading system that was so greatly extended during the early centuries of Islam in western Africa – with its main routes reopened to half the world, with the needs of camel transport ever more widely understood, with the wells of the Sahara constantly repaired and multiplied – brushed aside the Almoravid interruption and continued to gain in strength until the end of the sixteenth century. Then it finally levelled off in face of maritime competition and gradually was lost to sight in modern times.

Islam may therefore claim to have brought much to West Africa. A commercial map applying to the period

Opposite: Prayer in the Great Mosque at Jenne

of 1300–1600 shows many regions of the western continent, north or south of the desert, as being directly or indirectly linked with a worldwide commercial system built by men who recognized the essential unity of Islam, no matter how much they might at times contest each other's political authority. Throughout the Middle Ages it seemed natural to the religious leaders in Mecca to nominate a supreme representative or caliph in the Western Sudan, choosing for the purpose whatever powerful man might present himself from that quarter. And to the scholars of Cairo, Damascus, and beyond it seemed likewise natural that Mali, largest of the Sudanese empires, should be reckoned among the most important states of the Muslim world.

As elsewhere within the *umma*, a widening of conversion led to local variation and diversity of form. Although West African Muslims have often shown themselves of strict orthodoxy to the Quran, there was never a time when the actual practice of Islam did not differ, and sometimes differ greatly, from the customs of Egypt and North Africa. Ibn Batuta, visiting Mali in the fourteenth century, was shocked by such things as the nudity of unmarried women and the sociable self-confidence of wives, while the great brotherhoods of Islam such as the Qadiriyya or Tijaniyya have often taken special forms in the Western Sudan. On top of this, or rather underlying it, there was the constant rivalry and conflict between Islam and the religions of West Africa. Some converts became devout Muslims. Many more settled with their conscience by a more or less uneasy compromise. After 1010 King Kossoi of Gao felt it wise, and no doubt he also felt it necessary, to maintain non-Muslim ceremonies at his court. But this persisted. Even great rulers who became caliphs were obliged to do as much. The prestigious Askia Muhamad of Songhay (1493–1528) also supported non-Muslim ceremonies and festivals at his court. Such customs were similarly continued under another powerful Songhay ruler, Askia Dawud (1549–83). Those who came before him were expected to prostrate themselves and sprinkle their heads with dust, a custom already noted with distaste by the visiting Ibn Batuta two centuries earlier. Upbraided for this by a devout imam of Timbuktu, who observed to the Askia that he must be mad to allow such heathen customs at his court, Dawud is said to have replied: 'I am not mad, but I rule over mad, impious and arrogant folk. It is for this reason that I play the madman . . .'

We have already touched on this dichotomy between the Muslim towns and the non-Muslim or anti-Muslim countryside. Like other rulers in the Western Sudan, Dawud was faced in 'the Muslim question' with the most serious of all his many problems of political power. However devoutly orthodox he himself might have wished to be, however much he may have appreciated the literary, administrative and political advantages of Islam over traditional religion, he could not ignore the delicate balance of statesmanship that was alone capable of upholding him between the two sides. He had to consider on one hand his North African alliances and the interests of his towns and cities, while not forgetting, or not too far, the contrary alliances and interests of all those rural peoples over whom he also ruled, and often with a heavy hand. In this Dawud succeeded, like other outstanding rulers before him; but more than one Sudanese monarch came to grief in leaning too far one way or the other.

By contrast with this continually ramifying influence in the west, Islam in East Africa achieved no more than local influence. Yet what it did achieve was done with a memorable distinction. Conversion of island and coastal populations from Somalia in the north to Mozambique in the south, a process which had got into its stride by the twelfth century, helped to carry these trading settlements into closer partnership with the whole Indian Ocean community, instructed these East Africans in the manners and methods of long-range commerce and of ruling by the profits of trade, and endowed their developing civilization of the seaboard with a notably Islamic accent of its own. At one or two points, moreover, Arab settlement was sufficiently dense to mark a brief but interesting non-African presence. This may be seen, perhaps better than anywhere else, in the ruins of the once majestic Husuni palace on Kilwa Island. Believed by Chittick, its recent excavator, to have been built between about 1260 and 1330, this large place of commerce, residence and leisure on the brink of the Indian Ocean was equipped with lavish sanitary arrangements and an octagonal open-air bath, evidently supplied with fresh water, which has reminded archaeologists of Abbasid examples. For the most part, however, Arab settlers were quickly lost by intermarriage among Swahili or other communities. These accepted Islam and came to value greatly their membership in the Muslim world. But they retained their own languages, evolved their own literature, and built an urban civilization which remained emphatically their own.

Opposite: Dating from the fourteenth century and built in *pisé* and timber, the mosque at Jenne has been repaired and restored on many occasions up to the present century
Overleaf left: The Great Mosque at East African Kilwa; founded in the thirteenth century and extensively rebuilt by Sultan Muhamad (*c.* 1421–42)
Overleaf right: Rhodesia: ruins at Naletale. Many of the great stone structures of pre-European Rhodesia were embellished, as here, with ornamental patterns

4 Tropical Achievement

The great 'middle period' of the African Iron Age and its many cultures and political systems throughout Africa south of the Sudan – The kingdoms of the Rift Valley, of the stone-building peoples of the central-southern plateau, of the Luba-Lunda and other Congo states, and of the peoples of West Africa in the sixteenth century

A Mature Iron Age

'It seemed a perfect Arcadia', wrote Joseph Thomson when first traversing the green and temperate lands that lie to the north of Lake Nyasa. 'Imagine a magnificent grove of bananas, laden with bunches of fruit, each of which would form a man's load, growing on a perfectly level plain from which all weeds, garbage, and things unsightly are carefully cleared away.

'Dotted here and there are a number of immense shady sycamores, with branches each almost as large as a separate tree. At every few paces are charmingly neat circular huts, with conical roofs, and walls hanging out all round with the clay worked prettily into rounded bricks, and daubed symmetrically with spots . . .'

Perhaps the reality was less idyllic, as reality tends to be when looked at closely. Yet Thomson's travels took him near to the land of the Nyakyusa, and not even close inspection in modern times has altogether removed the Nyakyusa from Arcadia, or at any rate from something very like it. These are the people, after all, of whom Monica Wilson has reported a firm and primary attachment to *ukwangela*, the 'enjoyment of good company', the 'mutual aid and sympathy which spring from personal friendship' and imply 'urbane manners and a friendliness which expresses itself in eating and drinking together; not only merry conversation, but also discussion between equals, which the Nyakyusa regard as the principal form of education.'

Not all Iron Age peoples can have possessed such geniality and tolerance as the Nyakyusa, whose good fortune counted a fine and fertile countryside as well as immunity from the ruinous horrors of the East Coast slave trade in the nineteenth century. Others lived in harsh country and hungered every year, harried their neighbours or were harried in return, exacting tribute or being obliged to pay it, engulfed and barbarized in wars of migration and restless movement as northern peoples swept southward, or southern peoples thrust to the north. Yet the picture of old Africa as predominantly brutal and chaotic in its manners remains so widely accepted by the world at large – even to the point where many who question this picture are inclined to do so with a self-excusing air – that it may be good to remember the Nyakyusa and their love of peaceful argument, genial manners, and tolerance of error. They have not been unique in having these attitudes.

How far is the term 'Mature Iron Age' permissible? There is as yet no generally agreed periodization of African history such as exists for Europe with its convenient parcelling into Antiquity, Middle Ages, Renaissance and the rest. But the interpretation of African history, and its ordering into a meaningful sequence of events, requires a phasing process as much as any other history. So far as continental Africa is concerned – largely, Africa south of the Sahara – the thousand years before about AD 1000 were the period of the installation and gradual spread of initial Iron Age societies. This period may reasonably be called an Early Iron Age. In or around AD 1000 there occurs a series of events or developments, not confined to one or other of the regions of sub-Saharan Africa, which mark a change to a new period, although the terminal date is no more satisfactory than other dates of the same kind, and calls for as many reservations. By AD 1000 the North African states had long ceased to be primitive Iron Age societies. So had some of the societies of the Western Sudan, while Early Iron Age describes the Christian kingdoms of Nubia and Ethiopia no better. In general, though, a notably large number of societies in most regions had developed by about AD 1000 to the point where they could embark on forms of organization which were not only new, but were also a far-reaching realization of the potential which had been inherent within earlier forms. These were, in short, mature forms; and the gradual attainment of this maturity was carried into many fields of enterprise and effort.

This growing maturity of form is manifest in many directions. By 1400, for example, there were sculptors in wood, ivory, metal and terracotta in many African lands whose conceptual grasp of contemporary thought and belief had carried them to remarkable and daring experiments and styles. To be sure, the Mature Iron Age societies which produced such artists were still enclosed within an economy of subsistence, modified only by a varying though never dominant production for exchange. There was no revolutionary break. Yet these societies had mastered all the technical and ideological problems essential to their survival and could now, with a general development which gathered strength after about AD 1000, move towards fresh growth and even relative abundance. This they did in a number of ways.

They developed their methods of tropical or subtropical cultivation. They extended their systems of irrigation and of soil-conservation where these were needed. They brought into the realm of widespread knowledge a host of herbal cures. They became skilled in mining. By about 1500, Mauny tells us, the miners of West Africa had produced perhaps as much as 3500 tons of gold (and would produce as much again in 1500–1900); and they had done it, so far all the evidence shows, by methods of prospecting, shaft-sinking, extraction and refinement that were technical achievements of their own. In Southern Rhodesia, according to Summers, 'there is scarcely a modern gold mine . . . which is not on the site of an "ancient working"', adding that 'it has been deduced that originally the zone from the surface down to about 20 feet was exceptionally rich in gold, and it seems very probable that immense quantities were exported.' Copper was another important metal for noble decoration and exchange, and was greatly mined at many places; so was tin, enabling good brass alloys to be made; while iron

working, with the exception of a few rare groups such as Bushmen and the Guanche of the Canary Islands who had remained in a Stone Age culture, seems to have been practised by every people who could find the ore.

Being pre-scientific, these societies were still the home of magic and enchantment. They adopted magical or supernatural explanations for real phenomena they could not otherwise elucidate. Such explanations became interwoven with their religions, just as their religions were inseparably part of their process of social crystallization and self-identification. Magical and supernatural beliefs, in short, were necessary parts of the 'social cement' which held these societies together. This being so, they projected *systems* of belief, thought, and behaviour. That is why it is almost always wrong to conceive of Iron Age Africa as submitted to a chaotic or haphazard wizardry. On the contrary, Iron Age Africa was almost always submitted to a systematic wizardry having hard-and-fast limits, co-ordinates and rules. While they might temper this pre-scientific 'science' of community relations with a nicely shrewd scepticism – well displayed in the Niger delta proverb which recalls that once a spirit grows too violent, 'people can tell him the wood he is made of' – these societies depended for their survival on such rules being thoroughly understood and strictly applied. Nothing was punished so severely as their abuse: it was precisely for abuse of the rules of magical and supernatural belief and behaviour that witches were tormented.

Looking back on the way these communities were ordered, one may sometimes be as struck by the blind or squalid cruelty with which such rules could be applied as by the torments and ordeals of what Bishop Stubbs, but without irony, used to call 'the dear delightful Middle Ages' of Europe. Iron Age Africa was clearly not a paradise. Yet to isolate its darker side as evidence of unusual cruelty or natural human inferiority would be even more misleading than to suppose that the European Middle Ages knew only racks and thumb screws. If anything, the comparison between Africa and Europe is likely to be in Africa's favour. Throughout the medieval period most African forms of government were undoubtedly more representative than their European contemporaries; most African wars were less costly in life and property; and most African ruling groups were less predatory. So far as the comparison has any value, daily life in medieval Europe was likely to be far more hazardous or disagreeable for the common man and his wife.

Opposite: Top of an iron staff (*Oshun*) with a sculpture of a bird, possibly a swan, wrought from a single piece of iron. The staff, which is 4ft 7in. long, was a portable altar used for Ifa, a popular divinity cult

All these things, in any case, were part of their social context and have to be viewed as such. One might even say about Africa, if one wished to moralize, that they were a possibly unavoidable part of the price that had to be paid for man's being able to populate and master the arts of survival and expansion in this most huge and difficult continent. However that may be, the work of populating and mastering Africa was largely done by the later centuries of Iron Age maturity, a large and many-sided achievement in adaptation, new discovery, and bold initiative that may well be seen as the central and imposing contribution of Africans to man's general mastery of nature and the world.

Rift Valley Kingdoms

Early Iron Age cultures appeared in eastern and south-central Africa within a few centuries of their expansion along the Middle Nile and in northern Ethiopia, indicating a very rapid development of metal-using techniques once the necessary skills were known. Mere southward diffusion from Kush or Axum is probably too simple an explanation for this revolutionary advance. Correspondences between early metal-using cultures in eastern and central-south Africa do indeed point to a common source for all of them, but the probability here is that diffusion of technical knowledge from the north was accompanied by local invention. At all events these peoples had established a large number of farming settlements in the East African highlands, often using stone for their hut foundations, by the fifth or sixth century AD and perhaps earlier.

In later centuries, though probably not until after about AD 1300, these sedentary farming peoples were much disturbed, moved around and changed in their cultures by complex population movements on a major scale. A number of Bantu-speaking peoples seem to have dispersed in a generally southward and south-westward direction from the area of the Tana and Juba rivers on the fringes of modern Kenya and Somalia, although one tradition has it that they originated near Mount Kilimanjaro. Other Bantu-speaking peoples such as the Chaga are said to have originated there too. One authority places the arrival in central Kenya of the Embu, for instance, in about 1425, and of the Kikuyu in the Fort Hall area of Kenya in about 1545. To these Bantu migrations there were added many others by a number of non-Bantu peoples from the

north and north-east. All this helps to explain why the modern population map of eastern Africa shows a maze of peoples whose languages, appearance, customs and traditions go back to different roots in the distant past. Such was the complexity of this great incursion of diverse peoples over many years – 'movements on a scale', as Oliver has described them, 'which have not occurred in Europe since the Dark Ages' – that much about their history is still mysterious, and may probably remain so. As an example of the difficulties, there is the case of Engaruka.

Engaruka is a ruined town of many hundred stone-built huts or small houses terraced along the western slopes of Mount Ngorongoro near Tanganyika's frontier with Kenya, and about three hundred miles from the sea. In this remote place nothing is apparent to explain why Engaruka came into existence, and nothing to show why it lapsed into ruin. For anyone who cares to slash his way through the bush and thorn that overwhelm this extensive settlement, clambering terrace by terrace from its valley river to the ridge of the hillside where it terminates, there is only the insistent stumbling certainty of its presence, mutely unique in its acres of tumbled stone, its cairns and lines of house foundations, its scatter of level platforms, its hint of walls and paths half-buried in the grass and thorn.

Manifestly a product of Mature Iron Age development in these eastern highlands, and having some obvious cultural links with lesser settlements of the same general type, Engaruka is extraordinary both for its relatively large size and for the absolute silence which enshrouds its past: nothing but a little vague and dubious tradition has anything to say or to remember on the subject. No doubt it became the victim of some of those southward-moving peoples, forerunners of the Masai and other nomads from the north, who came into these lands during the Mature Iron Age and ruined much of their cultural fabric; but whether this was five hundred years ago or less remains a matter on which, at the moment, anyone may make his guess. Engaruka was in any case a point of Iron Age maturity, and remains, even today beneath its veil of bush and thorn, a powerful indicator to the depth and capacity of culture that lie behind the apparent simplicity of East African village life.

Elsewhere we can reach stronger ground, thanks to the survival of much traditional history and other useful evidence. The Early Iron Age farmers of Uganda, for example, had evidently acquired a simple form of

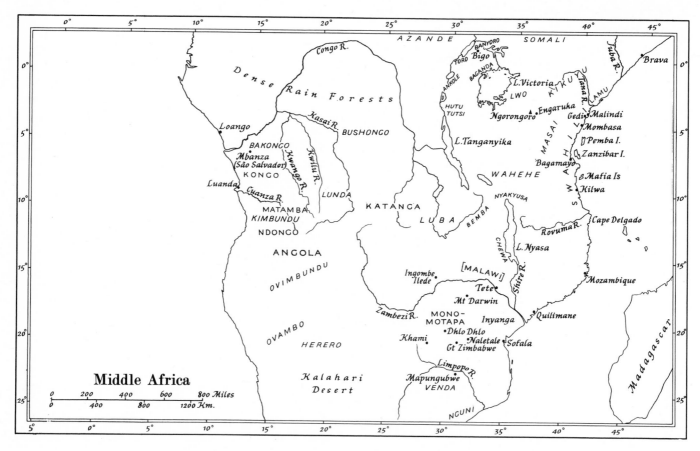

Middle Africa

government by chiefs during the thirteenth or fourteenth century. Some time after 1400 they were invaded by migrating groups of Lwo-speaking folk from the region of the Upper Nile. These Lwo were looking for good land. They found it in the pleasant country of Uganda where their ruling clans, supported by a large number of 'commoner clans' into which many local people were progressively absorbed, were able to impose themselves and to found states and dynasties of divine kings.

Being cattle-raising wanderers, these newcomers did not necessarily bring with them a higher level of culture than already existed in the East African lands where they settled. Often enough, as Engaruka suggests, they destroyed a great deal which they were quite unable to replace. Even from the little evidence that Engaruka has so far yielded, it seems clear that its builders and inhabitants had achieved a far greater mastery of environment, a far better use of labour and a much higher standard of living, than the wandering nomads who came from the north with their hunting spears and cattle shifting on the hoof. In Uganda, however, the newcomers settled down and introduced

new political forms, and their long surviving traditions indicate that with these they were successful in promoting long periods of peace and stability. One branch of the Lwo, for instance, founded the Bito line of kings who are remembered to have ruled over Bunyoro for eighteen generations. Another line of kings are remembered to have ruled over Buganda for twenty-two generations. The old kingdoms of Ankole, Koki and Kiziba have comparable traditions. Sometimes the process of political change, and the acceptance of rule by chiefs, has continued into very recent times. Even under colonial rule the chiefs of the Alur, another people of Lwo origins, were still extending their authority over neighbouring folk who had previously lived without any 'central government' of their own, but who now saw a new value in the arbitration of chiefs, accepted Alur chiefly rule without resistance, or even asked for it to be extended among them.

South from Uganda, along the splendid upland pastures which form the inland flank of modern Tanganyika, the same process of development into Mature Iron Age forms was repeated with the rise of the Hima and Tutsi kingdoms. Incoming wanderers,

Opposite: Iron Age Africans began building stone structures on the Rhodesian plateau as early as AD 1100. But these massive walls of Great Zimbabwe date from the Rozwi hegemony after AD 1500. It has been suggested that the conical tower (*top*) and the standing pillars of the 'acropolis' (*bottom*) may possibly reflect an East African influence linked with the gold and ivory trade. The buildings are in any case purely indigenous

Above: Ruins of the large stone structure of Khami near modern Bulawayo, almost certainly the residence of an important ruler, and probably built soon after AD 1700

Copper ingots in the form of crosses such as these from Ingombe Ilede were important in the trade of Central Africa for a long time before the coming of the Europeans. Each ingot is just over one foot in length

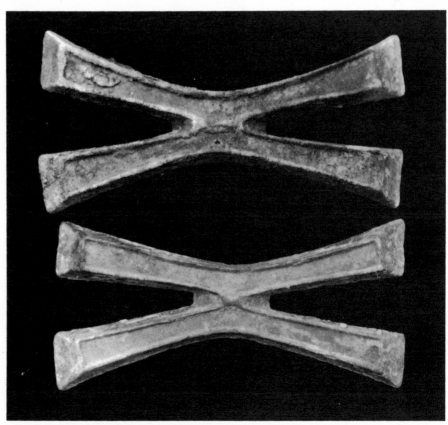

Opposite: Part of the outer wall at Great Zimbabwe

under strong chiefs, evolved new patterns of authority in combination with iron-using farming peoples who had previously lived in states that were far more loosely organized, or were organized so little as barely to deserve the name of states at all. There gradually crystallized a sharply hierarchical structure of society in which ruling clans were supported and supplied by subject clans or subject peoples.

As with all other such processes of ripening, there were gains and losses for different groups. While Tutsi nobles gossiped among their equals, sipping honeydew and arguing the wisdom of the ages, or leaned upon their spears while composing verse in praise of their courage, virtue, and authority, the humble Hutu laboured at their gates in producing food and bearing burdens. Yet the Hutu and their kind also had their benefits. The elaboration of these carefully structured kingdoms will have brought long periods when ordinary folk could feel free of the threat of invasion or warfare. For the Tutsi nobles and their like were under obligation to assume not only the responsibilities of government, but also those of defence. Just as the yeomen of medieval Europe preferred to bind themselves to strong masters, seeing in this their best assurance of safety and protection, so also did the farming peoples of these inland kingdoms think it wise to make themselves the tribute-paying vassals of men for whom warfare and government were a professional duty, as well as a guarantee of privilege. Rising in the fifteenth or sixteenth centuries, these Rift Valley kingdoms remained stable and independent until European colonial invasion overturned the world they knew, and left their peoples with the need to build another.

Around Great Zimbabwe

While it has long been known that the many large stone structures of the gold-bearing country between the Zambezi and Limpopo rivers (Southern Rhodesia or, as Africans now call it, Zimbabwe) were the work of indigenous African peoples, only in the 1960s was their chronology broadly established. Renewed excavations at Great Zimbabwe then showed that the early 'stone building culture' gave way in about 1450 to another though related culture which promoted much larger structures. Recovery of local traditions at about the same time indicated that this break and change corresponded with the rise to power of the Karanga people under kings belonging to the Rozwi clan. According to

Abraham, who has collected some of these traditions, this actually occurred in about 1440 when Mutota, king of the Karanga, organized a vast and victorious campaign of conquest designed to extend his rule over the whole inland plateau between the Zambezi and the Limpopo – the main gold-bearing area – and afterwards through Mozambique to the harbours of the East Coast trade.

All this was substantially achieved by Mutota and his son Matope, so that the latter became the most powerful sovereign in the central-southern continent during the 1470s, and was honoured as such by the rulers and chiefs of the East Coast ports. These called his empire *Wilayatu 'l Mu'anamutapah* after his indigenous title of Mwanamutapa, or lord of the conquered lands; and use of this title was duly taken over by the Portuguese who corrupted it to Monomotapa and believed, for a while, that they had found the empire of Prester John.

After the death of Matope in about 1480 this great system was riven by internal rivalries. Two of the Monomotapa's strongest 'barons' rebelled against the king's authority, and the first of these, Changa, established a separate state. This lay in the southern part of the domains of the Monomotapa, while the other, moving north to the region of Mount Darwin, continued to rule over the riverain lands of the Middle Zambezi and north-western Mozambique. Here the bold and enterprising Portuguese, coming up the Zambezi in the sixteenth century in search of gold and silver, set up permanent markets as far as the neighbourhood of Mount Darwin and tried to impose their military and political authority. In this they were partially successful, as elsewhere, by means of intervening on one side or the other of dynastic or 'baronial' wars. A decisive battle in 1628 enabled them to displace the ruling Monomotapa with a convenient nominee of their own, and a year later this virtual puppet, Mavura, duly signed a treaty which gave the Portuguese a free run in looking for minerals and, if they could find any, in mining and exporting them. This was the first Afro-European treaty of a 'concession type' which was to become common in later times.

Continuing over many years, Portuguese intervention – whether officially or by the hand of local settlers – went far to ruin the Monomotapan system of government, production and trade. In a valuable report of 1667 Barreto listed three reasons why so little gold could now be taken from these lands. They make sad

Opposite top: Benin: Part of the fortifications built by Oba Oguola at the end of the thirteenth century, and now overgrown by the forest. These ran round the city for twenty-eight miles
Bottom: An elder in the village of Fassi in Guinea, and also its blacksmith. Traditional methods of iron-working are still in use in some parts of Africa

171

reading. The first, he said, was the reluctance of chiefs to allow any digging for gold, lest the Portuguese should seize the land. The second was the lack of population. And the third, a constant theme in Portuguese rule, formed in Barreto's opinion the principal reason for decay: this was 'the bad Portuguese conduct' that drove people from their homes into exile in other lands.

Southward in later Mashonaland, a second Karanga state was ruled by kings of the Rozwi clan. These were the lords of Zimbabwe, Khami, Dhlo Dhlo and of other stone-built settlements. They fared much better. A few Portuguese came this way but never gained the decisive power they enjoyed in the north. Around 1690 they were driven out by Changamir Dombo, who considerably strengthened the Rozwi state; and they never returned. The seventeenth century seems to have been one of peace and progress, and it was now that the buildings of Great Zimbabwe, and others like them, received their greatest enlargement. Except among the eastern hills – at Inyanga and its neighbouring sites – there is little sign of defensive works in any of these structures. The hill-top 'acropolis' of Great Zimbabwe may have been a fort; just as probably it was a place of sanctity guarded merely from the profane. Khami near Bulawayo was certainly the dwelling of a powerful chief and possibly of a divine king, but it has nothing that resembles fortification. Naletale is much the same. Immune through many peaceful decades, and no doubt defenceless and largely disarmed, the Karanga were to be quickly and cruelly smashed and ruined by north-ward-moving invaders from Natal after 1800.

Further south again, beyond the Limpopo, the same kind of progress from early to mature Iron Age systems occurred with the so-called Mapungubwe Culture during the thirteenth or fourteenth century. Its peoples

took over the settlements of earlier Iron Age populations – established here in the Transvaal between AD 700 and 1000 – and built a new state (an outlier of the Zimbabwe Culture) of which little is known in detail. These newcomers, evidently Bantu-speaking folk from beyond the Limpopo, occupied the 'table tops' of a number of hills lining the southern bank of the Limpopo some 400 miles from the sea. Here they reproduced the skills and customs of their Karanga neighbours, working finely in cast and beaten gold, producing good hand-turned pottery, trading their products for Indian cottons and other Indian Ocean imports, and burying their kings with a wealth of golden ornament. Towards 1500 they were displaced by another set of rulers from across the Limpopo, a people called the Venda, who remained here until they too were ruined by the devastations of the early nineteenth century.

And the same state-forming process, in one degree or another, went on right across South Africa as far as its southernmost seaboard. Many new political systems appeared in the fourteenth or fifteenth century. Even as far as the mouth of the Umzimvubu river, only three degrees north of the latitude of the Cape of Good Hope, there was a place of trade between the peoples of Pondoland and sea-merchants from the Swahili coast. Almost the whole of south-eastern Africa was enclosed within Iron Age states formed by Bantu-speaking people whose remote origins had lain much further in the north.

These states long preceded the coming of the Dutch in 1652. Their institutions included the familiar vertical divisions of lineage and family-descent groups, as well as horizontal divisions into 'age-sets' and 'age-regiments' composed of men and women born at about the same time and bound to the same loyalties and duties. This two-way stratification of society was further complicated, as it was elsewhere, by horizontal divisions such as those between craftsmen and farmers, or between ruling groups and subject groups. There was the same divine kingship with its firm belief that the health and welfare of the king were inseparably linked with the health and welfare of the whole society. There were the same notions of spiritual identification with ancestors, of beneficial magic and harmful witchcraft, of methods of making war or keeping the peace. By at least 1400 the community of Iron Age ideas and structures reached from the fringes of the Sahara to the Antarctic-facing shore of southern Africa. It had almost touched its greatest possible geographical extension.

Left: The 'north gate' through the walls of Great Zimbabwe
Opposite: Mask of carved and painted wood made by the Bapindi of Congo (Height: 13¾ in.)

Harp of carved wood
made by the Azande,
who live in the north-
eastern Congo (Length:
17¾ in.)

Right: Head of Bakongo
nail figure, made of
wood and used for
magical purposes
(Height of whole figure:
20 in.)

Opposite: Bushongo
mask from the Congo.
Made of wood with
coloured beads, cowrie
shells, brass pins and
raffia, and nearly 9 in.
high, it was used for
ceremonies of the
Babembe secret society

In the Congo Basin

A few other examples may be useful of a socio-political evolution that was almost everywhere present in these central-southern regions.

The origins of the kingdom of Kongo, 'great and powerful, full of people, having many vassals', as the Portuguese described it four and a half centuries ago, are told in many traditions. Some of them say that the founders of this well-knit political system near the mouth of the Congo river had moved from the inland country beyond the river Kwango. Another and more likely version is that they came from the northern bank of the Congo estuary late in the fourteenth or early in the fifteenth century. This was again the pattern of a small but powerful intrusive group which imposed its superior organization on indigenous people. They conquered, intermarried, and gradually gained the upper hand of recalcitrant neighbours until by 1482, when the Portuguese captain Diogo Cão first anchored in the waters of the Congo, these Kongo people (or BaKongo, *Ba* being a prefix indicating the plural) had built a large and closely articulated state in the northern region of modern Angola. Their king in Cão's time entered willingly into trade with the Portuguese, exchanged ambassadors with Lisbon, and received Christian missionaries with curiosity if not conviction. In this way they opened with Portugal a brief but friendly period of partnership.

Early in the sixteenth century King Affonso of Kongo dictated many letters to kings of Portugal; here are the last lines and official signature from one of them

From his capital at Mbanza, which the Portuguese later baptized São Salvador, the divine king of the Kongo (also Christian in more than name after about 1506) ruled the metropolitan lands of his empire, the country between the Kwilu and Congo rivers. North of the Congo river were several small tributary states; southward lay several others. The Portuguese misinterpreted this lord-and-vassal hierarchy in terms of their own feudalism, and in 1512 presented the Mani-Kongo, the lord of these lands, with a list of noble titles which they thought he would do well to copy and which, to some extent, he did adopt. A Portuguese report of 1595 can thus describe the organization of metropolitan government as including the authority of 'six Christian dukes, who may even be called little kings . . . and as well as these there are Catholic counts and marquises who obey the king's orders with very strict obedience. He dismisses any of them who do not carry out their responsibilities, and replaces them by other men.'

At the beginning the Portuguese found it necessary and even desirable to respect the sovereignty of this strong kingdom and its neighbours. They presented themselves as friends and allies, just as they had done along the coast of Senegal, at the mouth of the Gambia, at Elmina and at Benin. They remained for some time content with this state of affairs, while extracting from Kongo the greatest possible number of captives for enslavement elsewhere. Yet almost from the beginning the overseas slave trade had its grim effect in violence and deepening despair. As early as 1526 the baptized King Affonso of Kongo is writing to his 'royal brother' in Lisbon that 'we cannot reckon how great the damage is . . . and so great, Sire, is the corruption and licentiousness that our country is being completely depopulated . . .' It made no difference. Slaving continued.

Events took a somewhat different course further south. Here, in the coastal country of the powerful Mbundu kingdom of Ndongo (whose king's title was *ngola*: hence the Angola of later times), the Portuguese ran into opposition and rejection. Inspired partly by a fixed illusion that the mountains of Ndongo possessed rich silver mines, they at first attempted the same tactics of peaceful penetration by which they had acquired indirect control of Kongo. Failing with these, they turned to outright invasion. From 1575 the wars went on for a weary century and more. Their little armies were repeatedly thrown back and scattered. Portuguese gangs roved the countryside, seizing captives wherever

Opposite: Bakongo wooden figure of magical significance depicting a man with a tribal mark from forehead to nose (Height: 6½ in.)

they could. Ndongo was steadily and disastrously depopulated. Shifting inland, its leaders set up a new state in Matamba, associated with the heroic name of Queen Nzinga, who fought the Portuguese for many years before coming to terms with them. By the 1680s the Kongo kingdom, like Ndongo, was far gone in ruin.

East of these Congo-Angola states were others of the same type, though varying in local structure and having no direct contact with Europeans. Many of their peoples, like those of the riverain populations of western Africa, were highly gifted in the plastic arts, while they shared with other tropical Africans their love of dancing and versatility in the use of rhythm. The Bushongo of the Kasai were among several who developed a fine art in raffia weaving, a skill that still partially survives. Their state appears to have entered its mature form, with divine kingship, a hierarchy of chiefs, some

division of labour and a complex ideology of moral and political behaviour, some four centuries ago.

As the exchange of goods between neighbouring peoples and eventually with the seaboard grew more important, there came a corresponding development in social organization. Thus the numerous Lunda peoples who live in a wide belt along the southern flanks of the Congo Basin undoubtedly went through a revolution in the early part of the sixteenth century. This is associated with the arrival among the Lunda of Luba ruling groups. These were able to profit from the new situation, perhaps because they themselves stood in the distant tradition of those ancient Luba kingdoms which had mined and traded so successfully in this broad region several hundred years earlier. By the late sixteenth century this Luba-Lunda complex had risen to some strength. And when the coastal demand for

During their long wars of invasion, the Portuguese met a formidable adversary in Queen Nzinga of Matamba (c. 1580–1663). In 1622 she went to Luanda on behalf of her brother, the king of Ndongo, in an effort to negotiate peace. When the Portuguese governor refused her a chair, she disdainfully called up one of her attendants and sat down as shown above

Opposite: Wooden mask from Cameroons (Height: 18 in.)

Congo: Head of a Baluba
effigy of dark wood, probably a
female ancestor-figure (Height of
whole figure: 18 in.)

Congo: Head of a Bakongo
wooden ancestor-figure of a
mother and child. Such figures
were commemorative, and were
placed on graves (Height of
whole figure: $13\frac{1}{2}$ in.)

ivory thrust its impact beyond the seaboard kingdoms, there came the rise of a Lunda empire under Luba chiefs whose skills included practice in the ivory trade. They founded a line of kings whose title was the Mwata Yamvo, and whose authority was buttressed by religious attributes and sanctions.

This new pattern of government in central Africa was evidently found effective, for similar states came into existence under the sheltering prestige of the Mwata Yamvos while often conducting, as later European travellers were to find, a vigorously independent life of their own. Soon after 1700, as a part of the process, this type of system appeared under strong local chiefs to the south of Lake Mweru in what is now part of Katanga and Zambia. Here there emerged a state that was ruled by a line of kings whose title was the Kazembe. Though in some sense a vassal of the Mwata Yamvo, the Kazembe appears generally to have seen in his vassalage little more than a guarantee of religious and secular authority by association with a ruler still more profoundly respected than himself.

Eastward again, amid the hill country toward the East African highlands and Lake Nyasa, there were other clusters of peoples organized in much the same way, and having much the same minor but persistent benefit from trade with neighbours. Here, too, the state-forming process originated in an Early Iron Age when trade was of minimal importance or none at all, but whose later forms of organization reflected a growing commercial factor. Thus the Chewa and Malawi (or Marave as the old travellers called them), the Bisa, Senga and others living south-west or south of Lake Nyasa, look back to a time, three or four centuries ago, when they were conducting useful trade with neighbours near and far. A Portuguese report of 1667 describes them as controlling the north bank of the Zambezi for six hundred miles from the Indian Ocean port of Quilimane, and as trading with the Portuguese 'in ivory, much iron, many slaves, and *machiras*, which are coarse cotton cloths in great demand in the country of the Monomotapa'. To some extent, therefore, the Malawi and their neighbours were commercial intermediaries between the Portuguese and the Monomotapan state along the middle Zambezi and to the south of that river. Though they are sometimes referred to as having formed 'the empire of Malawi', and may have worked together from time to time, it remains to be shown that they ever in fact organized a strong confederation among themselves.

How far did the trading enterprises of this period connect these peoples and their neighbours with the city-states of the East Coast? There is no doubt that an important trade route linked Kilwa with the northern end of Lake Nyasa. It was certainly used for a long time. Yet there is little to show what effect it had on the peoples through whose territory or near whose territory it passed. A little is known of the history of the interior of central and southern Tanganyika before the nineteenth century, and a little more may be guessed; in general, though, the impression is one of scattered or isolated peoples who lived on the margins of the pressures that were now developing around them. Largely because of the steady southward-drifting infiltration of nomad peoples originating in the Horn of Africa or along the Upper Nile, the Mature Iron Age in Tanganyika and Kenya was the scene of much conflict and confusion, as well as the overthrow of a number of settled farming communities or polities. Perhaps the greatest of these communities was that of Engaruka. When its history is finally unravelled, this tantalizing hillside ruin may throw useful light on this long period of eastern upheavals.

Yet migrations and incursions undoubtedly had a powerful impact throughout this region. Some of its peoples were successful in standing outside the region of nomad invasion, or at least of warding off attack. Old states remained stable here and there, while new ones were formed. But the repeated population movements seem to have had a widely disruptive effect, and new troubles were now added to them. These began with Portuguese piracy along the coasts. They were extended by the warlike pressures of internal migration. They were disastrously worsened for a number of peoples and states by the northward-moving Nguni invasions of the early nineteenth century, by the somewhat later East Coast slave trade, and by other such ruinous interruptions. But they were not everywhere present. And wherever slaving or other outside interference remained absent or of small importance, the stability achieved in the fifteenth and sixteenth centuries lasted until recent times. Such was the ordered condition of much of the inland country, even in the early nineteenth century, that goods could be carried from one side of Africa to the other. Two Afro-Portuguese dealers made the crossing from Angola to Mozambique in 1806–11 and proved that it was safe and easy provided one had the necessary permits. Hazards arose not from political chaos but from political organization: without the 'visas' of the Kazembe and the Mwata Yamvo, nothing could be done.

Living at the Katangan court of the Kazembe a hundred and sixty years ago, these traders found the land agreeably supplied with cereals, vegetables, fish and fruit, and the government strong and tolerant. The Portuguese traveller Gamitto, who arrived there in 1831, thought the Kazembe of his day a sensible man though very splendid in his style of life. Gamitto discovered all that 'ceremonial, pomp, and ostentation', as he put it, which were thought necessary to divine kingship. But the pomp was not an empty one. It stood for a power that was real. The chaos came later.

West Africa in the Sixteenth Century

Even a brief summary can do something to suggest the complexity and many-sided growth of western Africa during this period when the 'old society', the society of Iron Age maturity, touched or approached the peak of its achievement. Still more than elsewhere, one is confronted with the interplay of a multitude of peoples and political patterns, with the decline of ancient polities and the rise of others in their place, and with a wealth of oral and written record now more and more illuminated by the reports of visiting Europeans.

All this combines into a scene of arresting scope, its details painted with a riveting impression of reality, its dramas played out by kings and priests whose characters can sometimes be traced, its onward shift and movement turning on events whose meaning can often be defined. This was a period when the old civilization of western Africa, lettered or unlettered, had deepened to a profound self-confidence and social resonance whose returning echoes one may catch in many fields of effort, whether religious or artistic, political or economic. The mere bird's-eye view which follows here goes from west to east, moving from the shores of the Atlantic to the margins of the Congo forest.

Much of the western region, whether inland or near the coast, still showed the deep imprint of the old empire of Mali, itself in far decay but yet remaining strong enough in its ancient centres of Mandinka population to support a noble reputation. In Senegal the principal successor-state of Mali remained the Woloff empire, consisting of the three provinces of Walo, Cayor and Baol; these held the coast and much

of the near-coastal country between the Senegal and Gambia rivers. 'Here at the Senegal', reported Pereira in 1506, 'you find the first black people. This is the beginning of the kingdom of the Woloff, a hundred leagues long and eight broad', a lineal exaggeration, as modern cartography shows, but substantially accurate enough. 'The king of the Woloff', adds Pereira, again perhaps not exaggerating much, 'can put into the field an army of about 10,000 cavalry and 100,000 infantry. They go naked save for the nobles and men of honour who wear blue cotton shirts and trousers of the same material.'

North of the Senegal river were nomadic peoples who lived by a slave economy which was to persist into the present century. Though Berber and Soninke by origin, these Mauretanian peoples had come under the political control of southward-moving Arabs from Morocco during the fourteenth century. Loss of political control meant loss of local culture. These western Berbers, unlike their relatives of the eastern Sahara, gave up their own language and took to using Arabic instead, while at the same time adopting some other aspects of western Arab culture. All this was to have important consequences for the spread and nature of Islam in these western regions.

South of the Senegal and east of the Woloff states, in the Futa Toro along the banks of the river, lay the old state of Tekrur under rulers whose Soninke forebears had established themselves here, long before, during the later phases of the empire of Ghana. These paid tribute or at any rate a nominal allegiance to the king of Diara, once a tributary of Mali and now a tributary of Songhay. But there now occurred in Tekrur a change of a kind that was to become characteristic of much that happened in the grassland country of the Western Sudan after the collapse of Songhay in the 1590s. A people of the countryside, peasants hitherto strange to town life, came invading into Tekrur and built a new state.

Three hundred miles toward the east in the dry savannah lands of Termes and Nioro a group of Fulani cattle-breeders revolted against their allegiance to the emperor of Songhay, the famous Askia Muhamad, and set out to find a new home. Led by their chieftain Tengella, these wanderers began by a raid on Diara. Here they clashed in 1512 with a Songhay army under the Askia's brother, and Tengella was killed. There is some reason to think that these Fulani had been encouraged on their raiding path by the Mali emperor,

Altars at the ancestral shrine in the Oba's palace at Benin,
where the Oba offers to his predecessors

Detail of an altar in the Oba of Benin's ancestral
shrine, showing an Oba supported by his attendants

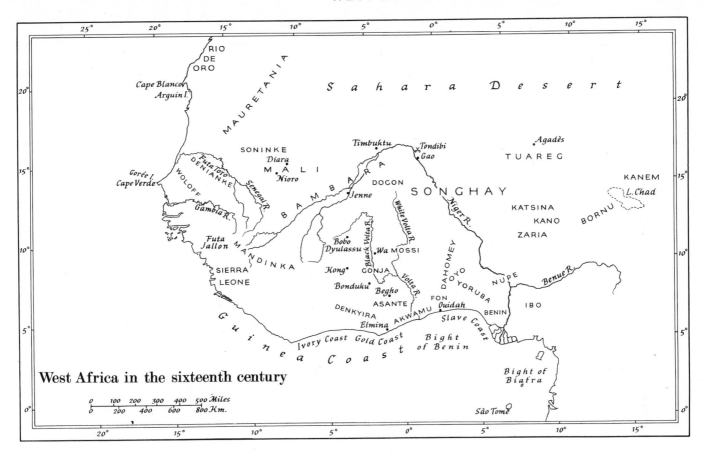

West Africa in the sixteenth century

seeking to undermine his Songhay rival. One of Tengella's wives, at all events, belonged to the Mali royal family. His son by this marriage, Tengella Koli, now assumed control and led his people southward into country that was still under Mali sovereignty. They arrived in Badiar, near the modern frontiers of Senegal and Guinea, and made common cause with a Mandinka group. Together these marched north-westward into Futa Toro. By about 1550 they had established there a new line of kings, the Denianke, who ruled in Futa Toro until 1776, when they themselves were displaced during the revival of Islam in the eighteenth century. Though not Muslim, the Denianke state may be regarded as the forerunner of many later states in which once-nomadic Fulani were to play a leading part.

South of the Gambia the Mandinka and related peoples remained in control of a country which had been theirs, or at least under their general influence, since time immemorial. These now began trading profitably with the Portuguese. Even 150 leagues up from its mouth, Pereira noted in 1506, ships' crews could carry on a good trade in cheap cotton goods and other items in exchange for gold. When these countries were at peace, he estimated, gold exports to Portugal were worth five or six thousand *dobras* of fine gold. Like so many other monetary calculations, this is vague enough; yet the total was evidently thought to be surprisingly satisfactory. Already the long-standing monopoly of the Western Sudan in trading West Africa's gold with North Africa and Europe had begun to be broken.

The same Pereira, like others after him, speaks of many small states along the eastward-bending coast towards modern Ghana. By this time the whole sea-board and forest country as far as Yorubaland and the empire of Benin was divided among a multiplicity of communities, sometimes closely linked to one other, which had built themselves into states ruled by chiefs or chiefly families. Their principal trade was in selling fish and other coastal products to their neighbours of the inland country, but the sixteenth century now called them to a maritime commerce which was entirely new. The coast of Guinea, as Dike has said, became for the first time a 'frontier of opportunity'.

Opposite: A dignitary of the city of Benin in 1964. A boy from his family acts as bearer of the ceremonial sword

Europeans found them keen men of business. Although interested in buying cottons and metalware, Africans could and did produce these goods for themselves. The Portuguése found their blue cottons worth buying for sale in Europe, while an English captain observed in 1556 how 'they can work very finely in iron', manufacturing spearheads, fish hooks and short swords, 'some of them as long as a woodknife and exceeding sharp on both sides.' Most of these little coastal states, accustomed to fending for themselves in fierce competition with their neighbours, were well able to defend themselves against European bullying, even though this was often tried; and their relations with visiting ships' crews were generally pitched in terms of alliance and partnership. John Hawkins turned this to his advantage in a slaving voyage of 1562. He struck up alliance with two kings of Sierra Leone so as to attack their neighbours, and was rewarded for the efforts of his soldiers with several hundred war-captives whom he carried to the Spanish Main and sold as chattel slaves for a handy profit. In later times there would develop a belief in Europe that only the climate and coastal fevers deterred European settlement along the coast. It was wide of the truth. The fevers, though not the climate, certainly cost many lives among Europeans who had developed none of the partial immunity achieved by local populations. But the real and enduring deterrent to any forced European foothold was the superior strength of African states until the nineteenth century.

Footholds secured by African agreement in pursuit of trading partnership were another matter. The Portuguese built Elmina Castle by initial consent in 1482, and against the payment of rent. Many other castles were afterwards built on much the same terms. From the African standpoint they were of merely local importance. What mattered to coastal Africans was not these minor European ventures but the major pressures of powerful states of the inland country. These inland or near-coastal states continued to dispute the control of central Guinea until the rise of the Asante empire in the eighteenth century. It was they, not the Europeans, who dominated the fortunes of the little seaboard states.

In the sixteenth century the main powers in central Guinea were still the old states of the Akan, exploiting their near-coastal or forest cultivation and trading in gold with the Dyula companies of Bonduku, Kong and other commercial centres to the north-west and north-east. Most of these states now fell within the orbit of two or three of their number. By 1650 Denkyira and

Akwamu were the powers that counted most. Yet the coastal trade with Europeans had its effect on the Akan and their neighbours, gradually and from small beginnings, in the same way as with the Mandinka further west. Little by little, the inland trade shifted round upon itself, as the sea-merchants grew more numerous; it was turned about-face, as Fage has put it, and began to look southward as well as north.

The foundation of Gonja, in the north-central part of modern Ghana, is a good illustration of the consequences. Towards 1550 the ruling mansa of Mali despatched a company of cavalry from the country of the Upper Niger into the grasslands north of the Akan country where the gold was mined. He was interested in the reasons why the northward flow of gold was beginning to run short. His pennoned riders, semi-professional, well equipped, the 'armoured fighting vehicles' of that day and age, bore southward from the region of Bobo and Jenne into the countryside of the Black Volta, west of the Mossi states, where they established themselves in the neighbourhood of Wa. Though unable to do anything about improving the flow of gold, they remained in these grasslands and founded several chiefdoms. Others of their fellow-countrymen are said to have joined them early in the seventeenth century, including a warrior-chief called Jakpa who was either an historical personage or the legendary personification of several such 'founding heroes'. To this day the imams of Wa in the old country of Gonja recall their origin in Jakpa and his trading companions, while the principal imam of Wa still bears the title of Dyula-mansa, 'lord of the Mandinka traders', or, as the Hausa have it, Shehu-Wangara, the 'sheik of the Wangara (that is, Mandinka) people'. The name of the modern city of Bobo-Dyulasso indicates the same background, for it means 'the house of the Dyula traders of Bobo'. Kong's history is another variant on the same theme.

Other large changes, still within the purely West African framework and owing nothing of importance to European presence along the coast, occupied the scene in what are now the Western and Eastern Regions of Nigeria, and in Dahomey. The late sixteenth century saw the rise of a new power among the Yoruba, that of Oyo lying just to the north of the deep forest. Its origin is remembered as the outcome of disaster. This occurred when the trading state of Nupe, north of the Benue river, conquered the Yoruba of Oyo around 1550, and drove their chief, headed by the Alafin or king of Oyo, into exile. When these came home again they set about

Opposite top: Bronze plaque from Benin representing the Amufi ceremony
Bottom left: Wooden box in the shape of a fish, symbol of Benin, ornamented with figures of the Oba with the attributes of a god (Length: 18½ in.)
Bottom right: Benin bronze relief of a leopard

Small Yoruba ivory carving
of a horseman, with a rich
brown patina. Probably
carved at Owo, western
Nigeria

Opposite top: Oba Akenzua II
in full regalia, including a
coral garment and headpiece,
on 24 December 1964
Bottom: Bronze and gilt hip
pendant, as worn by the Oba
of Benin

Ivory pendant, probably
worn on the hip, of the late
seventeenth or early
eighteenth century. It
represents an Oba with
attendants

organizing an army based on the cavalry which had made their northern neighbours strong. Alafin Orompoto is said to have begun with a thousand mounted men. His successors went further. They extended the principal of maintaining long-service troops who were composed of heavily equipped cavalry maintained by the state and quickly to hand in case of need; and in this way they made themselves unbeatable in the Yoruba lands to the north of the forest. By the end of the sixteenth century their rule was powerful throughout the thinly-wooded country to the west of the Niger as far as the hills of Togo, for they had also established themselves among the Yoruba of Dahomey – the Yoruba of Ketu – as well as bringing the Fon people of that country under their dominion.

The Alafins of Oyo were strong rulers for nearly two hundred years. Wherever their cavalry could operate, their power became legendary. To give an idea of the strength of the Oyo army, an Englishman resident in Dahomey was writing at the end of the eighteenth century, the Dahomey people (then tributary to Oyo) say that when the Oyo people want to go to war, their general 'spreads the hide of a buffalo before the door of his tent, and pitches a spear in the ground on each side of it. Between these spears the soldiers march until the multitude which pass over the hide have worn a hole in it. As soon as this happens, their general presumes that his forces are numerous enough to take the field'. The Dahomey people, he added, 'may possibly exaggerate, but the Oyo are certainly a very populous, warlike and powerful nation.'

They were also capable of building a large and long-enduring political system without the use of a literate bureaucracy. They extended the power of their Alafin over many of the Yoruba states to the north of the dense forest country, operating through a system of permanent officials whose powers may be likened to those of colonial commissioners or 'residents' in later times, but whose authority was deepened by their being able to act within the community of Yoruba language and tradition. The Oyo ruling families retained a king-making capacity, but their social and political organization absorbed many of the administrative advances of the sixteenth century. These included a sharper division of executive powers within the Alafin's supreme governing council.

South-east of the Yoruba, Benin was unaffected by the rise of Oyo but had troubles of its own. Oba Ewuare, who became ruler in about 1440, appears to

have strengthened the power of his dynasty. Oba Esigie strengthened it again after 1504. Yet the rule of Benin and its tributary states, like that of Oyo, was still a matter of delicate adjustment among an intricate hierarchy of chiefs rather than the expression of any individual will. This process of adjustment had formed a barrier against autocracy that was common to nearly all Iron Age systems in Africa. By the sixteenth century, moreover, Benin's trading community seems to have become strong enough to make its weight felt in government for the first time. Important changes were introduced by Oba Esigie, who reigned between 1504 and 1550. These reflected the growing importance of trade as well as efforts by the Oba to reduce the influence of his principal noblemen. 'Town chiefs' were created. Bradbury tells us that they were chosen from among those who had made their own way in life, achieving 'wealth, prestige and following through warfare, farming and trade'. But at the same time the 'peerage' was further watered down by the creation of 'palace chiefs' who owed their position to royal preferment, while the traditional Uzama nobles – the old 'earls and barons' of Benin – were deprived of their right of nominating the next Oba, this being now decided by primogeniture.

With all this the ruler of Benin grew more powerful within his immediate domains. Endowed with divine attributes, passing his days in the majesty and mystery of a labyrinth of decorated halls where he was surrounded by the tokens of his power, the Oba now stood for a concept and practice of kingship that were to make political adjustment fatally hard to achieve. When the Dutch took over the main European trade with Benin from the Portuguese in the seventeenth century, they found the king a very great man. His palace and apartments had galleries 'as big as those on the Exchange at Amsterdam', being supported by 'wooden pillars encased with copper where their victories are depicted', while the city had many wide streets and large houses. 'I saw and spoke to the king of Benin', a Dutch visitor remembered of the year 1702, 'in the presence of his great counsellors. He was seated on an ivory throne under a canopy of Indian silk. He was about forty years old and of lively expression. According to custom I stood about thirty feet away from him. So as to see him better, I asked permission to draw closer. He laughingly agreed.'

Unlike the Alafins of Oyo, who could always be deposed by their traditional nobles if they were judged

Opposite: Bronze head from an ancestral shrine, representing an Oba of Benin with coral collar and crown (Probably sixteenth or seventeenth century)

incapable of rule, the Obas of Benin gradually came to represent a petrifaction of authority and custom. Benin's royal sculpture in brass reveals this as well as anything else. After the great period of the sixteenth century, as William Fagg has pointed out, royal styles show an increasing heaviness and crudity of concept, loss of energy and experiment, and a notable decline in the quality of craftsmanship. There was indeed a growing rigidity in means and attitudes of government, and this, later on, was to make it doubly hard for the rulers of Benin to understand the nature of the European imperial challenge of the nineteenth century. The end of this ancient and famous state was to be a wretched one.

Northward of these forest and near-forest kingdoms, the political reorganization of the grassland country was now increasingly moulded by methods and techniques evolved or borrowed from those of the great Songhay and Kanem-Bornu systems. What M. G. Smith has called this 'double exposure of Hausa to influences from Bornu and Songhay' induced among the leading Hausa city-states, notably Katsina, Kano and Zaria, 'a period of intensive political and military development, as well as religious and economic change'. At Kano, for example, Sarkin Muhamad Rumfa (1465-99) took several leaves out of his Bornu neighbour's book. He formed new regiments under his close command. He glorified his kingship with new ceremonial. He built himself an imposing palace. And in line with the deepening stratification of the leading grassland states, reflected by these changes, he imposed new taxes and obligatory labour-service on the *talakawa*, the freemen of Hausaland. Now it was that were sown those seeds of Hausa discontent which were to ripen many years later into Fulani-led rebellion.

With reforms like these one may again trace the expanding influence of Islam. Though egalitarian in its spiritual teaching, Islam like Christianity went hand in hand with the practical dividing of rulers from ruled, rich from poor, and strong from weak. Many of its political and social teachings both fitted the deepening stratification of society and helped to carry it further. A place might still have to be made at court for the rites of the old religions; in practice, the kings ruled more and more by Islamic order and coercion, and less and less by the sanctity and ritual of local tradition. Hence the emergence of long-service regiments drawn from enslaved war-captives or others of servile caste: their loyalty would stick, or so it could be hoped, where royal

adherence to Islam had undermined the older lineage loyalties of 'divine kingship'. To Sarkin Rumfa and his like, again in M. G. Smith's words, 'the ritual support which the chief lost when he became Muslim was made good by new sources of power, especially by eunuch administrators and squads of slaves who could serve as guards, police, soldiers or messengers.' Local kingship fealty and the *levée en masse* were passing away in the grassland country. But the reasons for this were also the reasons why the states grew stronger, and why their productive power increased and their trade expanded.

Based on their flourishing towns, the centres of trade and craftsmanship, the Hausa states could now play an important role as distributing agents for much of the commerce of the eastern region. Travelling among them early in the sixteenth century, a youthful North African who was later to be captured by Christian pirates and baptized as Giovanni Leone, or Leo Africanus as he is generally called, found 'civilized handicraft-workers and rich merchants' in Kano, a city encircled then as now by a great wall of earth and timber, while the king of another Hausa state, Guangara, drew 'a great revenue from dealing in goods and from commercial taxes'.

Kanem-Bornu remained a large and influential state. Early in the sixteenth century its rulers regained much of their previously lost authority to the east of Lake Chad, and began encroaching on Hausa lands to the west. In 1580 there came to the throne a ruler who built a new empire. This was the renowned Idris Alooma (1580-1617), who raised Kanem-Bornu to a new eminence, carried further the process of administrative reform, opened embassies north of the desert, and entered into friendly relations with the Ottoman sultan of Turkey. In these and other ways the sixteenth century witnessed a summit of political achievement. There would now follow a long period of profound upheaval and transition to the modern world.

Opposite: The *Akairo-Mnowon*, or royal jester, at the court of Benin in 1964
Overleaf left: Terracotta head from a shrine in the brass-workers quarter, owned by the chief of the brass-workers of Benin
Overleaf right: Benin bronze relief representing a Portuguese

5 New Encounters

North Africa from AD *1100 until the European raids of the fifteenth and sixteenth centuries and the somewhat later Ottoman conquests – East Africa and its city-states along the coast during the early years of Portuguese discovery – West Africa and the coming of the European sea-traders – Growth and consequences of the Atlantic slave trade*

North African Invasions

Towards 1100 the Berber kings of the Almoravid line brought all Morocco and western Algeria within their rule, as well as the fifteen or so little states of Andalusian Spain and southern Portugal into which the Ummayad caliphate had previously sundered. This Arabized Berber dynasty now presided over a phase of great brilliance. This was brief enough, lasting only until the beginning of Christian Spanish conquest in the 1230s, yet it glowed with serenity and peace, with intellectual energy and artistic daring, and with much prosperity in town and countryside alike.

What the Almoravids had begun, the Almohads continued. Their story was much the same. Like the Almoravid kings, those of the Almohad dynasty drew their strength from the revolt of Berber peasants against kings, governors and traders of the towns and cities. Just as Ibn Yasin of Sijilmasa had called for a return to the pure teachings of the Quran, for an end to new forms of taxation imposed by rulers grown 'corrupt' through good living, liberal speculation, and all the 'laxity' of city life, so in 1125, proclaiming himself the Mahdi, did Ibn Tumart do the same, recruiting to his *ribat*, or hermitage, all those who were prepared to fight for a 'purified' order of society.

Descending from their hills, the *Muwahiddun* of Ibn Tumart, the Believers in One God, took the lead among the Masmuda and Zenata Berbers and quickly made themselves masters of Morocco. In 1147 the successor of Ibn Tumart, a Zenata called 'Abd al-Mumin, became Caliph of Morocco with his capital at Marra-kesh in the High Atlas. By 1159, invading eastwards, his armies had unified the Maghreb – Morocco, Algeria, Tunisia – for the first time in history and, at least until the times do alter, also for the last; while Almohad rule soon displaced that of the Almoravids in Spain as well. At the crossroads of a powerful state controlling all the southern trade routes of the western Mediterranean, the Maghreb blossomed once again. Cities like Fez and Tlemcen rivalled the urban beauty and learning of Granada and Cordoba, unsurpassed by now throughout the western world.

At home in these comfortable cities, the Almohad rulers and their governors soon followed their Almoravid predecessors. They too became adherents of all those things, 'laxity and corruption and religious liberalism', against which Ibn Tumart had raised his banners of revolt. Ambassadors of the English King John (1199–1216), visiting the Almohad sultan of his day, are said to have found him preparing for their visit by reading the letters of St Paul so that he could better argue the Muslim case; while the reputation of his military power was such that these ambassadors were even authorized, or so it is said, to declare John's readiness to accept Islam in return for Muslim aid.

This agreeable and tolerant civilization could neither resist the onslaught of hungry Christian knights, thundering down from the stony hills of Aragon and Castile, nor hold together within itself. In 1229 Tunisia broke away under its Hafsid governors. In 1235 a group called the 'Abd al-Wadids established a new kingdom of their own, weak and ravaged though it was by Beduin raiding and devastation, while Morocco after 1247 fell to the local rule of another Zenata family, the

Opposite: In 1375 the Majorcan cartographer Abraham Cresques completed the earliest of Europe's maps of West Africa. This detail shows the Emperor of Mali with his orb of gold. Off the west coast of the continent the complete map shows the galley of Jacme Ferrer, who set out from Majorca for the Rio d'Oro in 1346, but never returned

Marinids. Riven by these internal conflicts, incapable of finding any lasting solution to the rivalry of town and countryside, Berber civilization never recovered its strength and unity. Most of Spain was lost in the 1230s; Valencia in 1243, Seville in 1248, Cadiz in 1262. Only the little southern kingdom of Granada held out till 1492.

Having recovered in Spain and Portugal, the Christians passed to the assault of North Africa itself. In 1415 an expedition set out from the Tagus and captured the north Moroccan port of Ceuta, thus reversing for the first time in seven hundred years the northward tide of conquest across the Mediterranean. Launched now upon the wide world, the Portuguese would maintain their progress and drive their keels far to the west and south. But the early fifteenth century saw them fixed on less remote ambitions. After Ceuta there were other nearby ports inviting plunder. Slowly gathering strength and maritime efficiency, the Portuguese attacked and took Tangier in 1471 as well as Arzila and Larache. In 1508 they seized Safi and Argouz far down the coast. In 1513–14 they captured more Atlantic ports, while the Spanish in the western Mediterranean possessed themselves of Melilla in 1497 and other ports in 1508. Only with the decisive battle of al-Ksar al-Kabir in 1578 did the Sharif of Fez make an end to European hopes of conquest, and lay foundations for the revival of Morocco under his energetic son Mulay al-Mansur, Mulay the Victorious.

By this time a new power had made its mark in the eastern and central Mediterranean. Having established themselves in the Crimea and the Balkans as well as Anatolia, the Ottoman Turks had turned southward in 1515. In 1516 their Sultan Selim I (1512–20) acquired the plains of northern Iraq, engulfed Syria and Palestine, and secured a foothold in Algeria three years later. In 1517 the Ottoman armies occupied Egypt and evicted the Mamluk soldier caste which had ruled there since 1250. Suleiman the Magnificent (1520–66) thrust his famous cavalry and musketmen to the very outskirts of Vienna, enclosing most of Hungary and Slavonia within his domains. He also pushed westward through Africa, adding Cyrenaica in 1521, Tripoli in 1551, and a part of Tunisia, conquest of the latter being completed in 1575. With Morocco remaining under its Sa'adid rulers, the Ottoman frontier at the time of the battle of al-Ksar al-Kabir, in 1578, was established along the western boundary of modern Algeria, where it had indeed been in previous times.

What had happened, essentially, was that the Almohad empire in the Maghreb had broken down once more into the three main parts of Berbery which had existed since time immemorial; and the Ottoman conquests had confirmed this disintegration. For the generality of folk, little changed. Ruling from afar and indirectly, careful of the susceptibilities of their Berber vassals, Muslim like themselves, the Ottoman sultans were content to promote local kings or governors wherever convenient dynasties could be found. Their authority in Egypt was scarcely more foreign, after all, than that of the Mamluk generals who had preceded them. In Tripoli they set up Turkish governors who were expected to sustain good relations with local Berber rulers and keep the trade routes open. In Tunisia there emerged a line of Beys who had strong Turkish connexions but could also count on local support, and it was the same with the Deys of Algiers.

These tributary states of the Ottoman empire, strongly controlling the trans-Saharan trade at its northern terminals, well supplied with cereals and fruit and mutton from their fertile coast-long plains and hills, were harassed only by the activities of Christian navies, pirates and trading rivals. Traditionally described by these, but especially by their great competitors of Venice, as being little more than nests of pirates and ruthless sea-hawks, the North African polities were in fact a good deal more tolerant in their laws and easygoing in their customs than most of the European states of the day. The Protestant English, who were outside the influence of Catholic policy in the Mediterranean, admired their prosperity and made friends with them. Thomas Dallam found Algiers in 1599 'a great place of trade and merchandise', while Mainwaring, reporting on Tunis in 1616, spoke of it as a place where peaceful men were safe from molestation. 'In five months together, when I was coming and going there, I never heard of murder, robbery or private quarrel. Nay, a Christian, which is more than he can warrant himself in any part of Christendom, may on my knowledge travel 150 miles into the country, though he carry good store of money, and himself alone, and none will molest him.' Other visitors described these cities as being girt about with well-tilled market gardens and vineyards, and with white-walled farmhouses set amid groves of burdened fruit trees, while Algiers early in the seventeenth century was said to have as many as three thousand merchant families and two thousand shops.

Opposite top: Drawing by an unknown master showing the capture of the Moroccan port of Africha (Mehediya) in 1550 by the fleet of Charles V of Spain under its Genoese admiral Andrea Doria
Bottom left: Fragment of a carved tusk from Benin, with a relief representing a Benin warrior with a European
Bottom right: Rock at Matadi in the Congo estuary showing Portuguese inscriptions of 1488, including names of the great Portuguese navigator Diogo Cão and some of his men

AFRICHA

These states were invaded by the French in the nine-teenth century. How prosperous they had remained may in some degree be measured by the contents of the treasure of the Dey of Algiers, looted by the French in 1832 of 15,500 lb of gold and 220,000 lb of silver. How solidly their traditions of independence still held firm may be seen very convincingly in the long and bitter struggle they opposed to foreign conquest.

In the sixteenth century, however, it was the security and regularity of trade that suffered most. The western trans-Saharan routes by way of Morocco and Maure-tania were especially hard hit. Great market towns decayed. Sijilmasa, one of the biggest of them all, utterly failed to recover from the ravage of war. Yet this far-going ruin of the western routes was not repeated elsewhere.

Trade was interrupted along the central routes by the Moroccan invasion of Songhay and its immediate consequences, but a measure of general recovery in the wake of Ottoman conquest soon exercised a remedial effect. This was especially true of the eastern routes between the Fezzan and Bornu-Hausaland. It was now a duty of the Turkish governors of Tripoli to remain on good terms with the rulers of the Saharan oases, and with those of the Western Sudan whom they could reach; while Mai Idris Alooma of Kanem-Bornu exchanged ambassadors with the Ottoman sultan, and even imported Turkish technicians to in-struct a company of Bornu musketeers. The general effect, in short, was to shift trade from the western routes to the central routes, and, though in lesser degree, from the central routes to the eastern routes. By the eighteenth century the central and eastern routes were probably carrying as much trade as ever, together with an increase of slaves now demanded by rich Ottomans for their harems and households; but the old western routes, once the most important of all, were so far re-duced by the 1790s as to be carrying only one big cara-van every two or three years.

This temporary decline and permanent geograph-ical shift in the Saharan trade was a factor of growing importance in West Africa as a whole. Hand-in-hand with it went a vast expansion of the maritime trade from the coast of Guinea. Taken together, these changes soon combined into a comparative eclipse of the old Saharan trade. More and more it was the sea-going trade that really counted.

East Coast Disasters

Early in December 1497 three Portuguese vessels rounded the Cape of Good Hope and sailed into the Indian Ocean. Nine years earlier Diaz had come as far but had turned back. Quelling the fears of his men, da Gama held stubbornly on. He meant to reach India. Yet the brilliant discoveries for which he hoped began earlier than that. Five months before sailing for India, da Gama stumbled on a civilization neither seen nor known before by any European. Along the whole East Coast from Quilimane onwards, da Gama and his crews touched at city after city and were repeatedly astonished by their wealth and urban comfort, by their tall ships from unknown eastern countries, and by their commerce in gold and ivory with equally un-known African countries which lay behind the coast-long plains.

In truth these cities had flourished for some two hundred years before da Gama saw them. And their flourishing was no mere figure of speech. Even today one may stand among their ruins and remain surprised at the lavish wealth that could raise such palaces and dwellings, pave them with the carpets of Isfahan and Gujerat, line their walls with the swan-necked ware of Sung China or the floridly superb platters of Mesopo-tamia and Persia, and generally endow these cities with that air of world-experienced sophistication which the Portuguese, before rushing in to plunder them, had time to stare at for a moment and admire. 'Moorish' in the Portuguese records – for the Portuguese casually called any Muslim a Moor, however distant from Andalusian Spain or Morocco his place of birth might be – these cities and their peoples afterwards became 'Arab' in the books of European historians. In fact they composed a markedly African variant in the wide traditions of Islamic culture.

Their economic achievement was that of urban polities whose prosperity lay not in production but exchange. Kilwa in the south, Pemba and Mombasa in the north: these were 'city empires' in the same sense as medieval Venice or Genoa. Their genius lay in buying and in selling. They protected their monopolist positions by maritime enterprise which laid hold of key points for purchase or trans-shipment. Kilwa, for ex-ample, made sure of its overriding command of nearby rivals – notably of the important island-port of Kisimani Mafia – as well as of its firm dominion over Sofala, the principal export harbour for the gold of the inland country. They seem to have manufactured little or nothing for sale, but they must have had skilled craftsmen in metals, because some of them struck copper and silver currencies. There is also evidence that they grew cereals for export as well as for their own needs.

Very distant from any other centres of urban civilization, they do not appear to have developed a written literature, whether in Arabic or in Swahili using an Arabic script, until the seventeenth or eighteenth century, during their period of post-Portuguese recovery. But the quality of this later literature, some of which has survived, suggests that their unwritten work in epic and lyrical composition was copious and distinguished. For the Arabs of the north, coasting down this seaboard in the years of its prosperity, these were always cities of strange and surprising adventure, markets where a man might see marvels or make his fortune by some turn of luck or magic. To all of this the legends of the Thousand and One Nights, of Sindbad the Sailor and his kind, pay an eloquent tribute.

But their attention to the opportunities of commerce was anything but magical. Like the Venetian Council of Ten, the rulers of Kilwa and its sister-cities took a severely unromantic view of the needs and duties of monopoly. Knowing their harbours to be vital for the ships of India and Arabia, and their markets not much less important for the producers of the inland country, these kings and their merchant-councillors erected a mercantile system whose rigidly oppressive tariffs must seem impossibly restrictive today, but whose efficacy can be gauged by the relatively high standard of living these cities gradually achieved. Strong on the northern part of the coast during the latter part of the fifteenth century, the king of Mombasa imposed on all seafaring merchants who used his harbours an impost rate of great ferocity. For each thousand lengths of cotton stuff imported into Mombasa, he exacted a *mitqal* of gold (perhaps an eighth of an ounce), and then, says an early Portuguese account, 'they divide the thousand lengths of cotton into two halves; of these the king takes one half while the other remains with the merchant....' Since the cottons had come from India, this seems extraordinarily harsh. Yet the point here – as with early European trade on the Guinea coast – was that gold could be bought at prices which were extremely cheap, notwithstanding such duties, when compared with the values which this gold could realize when sold again in India and elsewhere.

Kilwa tariffs, imposed in respect of the southern stretch of the coast, were of the same high order. 'Any merchant who wants to trade in the city', runs the same Portuguese report, 'has to pay for an import duty of one *mitqal* of gold for every five hundred lengths of imported cotton, no matter what the quality. The king of Kilwa then takes two-thirds of the imported merchandise, while the third which remains with the merchant . . . is again valued, and pays another duty of thirty *mitqals* for every thousand *mitqals* in value.' Even then the patient Indian merchant had not finished with import tariffs. Moving on down to Sofala so as to buy his gold and ivory, he had to pay one length of cotton to the king of Kilwa (that is, to the king's agents) for every seven lengths he sold. Returning up the coast again, he was supposed to revisit Kilwa and pay another fifty *mitqals* in gold for every thousand *mitqals*' worth of precious metal that he had bought. If he tried to get out of paying this final five per cent impost by the device of sailing past Kilwa, but then stopped at Mombasa before setting out for India on the trade winds, he might have to pay the duty at Mombasa instead. Similarly heavy duties were applied to the export of ivory.

No doubt these exactions were often evaded by subterfuge or bribe. Until we have a fuller story from the Indian end, the details of the trade must remain something of a mystery. But what is clear and certain is that it greatly prospered. Through many centuries East Africa was a principal source of gold for Asia and Arabia, while East African ivory, valued for ritual or ceremonial purposes both in India and China, was irreplaceable. Bursting through the grey ocean doors upon this brilliant scene, the Portuguese almost at once began to loot and burn. They broke into city after city, sacking and stealing. Da Gama ravaged Mombasa. D'Almeida fired Kilwa. Da Cunha ruined Brava and Zeila.

On his first voyage da Gama had missed Kilwa. But Alvares Cabral sheltered there in 1500. Five years later the largest of all the Portuguese fleets that would ever sail for India, commanded by the future Viceroy d'Almeida, replied to this hospitality with war. A German or Hollander who was with d'Almeida has left an eye-witness account of it. They took this golden city of 'many strong houses several storeys high' without opposition from the surprised inhabitants, and as soon as this was done 'the Vicar-General and some of the Franciscan fathers came ashore carrying two crosses in procession and singing the Te Deum. They went to

Stone cross erected by Vasco da Gama at Malindi, Kenya

berrio

Nicolão coelgo

Two of the vessels that accompanied Vasco da Gama on
his voyage to India in 1497–8; that of Nicolão Coelho, and
that of Gonçallo Nuñez, which was destroyed by fire

gonçallo nunc

Criado de Vasq da gama depois daMao terpassado
ho cabo deboa esperança et ser pouco avante da agoda
de joo bras se Re partirão os mantimentos eagente
della pellas outras dacompanfia. edepois debespe
jada efe poserão fogo/

Dom Francisco d'Almeida — 1°

Dom Vasco da gama — 6°

Nuno da Cunha — 9

Dom frey Aleixo de Menezes — 36

the palace, and there the cross was put down and the Admiral prayed. Then everyone started to plunder the town of all its merchandise and provisions.' Two days later they set it on fire.

At Mombasa, says the same witness, d'Almeida 'ordered that the town should be sacked and that each man should carry off to his ship whatever he found: so that at the end there would be a division of the spoil, each man to receive a twentieth of what he had found. The same rule was made for gold, silver, and pearls. Then everyone started to plunder the town and to search the houses, forcing open the doors with axes and iron bars. There was a large quantity of cotton cloth for Sofala in the town, for the whole coast gets its cotton cloth from here. So the Admiral got a good share of the trade of Sofala for himself. A large quantity of rich silk and gold-embroidered clothes were seized, and carpets also; one of these, without equal for its beauty, was sent to the king of Portugal together with many other valuables.'

Writing in 1518, Duarte Barbosa remembers how da Cunha had treated Brava on the Somali coast. This 'great town of very fine stone and mortar houses' was 'destroyed by the Portuguese, who slew many of its people and carried many into captivity, and took great spoil of gold and silver and goods. Thenceforth many of them fled away towards the inland country, forsaking the town . . .'

This looting and burning need not have been fatal to these cities. Some of them, like Brava, did in fact recover quickly while others, such as Kilwa, knew another period of lesser but relatively fair prosperity after the power of Portugal had vanished from the scene. But what proved much more serious to them, and what finally undermined Kilwa and nearly all the other cities of the southern stretch of the coast, was the wrecking of the Indian Ocean trade.

Having stolen all the portable wealth they could find or carry – and this they did in parts of India as well – the Portuguese set about trying to reshape the ancient trade between western India and eastern Africa. In this they singularly failed. Having blundered through all that fine network of commercial intercourse, they found it beyond their strength or understanding to restore the customs and contacts of a score of enterprising countries. At one end of the network, they interfered grossly with the trade of inland Africa, or with such of it as they could reach by way of the Zambezi; at the other end, across the Indian Ocean,

they seized or simply ruined the import-export trade of India and Ceylon. They did their best to stop all maritime enterprise not conducted under their own flag or sovereignty, and although many Indian Ocean sailors and traders continued to evade them, Portuguese intervention gradually proved fatal.

Even so, the Portuguese might still have managed to remould this Indian Ocean trade to their own advantage if they had been able to supply it with enough ships. They manfully tried; but the effort was beyond their means. Portuguese records show a total of 1,231 sailings to and from India between Vasco da Gama's first voyage and the year 1612, or an average of about ten a year. Although considerable when viewed against the background of Portugal's comparative economic weakness, the number was far too small for any effective replacement of the manifold maritime operations in Asian bottoms which the Portuguese had interrupted or stopped. By as early as 1550 they were finding it very hard to supply the trade. Old ships grew unserviceable but were seldom repaired; the rate of new building slipped dangerously down. No fewer than sixty-six total wrecks were noted for the years 1500–1610, and other ships were lost through enemy action. After the first flush of loot was over, crews were almost as difficult to find as ships.

Ousted by the commercially thriving Dutch and afterwards by the English and the French, the Portuguese by 1650 could do little but cling to a few strong points such as Mozambique Island and Mombasa, or Tete far up the Zambezi and several inland markets of smaller value. In less than a hundred years of destructive effort they had gone far to ruin the work of centuries.

Further to the south, meanwhile, another arrival had set in train a series of events that would lead to modern South Africa. Outplaying the Portuguese, outsailing the French and English, the Dutch had entered the Indian Ocean in 1595, had consolidated their maritime enterprises in 1602 with the foundation of the Dutch East India Company, and now carried all before them. Far superior to the Portuguese in ownership of capital, commercial understanding, and knowledge of the world of trade, the Dutch lost little time in using the Cape of Good Hope as a way-station on their route to the Far East and back. In 1652 Jan van Riebeeck was landed there with orders to grow fresh vegetables and meat for Dutch vessels on the Indian Ocean route. Few in number and little noticed, these settlers were merely servants of the Dutch East India Company; and to

Opposite: Portraits of four of the Portuguese explorers, derived from a series of portraits painted in the hall of the Viceregal Palace at Goa in 1547. They show Francisco d'Almeida, Vasco da Gama, Nuno da Cunha and Aleixo de Menezes, and appear in a manuscript of 1646

207

begin with they all but starved. In an effort to remedy their helplessness, the Company decided in 1657 that the settlers should try their hand at farming on a bigger scale. Nine of their employees became landholders, 'free burghers' in the language of the day, each with thirteen acres and an exemption from all taxes on condition they could and would supply food for a minimum period of twenty years. Once again the experiment all but failed. Gradually, however, these new farmers adapted themselves. They found that the answer to their problems of production lay in using local labour at next to no cost. Soon they had turned the local Africans, who were Khoisan (Hottentots), into their slaves. The era of *apartheid*, of racial segregation and discrimination based on slavery or on very cheap African labour, had begun.

Even in these early years the accents of Boer preju-dice were clear enough. 'Their native barbarism and idle life', wrote Willem ten Rhyne of the Khoisan Africans of the Cape in 1686, 'together with a wretched ignorance of all the virtues, impose upon their minds every sort of vicious pleasure. In faithlessness, inconstancy, lying, cheating, treachery, and infamous concern with every kind of lust they exercise their villainy . . .' But in those early days, contrasting with later times, doubts cropped up from time to time. 'From us', commented Johannes de Grevenbroek in 1695, 'they have learned blasphemy, perjury, strife, quarrelling, drunkenness, trickery, brigandage, theft, ingratitude, unbridled desire for what is not one's own, misdeeds unknown to them before, and, among other crimes of the worst sort, the accursed lust for gold.' This was an aspect of 'race relations' which southern Africa's new settlers were quickly to forget.

Early in the seventeenth century the Dutch began to rival the Portuguese for maritime control of the kingdoms near the mouth of the Congo river. The drawing shows Dutch ambassadors being welcomed by King Alvaro II of Kongo

West African Adventures

Late on an August afternoon of 1578 a few score Portuguese soldiers got narrowly away from the bloody Moroccan battlefield of al-Ksar al-Kabir, leaving behind them some 25,000 dead and all hope of further invasion of North Africa: not for another three centuries would Europe repeat the effort here. Dying in the hour of victory, the Sharif of Fez was succeeded by his son Mulay. Faced with the need to rebuild his fortunes, the new king looked for new resources. Not surprisingly, he thought of Songhay.

Past years had already seen a Moroccan attempt to oust the Songhay rulers from their influence over the western trans-Saharan routes through Mauretania, and over places like Taghaza, the supplier of salt. Relieved of European pressure, Mulay now meditated conquest. Energetic and imperious, short of revenue and determined to obtain it, he decided that where merchants could go soldiers could surely follow. 'You talk of the perilous desert we have to cross,' he is said to have told his advisers, scoffing at fainthearts who urged him to desist. 'You talk of the fatal solitudes, barren of water and pasture. But you forget those defenceless and threadbare merchants, mounted or on foot, who regularly cross the wasteland which caravans have never ceased to traverse. Far better supplied than they, I can do the same with an army that will inspire terror wherever it appears.'

Yet he moved carefully, planning ahead. Three thousand yards of English cloth were brought to Marrakesh to line the tents of his best regiments. Fresh units were armed and trained with the most modern weapon of the day, a firearm called the arquebus that was capable of killing at fifty or even eighty yards, not much of a performance by later standards and yet one that would be scarcely bettered for another hundred years. In November 1590 the army of invasion marched out of Marrakesh under command of a Christian Spaniard, Judar, who had turned Muslim and had earned for his services the rank and title of pasha. With Judar went 1,500 Moroccan light cavalry and 2,500 arquebusiers and spear-carrying troops, most of whom were Christian or Muslim mercenaries from Spain, together with a transport train of 1,000 pack horses, 8,000 camels, 1,000 stablemen and 600 labourers. Crossing the desert in about twenty weeks, a remarkably good performance for so large a host of men and

beasts, this army met the Songhay forces under Askia Ishaq II (1588–91) at Tondibi, near Gao, and won an immediate victory. This success Judar owed mainly to his firearms and the better discipline of his troops; but he also seems to have been aided by divided counsels on the Songhay side.

Pressing into Gao and afterwards Timbuktu, the Moroccans were disappointed in their hopes of easy and profitable conquest. Gao proved to have little worth the looting. In Timbuktu they soon ran into trouble with its Muslim leaders. These had tended to welcome the Moroccan incursion as a means of reasserting their independence of Songhay overlordship. One of their Gao colleagues, Alfa Bukar Lanbar, is even said to have counselled Askia Ishaq II to abandon the field at Tondibi. But they were by no means content to accept Moroccan overlordship instead. Taking advantage of a moment when the Moroccan forces, now under Mahmud Pasha, Judar's replacement, had quit Timbuktu for another attack on Ishaq's still resisting army, the leaders of Timbuktu stirred up a revolt which was eventually settled only by Moroccan compromise.

There followed two years of profitless fighting up and down the Songhay empire as Mahmud Pasha sought to pin down his opponents and destroy them. In this he had some temporary success, and was able to regain Timbuktu in October 1593, when he at once set about breaking the political power of its religious leaders. Four months later Mahmud had most of these arrested, and sent the more rebellious in chains across the Sahara to Marrakesh. Among them was the famous Ahmad Baba (1556–1627), one of those sixteenth-century scholars of Timbuktu whose works still enjoy respect among the learned of the Western Sudan. After two years in a Marrakesh prison, Ahmad Baba spent another twelve under open arrest before returning to his native city in 1608. By then the Moroccans had relinquished any serious effort at close control there.

The task of exploiting Songhay proved beyond them. They tried hard, but succeeded only in completing the ruin of the empire. Their rule over Timbuktu and Gao proved stifling and disastrous: never again would these ancient cities see the restoration of their old prosperity. Much of the cultivated area around them fell waste as Songhay peasants fled from Moroccan control. Populations dwindled. The schools of learning were emptied of teachers and their students. The busy traffic of the Western Sudan was for long disrupted as revolt after revolt swept through these Middle Niger lands. There followed a decisive shift in power from the peoples of the towns to those of the countryside.

Effective Moroccan control, even of Timbuktu, came to an end early in the seventeenth century when Sultan Mulay Zidan, Mulay's successor, complained bitterly that the whole enterprise had cost 23,000 Moroccan lives and decided to cut his losses. The government of Timbuktu devolved to a local pasha who was at first appointed by Marrakesh and owed the Sultan a close loyalty; but gradually the ties slipped and were lost as the Timbuktu Moroccans, little reinforced from home, married with local women and lost their identity. The records show no fewer than 156 pashas in 160 years. By the end of the eighteenth century they and their *arma* community, as this Moroccan-Songhay mixture was called, possessed no more than a shadow of their old authority.

But the Songhay empire was beyond recovery. Although the southern provinces remained under the command of Songhay chiefs, the region of the Middle Niger – crucial for the trading connexion – was left to the push and pull of local pressures. Prominent among these were the efforts of the Saharan Tuareg to win grazing land along the north banks of the Niger and to milk its cities of tax and tribute, while south of the river there were other peoples, Dogon and Mossi and Bambara, with similar ambitions. The year 1600 may be taken as a major turning point throughout these lands. The old history of the medieval Sudan had ended. A new period had begun.

There were other adventures along the coastland as European sailors came over the horizon. By contrast with the vast upheavals of the inland country, these coastal operations were still of small importance. Yet they marked the gradual outset of other changes which were to prove, in the end, of still more formidable influence for West Africa than the overthrow of Songhay.

Early European voyages down this coast were little more than an extension into ocean waters of the piratical manners of the Mediterranean. They are usually said to have begun in 1441, when Antam Gonçalves seized 'two Moors' who were no doubt Sanhaja Berbers on the coast of Rio d' Oro, north of Senegal, and took them with some other captives back to Lisbon. Two years later Nuno Tristão carried out another little raid near Arguin, somewhat further to the south. Other pirates quickly followed. Their forays against defenceless fisher families or cattle nomads were, as the records show, anything but glorious.

Somewhere south of Arguin, where the long biscuit-brown edge of Saharan Africa crumbles into Atlantic surf and spray, a certain Fernandes went ashore with two swordsmen and met five women walking near the beach. These, say the Portuguese annals, Fernandes and his bullies 'took with right good will, as something that increased their capital without toil; and led them with other captives to their ships.' Southward again, lying off and on the rising land near Cape Verde, another captain not long afterwards put seven men into a ship's boat and 'ordered them to row along the coast. As they went, these men caught sight of four Guineas seated by the water's edge. Seeing themselves unnoticed, six of the men in the boat jumped ashore, hiding themselves as well as they could until they were near to the Guineas, when they began to run to capture them.' But the 'Guineas', at least on this occasion, ran faster and escaped.

Violence and deception were never to be entirely absent from the Guinea trade in sailing ships throughout its four centuries of vivid experience. Yet the hit-and-run raiding of early voyages soon gave way to a more or less regular partnership in trade. The Europeans were in any case far too weak, and the Africans too strong, for violent methods to offer a satisfactory profit on these hazardous expeditions. Here along the Guinea Coast there were no rich cities to be pillaged and put in fee, but only a string of fisher hamlets and little states whose warriors were capable of beating off any attack that could be mounted through the surf.

Soon after 1445, accordingly, the Portuguese built a little trading fort on Arguin island just south of Cape Blanco, near the site of the modern Port Etienne; and 'henceforth the affairs of these parts were treated more by trafficking and bargaining of merchants than by bravery and toil in arms'. A Venetian who sailed on this coast in 1456 could note that the Portuguese at Arguin were already buying and sending back to Lisbon about one thousand slaves a year, and this within a dozen years after Gonçalves had taken the first captives. What had really happened was that the Portuguese, having sailed round the Muslim monopoly established along the North African coast, had now entered the trans-Saharan slave trade by the back door.

Their next effort was to get themselves into other forms of trade, especially in ivory and gold. By 1472 their ships had sailed as far as the Bight of Benin, and brought back news of large and wealthy kingdoms near the seaboard. In 1482, as part of the Portuguese

Opposite: The famous Cantino chart of 1502, marked with the crosses that the Portuguese explorers set up along the shores they visited, as well as with a great deal of coastal information

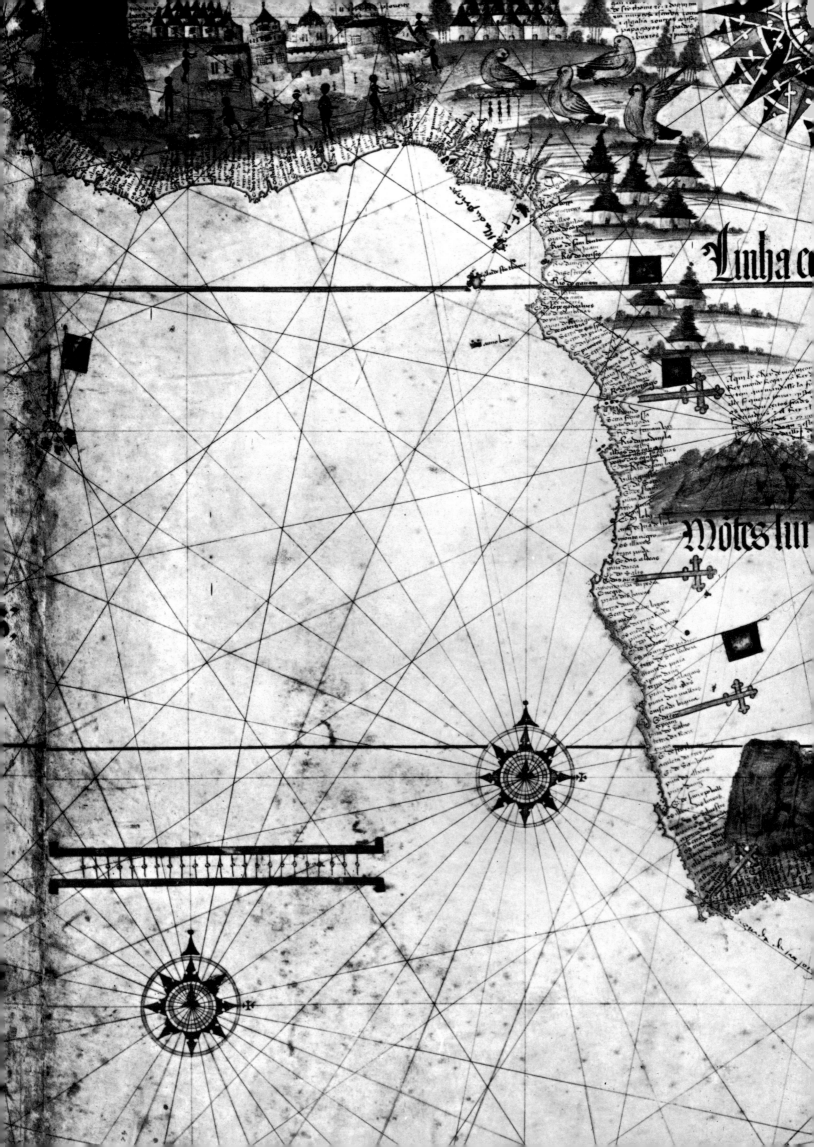

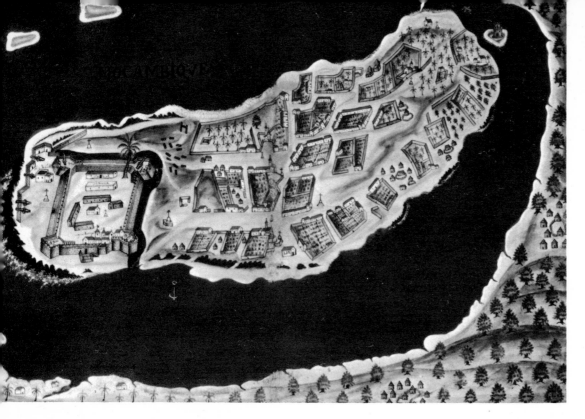

Plan of the island of Mozambique from a
Portuguese manuscript, showing the fortress,
houses of African and European types, and
numerous churches and crosses

Right: Bust of Antonio Nigrita, ambassador
from the kingdom of Kongo who died in
Rome in 1608, by Francesco Caporale. From
the Baptistry chapel of Santa Maria
Maggiore, Rome

Part of a Portuguese map by Diogo Homem
(1558) showing the Nile valley and Ethiopia,
with Prester John enthroned

plan to secure a safe way-station to the East while taking full advantage of local opportunities for buying gold and other goods, a local chief at what was to become Elmina (at the western end of the coast of modern Ghana) was asked for land on which to build 'a house' for the storing of merchandise. Assenting, he was surprised to find the Portuguese erecting what was obviously much more than 'a house' and that they were building it, moreover, on a piece of land traditionally held as sacred. The Portuguese account of this affair says that Azambuja, who was in command, managed to buy himself out of the fighting which then ensued and that 'the work was pressed on so fast that within twenty days the walls of the fortress were built up to their full height, and so was the tower . . .' After this Azambuja remained 'in the castle for two years and seven months, during which he set up a gallows and a pillory and made other ordinances and agreements with the Negroes to the great honour and service of the king of Portugal', and not neglecting, as a salutary warning of what was to come, to burn down the local chief's village.

Though it would long remain without much significance for the inland country, this early trade upon the coast expanded with surprising speed. From the first it fell into a geographical pattern that was to hold good in later times. Three main areas of useful contact were recognized. Westward, there was the long coastline between the mouth of the Senegal and Sierra Leone; and here, 'when the trade is well organized', Pereira was writing in 1506, 'we can look every year for more than 3,500 slaves, many tusks of ivory, some gold, fine cotton stuffs and numerous other goods.' In this 'windward' region, so-called because the prevailing winds blew from the west and south-west, trading contact was with Dyula merchants operating from their markets in Mali, with the Woloff states in Senegal, and with a host of little chiefdoms along the coast.

Next there was the central region based on Elmina Castle and other such coastal stations established by African agreement and against the payment of a yearly rent. Into these a little of the gold trade of the Akan forestlands now began to flow. The Portuguese were able to expand their trade here by augmenting the supply of porters, bringing in for this purpose a continual flow of slaves purchased at Benin and selling these for gold to their African partners in business, who also used them as mining labour. Here this new connexion promised so well that the English and the

French began pushing their way into a trade which the Portuguese, arguing Papal consent to their monopoly, regarded as entirely their own. There was much skirmishing at sea, but the interlopers could not be stopped. An early English voyage of 1553, consisting of two ships and a pinnace, brought back 400 lb of gold to London river, 36 barrels of peppercorns and some 250 tusks, the English being surprised to find that a basin of brass or copper could be exchanged for gold to the value of as much as thirty pounds sterling in the currency of the day.

Eastward lay a third region of trade, the empire of Benin. This commercial contact dated from 1485 when d'Aveiro was received at court and opened diplomatic relations between the King of Portugal and Oba Ewuare. Here the export trade was largely in peppercorns, later supplanted by a better product found in the Far East, as well as in ivory and in slaves for sale at Elmina on the Gold Coast. The Benin trade in peppers and ivory was entered by the English in 1553, but English and French vessels were few in these waters until the seventeenth century, and even then it was the Dutch who took the lead.

Eight hundred miles further down the west coast, Diogo Cão paralleled the diplomatic efforts of d'Aveiro at Benin by visiting the court of Mani Kongo, ruler of the Bakongo empire near the estuary of the Congo river. Here too envoys were exchanged and Portuguese missionaries allowed to settle at the capital. For a while, as at Benin, all promised well for this new partnership and alliance. 'Royal brothers', African and European, dictated polite letters to each other and exchanged their thoughts about the future. But the courtesies were not to last.

The Atlantic Trade

Passing through Cairo in the 1320s on his way to Mecca, the great Mansa Musa of Mali had told a dramatic tale of maritime adventure. He said that his predecessor had sent two big expeditions, one of four hundred ships and the other of two thousand, across the ocean in order to discover what lay the other side, but only one of these ships and its crew had ever returned. Even if these expeditions really took place, it is clear they were altogether exceptional. The coastal peoples of West Africa were skilful in building large canoes for inshore fishing and at handling these across thundering surf; but this was the obvious limit of their need. Until the coming of the Europeans, they faced an empty ocean. In this respect, of course, they were very differently placed from the Swahili peoples of the East Coast, who had long since learned ship-building and sailing skills from the Arab and Indian sailors of the Indian Ocean.

During the sixteenth century, however, there evolved in the Atlantic a trading community that was parallel to the much older and in many ways vastly different system of the Indian Ocean. From 1500 onwards the western seas were increasingly traced by sailing ship routes linking western Africa to western Europe, and soon afterwards to the eastern seaboard of the Americas and the islands of the Caribbean. In this new trading community West Africans played almost from the first an indispensable part. Their participation was not in the carrying trade itself, which remained a European monopoly of skill and ownership. But it was none the less vital to the whole system, and it forms an important aspect of the history of many African peoples.

Aside from unruly outbreaks here and there, European piracy along the Guinea Coast had given way to trading partnership well before 1500. But the partnership took a very different shape and meaning from that of eastern Africans with the Asian traders of the Indian Ocean. There along the East Coast, so far as all known records indicate, slaving remained a minor aspect of trade or one that was sometimes altogether absent. None of the Arab writers of the medieval period speaks of the slave trade from East Africa as being of any importance, and some of them do not mention it at all. If slaves were wanted they could be needed only for household work, for there was no plantation system in the East which could absorb large quantities of manual labour; and the number required for household work could never be enormous.

At first it was the same in the west. Though the Portuguese might be taking home several thousand slaves a year, they were still only supplementing the supply of domestic labour fed by an already existing and profitable trade in European slaves. So profitable had the Venetian Republic found its sale of Christian slaves to Egypt and other Muslim countries, indeed, that its merchants had not been deterred even by Pope Clement V's edict of excommunication for this offence, nor by his authorization to all other Christian peoples to reduce the Venetians to slavery in their turn.

But this use of slaves and slave labour, familiar in medieval Europe as in Africa, became an altogether different matter once the Americas were discovered.

Only hard work could open mines and make plantations flourish; and work was the last thing envisaged by the conquerors, at least for themselves. Yet even if Portuguese and Spanish soldiers and settlers had cared to labour in mines or plantations, they were desperately short of the necessary skills. They knew nothing of tropical farming; and, although they had miners of their own at home, these were few and could seldom be spared. Consequently it became necessary to find labour; and, if possible, skilled labour.

They started by impressing the 'Indians' – the native peoples whom they found – and the results were appalling. When Hispaniola was discovered 'it contained 1,130,000 Indians', a Spaniard well-placed to make this guess was writing in 1518. 'Today their number does not exceed 11,000. And judging by what has happened, there will be none of them left in three or four years' time unless some remedy is applied.' The remedy, in fact, had already been found. European slaves being in too short supply, and Amerindians incapable of filling the need for labour except with their corpses, recourse was had to Africa. Within a few years of Columbus' first voyage in 1492 the Spanish were taking West African slaves across the Atlantic: few enough to begin with, and yet sufficient to cause the governor of Hispaniola to complain in 1503 that too many Africans were escaping and 'teaching disobedience to the Indians'. They were also breaking away from enslavement in sudden and successful revolts, terrifying the local settlers; and it would be better, the governor thought, not to send any more. But no such counsels could prevail over the pressing need for labour.

Two years later, in 1505, a caravel sailed from Seville with seventeen Africans and some mining equipment. Five years after that the sale of Africans in the Americas was legalized by the Spanish crown. In 1516 Spain received its first shipment of slave-grown sugar from the Caribbean; and in 1518 a ship in Spanish service carried the first cargo of Africans directly from the Guinea Coast to the Americas. With this there opened a regular slaving system which was to endure for three and a half centuries, and convey across the ocean some tens of millions of Africans as well as causing the death before departure of many other millions. This peculiar form of trade, immensely valuable to western Europe but increasingly disastrous for western Africa, was to overshadow the whole commercial system of the Atlantic Ocean. It formed the major factor of difference, in so far as Africa was

Opposite: Ghana: the west bastion at Cape Coast Castle

Fort Jesus at Mombasa, greatest of the old Portuguese
citadels along the East Coast. Begun in 1593, but not
completed until 1639, this fine structure is a product of
Renaissance theories of fortification. Well preserved, today
it houses an excellent museum of antiquities

concerned, between the Atlantic system and its older counterpart of the Indian Ocean.

One may turn aside for a moment here and look at the conditions under which this overwhelming tide of forced emigration became so large a part of the African scene. While ashore on Grand Canary in the 1550s, John Hawkins of Plymouth heard not only that 'Negroes were very good merchandise in Hispaniola', but also that 'store of Negroes might easily be had upon the coast of Guinea.' Why easily?

The answer lay in the social systems of Africa. Like other systems based on economies of subsistence which were qualified but not essentially changed by a certain amount of production for trade, these had no wage-labour of any regular kind at their disposal. Having no labour market, they functioned either by organizing men and women of certain 'age sets' – men and women born at about the same time as each other – for traditionally accepted forms of labour, such as porterage among forest peoples who had no draught animals; or else by imposing free-labour services on certain groups and individuals. The latter might arrive at their servile condition through conquest, capture in war, or punishment for crime. More often, though, they would be peasants whose status differed little in essence from that of the serfs or villeins of medieval Europe, and who were regarded as inseparable from the land they tilled. As in Europe, it was customary to use such people for household or military services, for the accumulation of food or handmade goods, and for gifts or a means of exchange. In 1493, for example, the new emperor of Songhay, Askia Muhamad, inherited from his predecessor a number of 'slave peoples' whose slavery consisted in the obligation to provide certain stipulated goods or services. Blacksmiths had to provide spears, fishermen had to deliver fish or canoes or canoe-crews, cattle-breeders had to bring in forage or cattle, others had to perform household services.

There is no doubt that this use of slave or wageless labour increased after the fifteenth century. It was one of those aspects of Iron Age growth which steadily transformed the old equalities into new forms of central power and privilege. Kings imposed heavier labour-services, accumulated wealth in kind through wider use of slave labour, and raised slave armies to protect their authority from lineage rivals, usurpers, or popular revolt. All this, going hand-in-hand with the growth of trade and the expansion of money-currencies but generally stopping short of early forms of capitalism,

occurred in the Western Sudan from at least the time of Askia Muhamad. Later it spread southward into the forest regions under the Alafins of Oyo and the powerful kings of eighteenth-century Asante.

Yet these slave or 'wageless workers', one should note, were seldom or never mere chattels, men without rights or hope of emancipation. They might be bought and sold, given away and accepted as gifts. Yet their condition was different from that of the African chattel slaves who would labour in the Americas. They were not, as these were, outcast in the body politic. On the contrary, they were integral members of their community. Household slaves lived with their masters, often as members of the family. They could work themselves free of their obligations. They could marry their masters' daughters. They could become traders, leading men in peace and war, governors and sometimes even kings. 'A slave who knows how to serve', ran the old Asante proverb, 'succeeds to his master's property.'

These systems, then, were not 'slave-based economies' such as had existed in parts of Europe or Asia. They lacked the wholesale alienation of land into private ownership that could deprive the mass of people of their independent livelihood. If they had many forms of currency, notably the cowrie shell, these remained marginal to economic life as a whole. While skilful in trade and trading techniques, their merchants were by no means numerous or strong enough as yet to play a dominant role in the state. Horizontal divisions in society were increasingly apparent and important; but they could exercise political and economic influence only at certain points and in certain situations, none of which was capable of transforming these economies from subsistence systems to full-blown 'money-and-market' systems.

In the context of slavery, however, these systems manifestly provided many forms of obligatory servitude. Some men had much power and status, while others had little; and those who had little were increasingly, as the process of horizontal social stratification continued, at the service of those who had much. Comparatively large numbers of men and women became 'disposable' for one reason or another, mainly by capture in war or sentence of the criminal courts. And it was out of this situation that the trans-Saharan slave trade, and afterwards the infinitely greater trans-Atlantic slave trade, were born and made to flourish. However deplorable it may appear in the light of what happened later, this 'disposing' of 'persons of inferior status' can have seemed no more shocking or immoral to 'persons of superior status' in Africa than the arbitrary sacking and starving of workers seemed to the English employers of the industrial revolution. The one form of servitude appeared as 'natural' as the other.

Neither buyers nor sellers therefore found it strange that a demand for slaves should be met wherever the balance of interest led that way: meeting this demand, indeed, became part of the traditional economies of those concerned, whether they hailed from America, Europe, or Asia. Who generally bought and who generally sold was determined for the most part by the relative strengths of the economic systems in play. During the early Middle Ages the flow of slaves had gone from Europe to the Muslim states of the Near East and Egypt in exchange for the finished goods of those then more advanced regions; later, with Europe growing more developed, the flow was reversed and went from Africa to Europe. Only with the coming of wage-labour was slaving brought to an end; and wage-labour during many of its early years, characteristically for the attitudes out of which it had grown, imposed conditions which were seldom better and were sometimes worse than the outright enslavement of old.

The point to be noticed here is that the early sale of Africans to European sea-merchants departed in no way from previous practices of exchanging servile persons within Africa, or, indeed, within Europe. The only difference was that the slaves were sold for transport oversea instead of transport overland, a change that was of no importance (at least for many years) to the traditional economies and social systems either of sellers or buyers. And had the European demand remained at the minor level of interest where it stood before the American discoveries and enterprises, the slave trade with West Africa could never have exercised any major influence on the course of events. But the American discoveries changed everything.

Not only were Africans plentiful. They were also skilled in tropical farming and mining, being in these respects far superior not only to the Amerindians but often to the Europeans as well. As the years went by, they became so valuable and their rapid replacement so necessary, because of the hardships to which they were ruthlessly submitted, that the Portuguese from Brazil were even bringing gold to the Gold Coast, during the eighteenth century, in order to purchase with it slaves who could not otherwise be had. 'There remains only to tell you', wrote an English buying agent on the

Gold Coast in 1771 to his directors in London, 'that gold commands the trade. There is no buying a slave without one ounce of gold at least on it . . . Formerly, owners of ships used to send out double cargoes of goods, one for [buying] slaves and the other for [buying] gold. If slaves happened to be dearer than usual, the cargo for [buying] gold was thrown into the slave cargo in order to fill the ship. On the other hand; if slaves were reasonable the gold cargo was disposed of for gold and ivory at a profit of thirty, forty, or fifty per cent . . . How strangely things are reversed now . . . [when] we scarcely see a ship go off with her complement of slaves, notwithstanding her cargo [is arranged to allow for payment of] eighteen to twenty pounds sterling [per slave] on the average . . .'

By this time the trade was thoroughly engrained in the commercial system of the coastland. Its customs and regulations were almost a matter of tradition. From selling a few slaves in the early years, the Africans in the business – a 'business of kings, rich men, and prime merchants', as Barbot called it in the 1680s – found themselves gradually edged and pressured into providing more and more. Far outstripping the early demand for household slaves and domestics, the business now called for enormous numbers. These could be provided, as we shall see, only by warfare and capture, so that from the middle of the seventeenth century it is usually more accurate to speak of this trade as dealing in captives and not in slaves. Increasingly, the victims were prisoners-of-war whose enslavement began only with their sale to Europeans: few, any longer, had been slaves before they were sold.

Some of the 'kings, rich men, and prime merchants' who had lightheartedly embarked on selling 'common folk' to the Europeans soon found reason to hesitate. The Kongo king Nzinga Mbemba, baptized soon after 1500 as King Affonso I, had welcomed the Portuguese who came with promises of trade and useful knowledge, and made them many gifts of household servants and other persons of servile condition. But he found the Portuguese appetite for slave labour, whether for growing sugar on the offshore African island of São Thomé or for transport to Brazil, entirely insatiable. Portuguese agents rode roughshod over his authority among the coastal chiefs, dealing separately with each rather than through his own agents, and carrying off anyone they could get their hands on, including members of the king's own family. They spread such 'corruption and licentiousness', this Kongo king complained in a

Opposite: Though built by the Portuguese in 1482, the famous castle of Elmina in Ghana passed into Dutch hands in 1637. In the background of this picture is a market chamber where slaves were sold. The wrought ironwork in the foreground bears coats of arms and a monogram of the Dutch royal house

letter to Lisbon of 1526, 'that our country is being completely depopulated.' Two centuries later a king of Dahomey even offered to allow Europeans to establish plantations along the coast if they would cease to carry men away. There were other such attempts but none of them availed. To obtain European goods, especially the firearms whose use was now spreading through West Africa, it was necessary to meet the European demand for captives; and if one local chieftain or 'prime merchant' should refuse, his rival or neighbour would undoubtedly comply. Only a major shift in European demand could have brought the traffic to a close.

Brutality grew worse after about 1650 when the trade got into its stride. Coarsened by dealing in men, women, and children whose value was only what they could realize for cash in the Americas, and whose fate promised only a quick death or perpetual servitude, the sailing-ship captain soon came to treat his captives like cattle. He bought them for size or strength or handsomeness, applied crude tests for ensuring that the goods were 'as per invoice', crammed and chained them in stifling misery below decks, and sailed for the Americas with such slow speed as he could muster, hoping that losses on the way would not exceed ten or fifteen per cent.

'As the slaves come down to Ouidah from the inland country', Barbot wrote of the familiar scene, 'they are put into a booth or prison, built for that purpose near the beach, all of them together; and when the Europeans are to receive them, they are brought out into a large plain, where the ships' surgeons examine every part of every one of them, to the smallest member, men and women being all stark naked. Such as are allowed good and sound are set on one side, and the others by themselves: these rejected slaves are called Makrons, being above 35 years of age, or defective in their lips, eyes, or teeth, or grown grey; or that have the venereal disease or any other imperfection.

'These being set aside, each of the others passed as good is marked on the breast with a red-hot iron, imprinting the mark of the French, English or Dutch companies so that each nation may distinguish their own property, and so as to prevent their being changed by the sellers for others that are worse . . . In this particular, care is taken that the women, as the tenderest, are not burnt too hard.' A week or so later if ships were to hand, or many weeks later if they were not, these luckless captives would start the 'Middle Passage'

across the ocean, and with this again there were traditions of outrageous brutality. Every ship's captain feared revolt on board, and with good reason, for revolts were many. He would normally cause all his slaves to be chained below decks, sometimes bringing them up into the air once a day and making them jump about to restore their circulation. This was thought so necessary for health, the House of Commons was told in 1789, that the prisoners were 'whipped if they refused to do it'. Anti-slavery campaigners rightly pointed to the horrors and demoralization of these terrible voyages. They canvassed seamen in the great slaving ports of England and came back with gruesome evidence. 'Men on their first voyages usually dislike the traffic', Clarkson found after researches in Liverpool and Bristol. 'But if they went a second or third time, their disposition became gradually to be accustomed to carry away men and women by force, to keep them in chains . . . and to behold the dead and dying.'

American advertisement for the sale of slaves in 1784

Opposite top: Cape Coast Castle: its name corrupted from the Portuguese *Cabo Corso* (Short Cape), this was Britain's main fort on the Gold Coast. Its basic structure was built in the second half of the seventeenth century, being raised on the foundations of an earlier Swedish fort called Carolusborg *Bottom*: Drawing of the fortifications and city of Algiers (1668–9) by Wenceslaus Hollar, the Czech artist who held an appointment at Tangier in the service of the British

The degradation went beyond the slaving ships and plantations. Ramifying through European and American society, it formed a deep soil of arrogant contempt for African humanity. In this soil fresh ideas and attitudes of 'racial superiority', themselves the fruit of Europe's technical and military strength, took easy root and later came to full flower during the decades of nineteenth-century invasion and of twentieth-century possession of the continent. Even men and women of otherwise thoughtful and generous disposition came to think it well and wise that Africans should be carried into slavery, since they were carried at the same time, it was said, out of an 'endless night of savage barbarism' into the embrace of a 'superior civilization'.

But other men and women disagreed. British and French abolitionists played an admirable part in bringing the trade to an end. Often treated by their opponents as subversive revolutionaries who should be hounded from society because, in wishing to destroy a valuable national trade, these abolitionists had clearly 'sacrificed their national feelings', they undoubtedly hastened the day when slaving was declared illegal. Men like Sharp, Clarkson and the Abbé Grégoire deserve the more honour because their task appeared so hopeless. In 1775 the British Secretary of State for the Colonies, a certain Lord Dartmouth, could still tell Parliament that his Government was unable to allow a check or discouragement 'in any degree' to a 'trade so beneficial to the nation'. Thirty-two years later, all the same, another British government forbade any British ship to carry slaves; and the abolitionists could rightly claim that the victory was theirs.

Yet it was not, of course, only theirs or essentially theirs. Great changes in society may be hastened by good will; they have their origin in deeper pressures. The truth was that predominant British interests were no longer the same. The times had passed, as Eric Williams has explained in his classic study of this subject, when King Sugar could rule the day at Westminster. Having embarked on manufacturing industries at home, the British were more interested in their own labour market than in any that might exist elsewhere. By the final years of the slave trade in British bottoms, its main work was finished. The capital it had helped to accumulate and nourish by the triple profits of the 'triangular trade' – cheap goods to West Africa for the buying of captives, slaves to the Americas for the buying of sugar and tobacco, and these in turn to western Europe for cash – had gone far to float the in-

dustrial revolution off the shoals of doubt and speculation. Europe changed. And when the British and the French next looked for adventures oversea they went in search of raw materials, prestige and military advantage, and not in the least for slave labour.

A massive aid to the founding of mechanical industry: such was the main result of the oversea slave trade for western Europe. What the African chattel slaves had begun, the European wage slaves of the late eighteenth and early nineteenth centuries continued. Across the Atlantic the results were very different, but in any case so great as to be knitted deeply into the fabric of daily life in every American land or island except Newfoundland or Canada. By 1800 half the population of Brazil was of African origin. There was not a single Latin American or Caribbean community without its numerous Negro or partly Negro component. Many of the more prosperous North American states relied on Negro labour. And such was the rate of replenishment from Africa, following the rate of mortal wastage of the slaves, that these Negroes were for the most part much more than 'Africans by descent'. They were often Africans *tout court*. At any rate up to 1800 the rate of mortality was such that whole 'slave populations' had to be replaced every few years. More than half the soldiers of Toussaint Louverture and Dessalines, those rebels who carried through the anti-slavery revolution in Saint Domingue and defeated the armies of Napoleon and afterwards the armies of Britain, had made the Middle Passage and were 'first generation Americans'. To omit these peoples from the scope of African history would be like excluding the early New Englanders, Australians, Canadians and New Zealanders from the history of Britain.

On Africa itself, the home and source of all this slave labour, the long-range effects of the Atlantic trade remain harder to evaluate. They were undoubtedly very great, and far transcended the effects of other slave trades. The trans-Saharan trade in human beings never achieved a volume that could have any large consequence for West African society, however painful might be the individual consequences; while the Indian Ocean or East Coast trade in slaves was of even smaller significance up to the 1840s, though its influence for evil in the relatively brief but disastrous period of about 1840–80 became frequently extreme. In contrast with these, the Atlantic trade had grown to such a size by 1650 that for at least two centuries it did unquestionably bring a major influence to bear on

Opposite: Old trading houses in Calabar, for long a principal centre of trade in the Niger delta

View of the town on
Gorée Island, off Cape
Verde, an important
selling-station for the
Atlantic slave trade

The 'Middle Passage':
from a nineteenth-
century print

Inspection and sale of an
African captive in
exchange for firearms
and spirits

many coastal and near-coastal peoples from the mouth of the Senegal to the southern borders of Angola, a territory of varying and generally narrow width but more than three thousand miles in length.

Although depopulation might seem the most obvious effect of a trade which probably involved the deportation or death of several tens of millions of Africans over three or four centuries – estimates have varied between thirty millions and one hundred millions – a good deal of evidence suggests otherwise. It is perfectly true, as Hrbek has lately argued, that African populations (so far as anyone can guess) seem to have grown by 1900 much less rapidly than European, American or Asian populations. But to infer conclusions about the slave trade from this is to overlook two objections: first, that the African estimates (as recent counting in Nigeria and Ghana strikingly confirms) have probably been far too small, and secondly, that a number of African populations suffered disastrously from the upheavals and invasions of the years 1800–1900.

Some peoples must certainly have lost much of their strength to the slave trade. Wherever slaving struck at a people who were comparatively few or economically weak, it left an empty land: here the right comparison is with the forced emigration of peasants from the Scottish Highlands during the nineteenth century, an operation from which the population and economy of that region have yet to recover. But the parallel with emigration from Europe can also be extended to more populous countries and stronger societies, and the conclusion will be different. It seems unlikely, for example, that there was any more serious effect on the birth-and-survival rates of Iboland, through the forced emigration of the slave trade, than on those of southern Italy, Ireland, or England itself through an emigration forced not by outright violence but by hunger and unemployment.

Depopulation of Africa there undoubtedly was; but the main damage lay elsewhere. Essentially, the Atlantic trade was a large and long-enduring exchange of cheap industrial goods, mainly cottons and metalware and firearms, for the 'raw material' of African labour. (The inverted commas are also necessary because the labour was in fact often skilled in those very techniques most required in the Americas: tropical farming and metal-working.) Every question of humanity apart, this trade struck at Africa in two ways, both of which meant impoverishment. By flooding Africa with cheap substi-

tutes it undermined the local production of cotton goods and metalware, and helped to prevent any industrial expansion even at the handicraft stage. In the sixteenth century the Portuguese had imported the cotton stuffs of West Africa for sale in Europe; now the flow was reversed. Secondly, the Atlantic trade deprived a large number of African societies of many of their best producers, the youngest and strongest of their men and women; and it did this not spasmodically but regularly over a long period.

One may therefore regard the oversea slave trade as an early type of colonial economy, of the exchange of European goods for African raw material, and as one of the reasons why early forms of capitalism failed to develop in Africa until the latter part of the nineteenth century. No one can say how far African societies could or would have moved into cash economies and industrial methods of production if their early partnership with Europe, the partnership of the sixteenth century, had continued into later times. Yet there are some interesting pointers to an answer. When living in Kano a century ago, Heinrich Barth observed that handicraft production of textiles had reached such a high degree of 'cottage industry' as to be able to supply the whole of the Western Sudan from Senegal to Lake Chad. Far outside the slaving network of the Atlantic trade, Kano had clearly developed to the point where early capitalism could begin to emerge.

Later on, even within that network, a number of African societies adjusted to forms of capitalism with remarkable speed. They changed over from selling slaves to selling palm oil, cleared plantations of their own, traded enormously by credit, accumulated large reserves in cash or goods, even embarked on the business of chartering ships and crews. With Europe needing more and more soap as her factories grew in number and her cities in filth, palm oil exports from the Guinea Coast expanded from a few tons in 1800 to several thousand tons a year by the 1830s. This was not yet industrial production. But it was certainly an approach toward capital accumulation, the necessary parent of industrialism, such as had never been possible in slaving days.

If the economic effects were generally bad, some of the political effects surpassed them. Because the demand for slaves far exceeded the supply of those who actually lived under servile conditions – whether from capture in war, from sentence of the civil courts for crimes of one kind or another, or from any other reason – it was necessary to supply captives. And since African kings and merchants were generally hindered by their own social norms or political expedience from supplying their own people – though they certainly sold their political rebels, as being 'criminal', in much the same way as European governments transported theirs across the seas – they could obtain sufficient captives only by warfare or violence. Knowing that without captives they could not hope for European trade, the chiefs of the Niger delta armed their great canoes and sent them on expeditions into the populous inland country. The lords of near-coastal states plundered their tributary peoples for the same purpose. Wars and raids multiplied. At the same time a close-knit system of commercial interest ensured the buying of any captive who was brought for sale. If many regretted the trade which had led to this, none could long withstand its pressures. Among these pressures, the need for firearms and ammunition now became the foremost.

By 1700, if not before, few coastal or near-coastal kings or chiefs could feel safe in their country without a supply of troops equipped with firearms. Only with these could slaving wars be carried on and European trade assured; only with these could the slaving raids of their neighbours be resisted. Incapable as yet of manufacturing their own firearms, African kings were obliged to buy them from the Europeans. But the Europeans would sell them only in part-exchange for slaves. So the need for captives led to the need for firearms; and the need for firearms led to the need for still more captives, and still more firearms, in a vicious circle there seemed no means of breaking. Many of these coastal countries became gradually enmeshed in a spiral of mounting violence.

The Dutch agent at Elmina explained the roots of the system in a letter of 1701 to a friend in Amsterdam. Having described the skill with which Africans managed their 'muskets and carabins', Bosman wrote that: 'Perhaps you will wonder how the Negroes come to be furnished with firearms? But you will have no reason to do so when you know that we sell them incredible quantities, thereby obliging them with a knife to cut our own throats. Yet we are forced to do it. For if we did not sell firearms, the Negroes would be easily provided with them by the English, Danes, or Brandenburghers. And even if we [the official trading companies of these nations] could all agree not to sell firearms, still the English and the Dutch interlopers [private traders] would abundantly do so. In any case, since gunpowder

and firearms have been our chief selling goods for some time now, we should have done a poor enough trade without them . . .'

But what was true of firearms on the European side was likewise true of captives for enslavement on the African side. If one king refused to supply them he knew that his neighbour might not be so delicate. Even if all the kings could have agreed against supplying them, still there would have been plenty of individual operators to fill the need. And since slaves were what the Europeans chiefly and urgently wanted, no king or merchant along the coast could have hoped for anything but a 'poor trade', as Bosman puts it, without making his contribution in captives. Europe and Africa were thus involved in a trade that was morally degrading for both but was also, for Africa, often economically destructive and sometimes politically disastrous.

A group of captives being taken to the coast for sale as slaves

Mende mask, *Bundu-doble*, from Sierra Leone. This was used by the Poro society and represented the society's protective deity

Kono bearded mask, *Niamu*, from the N'zérékoré forest in Guinea. It is used by initiates of the sacred forest and may not be seen by women and children

6 Towards Crisis

*General outline of the history of the seventeenth and eighteenth centuries –
Emergence of new states in the forest and coastal lands of West Africa; in
the Niger delta; in Oyo, Dahomey and Asante – The Western Sudan after
1600 – The Bambara states – The Muslim revival movement both in
Western and Eastern Sudan up to the 1890s – East Africa, including
Madagascar, after the Portuguese ravages – South Africa and the Zulu
empire – The condition of Africa in the nineteenth century*

The Seventeenth and Eighteenth Centuries

Just as the sixteenth century may be regarded as marking a certain point of climax in the history of old Africa, at any rate to the south of the Sahara, the long period which followed may best be understood as one of transition – of several stages of transition – to the situations and problems of regained independence in Africa today. This is not to say, of course, that Iron Age structures had fully realized their inner potentialities of growth by 1600, nor that the years which followed saw nothing but the gradual decline of 'classical structures' until, with the 1950s, a new world could break its way through colonial doors: on the contrary, some of the 'classical structures' continued to evolve and expand. Nor was there at 1600 any more obvious break in continuity than at most other convenient dividing-lines in history. Life for a majority of folk went on much as before. The old traditions held firm. Families of ancestors, vanished from this world but well remembered, continued to give self-assurance and identity to their descendant peoples. The ancient customs were observed.

Looking back, though, one can see that new elements were at work. However obscurely or indirectly, more and more populations were now drawn within the orbit of a continental crisis, slowly gathering, slowly widening, of unexampled magnitude. This is especially true of the peoples who lived south of the Sahara. Up to the sixteenth century their civilizations had evolved out of their own unfolding dynamic in large though never complete isolation from the outside world. They had reacted in a variety of ways to the influence of the outside world, as the trading records most obviously show, but the reactions had been very much their own. They had built up new polities and systems of self-rule, but these had followed an emphatically African pattern. The many new answers they had found to many new problems of everyday life had developed within an indigenous framework little shaped by foreign pressure or example. Even where the universal religions of Islam and Christianity had made some headway these had rapidly acquired an African accent and appearance. 'Out of Africa there is always something new', ran the old Roman tag; and it was echoed down the years by men who observed that whatever came out of Africa did indeed seem different from anything they had previously known.

This 'African Middle Ages' – this Mature Iron Age, as I have suggested we may call it – came to an end around 1600, and there now began an equally lengthy period that was to include European colonial invasion and its aftermath. The actual 'point of change', if any such moment of break can be sensibly extracted from a process so very complex, occurred at different times in different places. For the Western Sudan it may be placed in the 1590s with the destruction of Songhay. For the Guinea Coast it came a little later with the wide expansion of the Atlantic trade. For the East Coast it struck as early as 1498 with the arrival of Vasco da Gama and the years of ruin that immediately followed. For North Africa, less identifiable than elsewhere, the 'point of change' may be thought to occur at the Ottoman conquests of the early and middle sixteenth century, while for southernmost Africa it can be fixed as late as 1652, when the Dutch made their first small settlement on the Cape of Good Hope.

Whether early or late in the sixteenth or seventeenth century, large regions of Africa were now pulled ever more closely and continuously into the affairs and ambitions of a rapidly changing world around them. Reservations must always be necessary in any statement as bold as this; yet the period which now opens, even when allowing for such reservations, does indeed appear to support this dominant and deepening trend. Africa is carried by successive stages into an ever greater economic and technological inferiority over against the industrial nations, and finally into a continental subjection which goes on until the 1950s. Then at last Africans can face the direct challenge of all those post-medieval skills which have fashioned the modern world, and formed a common ground for human equality.

This Age of Transition is therefore one of slow revolution, of gradual movement and enlargement in the forms and limits of Iron Age society – pre-industrial, non-scientific, based on economies of subsistence – to the threshold of full participation in the knowledge and techniques of the world of today. It is an Age of Transition which obviously still continues in these present years. Just as clearly, it is one that has displayed the resolution, or attempted resolution, of many inner conflicts and contradictions. Some regions suffered disaster. Others built new and effective systems of self-rule. Yet all of them, early or late, directly or indirectly, were caught within the same great underlying crisis of many-sided change.

New States in Guinea

Allied to the arms trade, the Atlantic slave trade had disrupting consequences which gradually spread after 1650 from the seaboard to the lands immediately behind the coast. Yet it would be wrong to exaggerate these consequences. The disruptions they caused at certain points along the coast and near the coast were undoubtedly very great. Further inland, however, these disruptions were either almost absent until the nineteenth century, or merely ancillary to other and much greater conflicts of political and economic power and interest. There was increasing warfare and insecurity in near-coastal West Africa. But to see this merely as the imposed result of slave raiding and 'tribal fighting' is to fall into the old Europo-centric myth of pre-colonial chaos or stagnation. In truth, this warfare

should rather be seen as the outcome of power conflicts, state conflicts, which were as politically intelligible as those of contemporary Europe.

And where some peoples lost, others undoubtedly gained. 'There is', remarked Pereira in 1506, writing of the long low line of mangrove swamps that leads away south-eastward from the river of Benin, 'no trade in this country, nor anything from which one can make a profit.' So it would remain for another century. The scattered peoples of this water-logged delta of the Niger, mainly Ijaw, had nothing to offer but fish and salt; and no ships crossed the ocean for salt and fish. But when they crossed the ocean to buy captives, the position in the delta singularly changed. For behind the delta villages on their tufts and clumps in the swampland lay the fertile country of the Ibo, one of the most densely populated areas in all Africa.

During the sixteenth century the population of the delta began to grow for a number of reasons. Refugees arrived from the wars of Benin with its tribute-states or rivals. The chance of trade with sea-merchants attracted others. Little states began to take shape at the mouths of the estuary. Gradually these became partners in trade with Europeans. Often their organization took highly original forms, reflecting in this their great diversity of peoples, Ijaw and Jekri and Oron, Ibo and Ibibio, Edo and many more. What became vital to the stability of a Niger delta state was not to find means of expressing and safeguarding ethnic separateness, for any such course would soon have ruined its unity and welfare, but to find ways of knitting different peoples into a new community.

This was skilfully achieved. Delta society became something entirely new in West Africa. In these small republics and monarchies the most powerful traditions and customs of previously separate identity were set aside in favour of new techniques of union. Foremost among these techniques was the 'canoe house', a kind of co-operative trading corporation governed by men of strong political authority, sometimes numbering a few hundred people of varying ethnic origin and social status, sometimes numbering many thousands. At Brass, Bonny and elsewhere, at the four main towns of Old Calabar in the Cross river, there emerged political and commercial systems of great resilience and originality where, in earlier times, none but little groups of fishermen had lived.

In this there was both development of potentialities inherent in Iron Age society, and, by the influence of

Opposite top left: Asante wooden dolls (*Akuaba*). These carved figures with small highly stylized bodies and large flattened heads were carried on their backs by women who wanted to have a baby (Height: 14¾ in. and 15½ in.)
Top right: Ghana: Top of a state umbrella from Akwapim: carved figure of a man seated with a bowl of food in front of him (Height: 8 in.)
Bottom: Stool of carved wood from Cameroons (Height: 15 in.)

Gold-plated Asante stool, a copy of the reigning Asantehene's (Sir Osei Agyeman Prempeh II) personal ceremonial stool, which will be blackened on his death and kept in the stool house to his memory. Each leg of the stool incorporates a knot of wisdom, traditionally symbolizing the Asantehene's resolve to rule with wisdom, and not through the power of the sword. The stool stands about eighteen inches high

An Asante boy carving a traditional stool

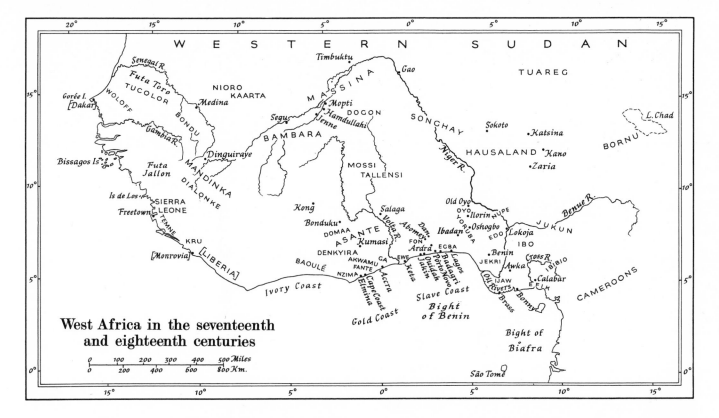

West Africa in the seventeenth
and eighteenth centuries

European trade, a certain adaptation to new forms that may possibly be called early capitalist. Traditionally, government and trade in the Delta had rested with the authority of lineage-groups that were little interested in economic expansion. As elsewhere in Iron Age Africa, the production of a food surplus had supported the emergence of many specialist workers who produced not food, or little food, but useful articles instead. This specialization in the Delta had seen the development of groups concerned with wood-carving, smithing, salt-making, potting, trading, divining-and-doctoring, and many other useful activities. But these specialists had remained for the most part within the limits of a subsistence economy: they produced for immediate needs and not for accumulation.

With the eighteenth-century development of the 'canoe house', however, accumulation became to some extent a deliberate aim in itself. What an enterprising man in the Delta would be likely to attempt now would be to buy or otherwise attract enough dependants to man a war canoe, a vessel requiring up to eighty or a hundred rowers and fighters, so as to embark upon the slave trade in a regular way. 'A potential founder of a canoe house', G. I. Jones points out, 'could use his wealth to buy more dependants; and the work of these

dependants in turn produced more wealth to buy still more people. It was a cumulative process . . .' Having thus 'filled his canoe', in the saying of the time, he would apply for acceptance as the chief of his own canoe house or trading corporation. If the established canoe houses found it in their interest to help him, they would recognize him as a trading chief.

In these and other new ways the city-states of the Delta built their commercial strength on strict monopoly of the coastal trade. No doubt there are parallels here with the history of the East Coast city-states, although these dealt mainly in ivory and gold, and not in slaves, and little is known of how they actually did it. In the Delta, however, the long Afro-European partnership has left copious records. They show clearly how these ingenious systems worked. Well armed, the Delta states saw to it that the inland peoples respected their monopoly. Perfectly capable of uniting among themselves when the need arose, they repeatedly forced the ships' captains and supercargoes of several European nations to pay scheduled taxes, to honour local customs, to moderate prices, and generally to treat as equals men like King Pepple and King Eyo and others of their energetic sort.

For their own law and order, and the needs of their

233

commerce, they relied on an adaptation of traditional sanctions. Among the Efik of the Old Calabar towns, for example, the effective government of society became that of Egbo, the 'leopard society'. Men of substance were organized at several levels of authority, commanding the obedience of men of lesser substance, to the point where Egbo could administer laws and apply punishments, settle disputes, organize business agreements, and act as an effective civil power. Reflecting its great concern with trade, Egbo was not an aristocratic or ancestral organization but one whose several grades of membership could be entered by meeting a fixed scale of payment. Its hierarchy of authority was thus achieved by means closer to those of the City of London than the House of Lords. It was a flexible system designed to meet the needs of a new type of society.

The trouble with these prosperous little states was that their trade was built largely on the sale of captives. 'All that vast number of slaves which the Calabar Blacks sell to all European nations', observed Barbot in the 1680s, and much the same observation would be true for another century and more, 'are not their prisoners of war, the greatest part of them being bought by those people from their inland neighbours.' Or when the inland trade faltered, as it sometimes did, the strong 'houses' of Bonny, Brass and other city-states would simply arm their war canoes and send them upstream to kidnap on their own account. Hence it came about that the ending of the slave trade, gradually from 1807 onwards, plunged some of these city-states into a crisis from which they found it extremely hard to emerge. Others among them, seeking new outlets, embarked on plantation economies of their own and began exporting palm oil. But even these, very successful though they often were, failed to escape the general crisis of the region, since by this time the pre-colonial movement of British territorial encroachment had begun.

Elsewhere along the Guinea coast the Atlantic partnership had varying but more or less comparable effects. Other little states prospered along what Europeans called the Slave Coast – the seaboard of modern Dahomey and Togo – and were active in the seventeenth-century slave trade. 'So diligent are they', Barbot remarked of Ardra and Jakin and their neighbours along this coast, 'that they can deliver a thousand slaves a month.' Though generally tributary to Oyo, they contrived a fair measure of independence until the 1720s when, as we shall see, they became involved in the great battles of the inland country.

It was much the same on the Gold Coast, the seaboard of modern Ghana. Here the growing maritime trade was conducted by Europeans, mainly English and Dutch and Danes, through some forty castles established on the coast with local consent and against the payment of a fixed rent; and from all this a dozen coastal states, led by the Ga, Fante and Nzima, drew steady profit. But here too, as we shall see, the balance of power turned not on European influence or presence, but on the varying fortunes of large states and empires in the inland country.

Further westward, beyond the inhospitable coastline of modern Liberia, the good harbours of Sierra Leone were likewise the scene of political development based increasingly on the opportunities of maritime trade, though little disturbed by the affairs of the lands behind them. Beyond these again the northward-trending coast of the modern Republic of Guinea, Gambia, Senegal – the coastland that Europeans came to know as Senegambia – continued to be dominated by the Mandinka, Serer and Woloff but acquired some special characteristics of its own. These were later to be of great importance, in that Europeans established themselves here on a number of 'sovereign' islands, such as Gorée near modern Dakar.

While these small states along the coast were reinforcing their trade and evolving new means of exploiting their contact with the European sea-merchants, large changes were under way in the lands behind them. There, repeatedly, Iron Age society wrestled with new factors. These were visible in more advanced techniques of government and warfare; in larger commercial ambitions (though still linked mainly to the northern and not the maritime trade); in the drive for greater political power coupled with a need for more abundant revenue from tribute and taxation; and, as seems likely, in the pressures imposed by steadily growing populations. These new factors brought new and widening struggles for supremacy. And these are the struggles that dominate the whole complex story of the forest and near-forest lands of western Africa during the two centuries between about 1650 and 1860.

More and more enclosed within its stifling divine kingship, the once prestigious empire of Benin plays surprisingly little part in all this. East of the Niger the Ibo were always too strong for it. And west of Benin there was the Yoruba empire of Oyo, far exceeding it in size and strength. Based on Old Oyo, in open country where their heavy cavalry could operate, the Alafin

Opposite: Hands and robe of Nana Owusu Sampa III, Omanhene of Akrokerri, during the yam festival celebrations

and his nobles now had dominion over many of the Yoruba states as far southward as the dense forest near the coast, a region where their power never securely ran. They greatly expanded this power in the eighteenth century, conquering much of modern Dahomey where open country comes right down to the sea, and dealing with Europeans through Porto Novo, which they dominated.

This large and orderly empire, administered by a non-literate but highly integrated system of chiefs and sub-chiefs, fed by revenues of tax and tribute from many prosperous farming peoples and defended by its cavalry as well as by its prestige, formed a political achievement of impressive size and scope. Little interested either in the slave or firearms trade, at least until the late eighteenth century, Oyo was able to prevent this commerce from inflicting much damage in Yorubaland. After enduring for nearly a century and a half it fell apart for detailed reasons which are still in dispute, but which probably derived from its having overgrown its strength. The first clear blow came with Dahomey's successful refusal to pay tribute in 1818. There quickly followed a damaging war of succession, and then, most fatal of all, an invasion of Muslim-led cavalry from the new Fulani empire in Hausaland.

These armies destroyed Oyo influence north of the Niger-Benue line, detached Ilorin from Oyo loyalty, raided and ravaged the northern Oyo towns and thrust many thousand Oyo subjects southward into the refuge of the forest. After 1840, when the northern invasions were finally halted at Oshogbo, the power of Old Oyo was gone. Efforts were made to re-establish it from a new capital further south, also called Oyo, under Alafin Atiba, 'a tall, charming, soft-spoken man, an imaginative conservative', in Ajayi's words, who was 'a little pathetic in his undying belief in the force of tradition in a world of revolutionary changes'. These efforts failed. From 1840 onwards until British invasion, the lands of the Yoruba were the scene of a tremendous struggle for power between the successor-states of Oyo. In this Ibadan gradually took a hard-fought lead. And then the British, profiting from these rivalries, came in with military expeditions and fastened a new kind of unity on these divided lands.

The inland and coastal country of Dahomey, west of Yorubaland, was the scene of a comparable struggle for power with the Fon state, based on Abomey not far from the coast. The Fon were eventually able to achieve a supremacy which lasted until French invasion at the end of the nineteenth century. This Fon state also had new characteristics of its own. It was organized on strongly military lines, its hierarchy depending not, as in Oyo, on membership of an aristocracy but on service to the state. Taking its rise at about the same time as Oyo – and here, once again, one may presume the driving pressures of Iron Age growth – the Fon were for a long time both tributaries of Oyo and victims of slave-raids by the city-states of the Slave Coast. Early in the eighteenth century, however, they grew strong enough to make a bid for independence from Oyo, and to forge their own partnership with the sea-merchants. Under Agaja (1708–32) they captured the coastal markets of Ardra (Allada), Ouidah (Whydah or Fida) and Jakin and thus brought themselves into direct contact with the source of firearms. Agaja seems also to have wanted to cut down the export of captives from which his own people had suffered: from this time onwards, at all events, the Slave Coast began ceasing to deserve its name. A regular supply of firearms, coupled with growing power in the inland country, brought the Fon to the height of their power under Agonglo (1790–7) and Ghezo VIII (1818–58). They could now at last turn the tables on their Yoruba overlords. Refusing the tribute demanded of them by Oyo, they invaded eastward into Yorubaland, making two great raids on Egba country.

Westward of Dahomey, meanwhile, a third great area of conflict had opened in the central and coastal lands of modern Ghana. Here again the same internal factors of political and economic rivalry came to a climax in the long and remarkable supremacy of the Asante empire.

By about 1650 the gold trade of the Akan forestlands, still facing largely to the northward, was divided among a number of producing and trading groups of Twi-speaking folk. Bono survived in Takyiman. East of it was Domaa. South of Domaa lay a number of fragmentary Akan peoples under tribute to Denkyira, then the strongest among them.

Two lines of development now emerged. After 1700, Denkyira was increasingly submerged by the rising power of Akan groups who called themselves Ashanti, or, as I shall write this word in line with modern West African usage, Asante. Secondly, though beginning a little earlier, the south-eastern part of modern Ghana saw the rise of the strong state of Akwamu. Under their famous king Ansa Sasraku, the Akwamu successively enclosed the Ga cities of the coast, Great and Small

Opposite: A traditional ruler of the Akan in full ceremonial dress. The little boy is his *okra*, an embodiment of his soul or spirit

237

Accra, and other states to west and east. By 1702 the king of Akwamu had more than nominal overlordship through some two hundred miles of country and coastland between the Fante state of Agona, his main vassal on the west, and the Slave Coast city-state of Ouidah, his distant though briefly-held boundary on the east.

Akwamu maintained its primacy among the states of the Gold Coast and Togo seaboard through nearly half a century. Challenged by the Danes at Christiansborg, soldiers of Akwamu seized the castle and held this for a year, trading under their own flag, until handing back the castle to the Danes in exchange for a smart ransom. Yet their political organization rested on no sufficient principle of unification. So long as the king's armies were loyal and successful, his vassals fulfilled their obligations and paid their tribute. Otherwise they remained little more than a collection of defeated neighbours awaiting their chance of relief. No such empire could long withstand the fissuring pressures of new rivalries. These soon appeared from the inland country. Jostled by the Asante, now nourishing imperial ambitions of their own, another Akan group or rather three groups, the Akim branches of Abuakwa, Bosume and Kotoku, began pushing into Akwamu territory from the north-west. After many battles the Akim made good their penetration. Akwamu by 1731 had practically vanished from the scene.

With Asante, though, the story is notably different. Emerging in the latter part of the seventeenth century, the Asante Union deserved its name. It was far more than a collection of defeated neighbours, though in course of later expansion it became this as well. After 1700 the Asante turned themselves into a group of peoples so closely self-identified that they were at once called a nation by European observers, and became sufficiently powerful and tightly organized to rule the greater part of modern Ghana for nearly two centuries.

Like the divine kingship of the old Mesopotamian legends, the mystical bond of the Asante groups of the Akan or Twi-speaking people of central Ghana 'came down from heaven'. This happened when the priest Anokye caused the Golden Stool of Asante to alight gently upon the knees of King Osei Tutu. The Stool became the sacred object which symbolized not only the union of separate traditional groups and loyalties but also the guarantee of their united wealth and welfare. So long as the Golden Stool was safe its adherents would prosper: but the condition of this safety was unity, and it was precisely the close-knit union of these

groups which most distinguished them from their neighbours. Beyond this legend there is the evidence, misty and yet persuasive, of a conscious effort to weld together those who would otherwise, if left apart, have fallen to the continued exploitation of their more distant neighbours, Denkyira or Domaa. Thus it is known that Osei Tutu enacted laws by which all previous and separate traditions must be forgotten, or at any rate consigned to silence. With these laws of 'common citizenship' every man of the Asante Union, publicly at least, was to place loyalty to the Golden Stool above all else.

Behind this legend there lay in any case a network of new commercial interests. Those chiefly families who led the Asante Union appear to have come from country to the southward. Perhaps they had looked for new land with which to grow new crops. Trans-Atlantic maize, sweet potatoes and pineapples were now spreading through West Africa with increasing fruitfulness. Or perhaps they had wished to fasten on the profits of the gold trade. Undoubtedly the gold trade became central to their polity. It is even reasonable to see in the Golden Stool a sort of livery or corporation badge of loyalty and function in this trade. So long as the Asante held the upper hand over the gold trade, they would prosper; and the condition of their holding it, quite certainly, was their unity of action.

Facts about the Asante Union begin to become available around 1700, thanks largely to the survival of records made by the English and Dutch trading companies along the Gold Coast. Putting these together with Asante tradition, it seems clear that Osei Tutu died at an advanced age in about 1712, having completed the forging of Asante groups into a nation and successfully thrown off the overlordship of Denkyira. Under Opoko Ware (1720-50) and his successors, Asante became the greatest power in the central forestlands, dominating the Gold Coast and part of the Ivory Coast, and trading extensively with the Western Sudan as well as with the Dutch at Elmina and the English at Cape Coast. Only with the reign of Osei Tutu Kwame (c. 1801-24) did the European element enter in any large degree into Asante strategy and foreign policy. But with the second half of the nineteenth century, this European element came gradually to overshadow the future and led, eventually, to British conquest.

The European cloud was at first a small one on the ocean skyline. In 1637 the great Portuguese castle at

Opposite: Double blade of a ceremonial sword from Akwamu, Ghana. This forms an important part of a chief's regalia, and is symbolic of his authority at an installation or enstoolment ceremony (Width of blade: 18½ in.)

Two finger rings (*nkaa*) and three wrist or knee bracelets (*nfre*) of the Asantehene. The top ring takes its name, *Kotoku Saa Bobe*, from the serval, which though neither leopard nor lion will not spare its prey. The ring with an elephant signifies the omnipotence of the wearer. The *nfre* are strings of precious beads and gold jewellery

Hilt of a ceremonial sword of gilded wood and iron from the Adanse area of Ghana, in the form of a woman's head. Used by king's messengers and Asante court officials

Elmina had passed into Dutch hands. Soon after this the rent agreement for Elmina, called 'the Note', had become the possession of the king of Denkyira who had taken the Dutch into peaceful trading partnership. This 'Note' was among the spoils acquired by Asante in its defeat of Denkyira after 1700. From now onwards the Dutch were lessees of Asante, not Denkyira, and so came to regard Asante as their principal trading partner. But their English neighbours at Cape Coast, by contrast, were lessees of the Fante, a coastal group of the Akan who were unwilling to admit their vassalship to Asante. In 1805 the Asante came down with their armies to subject the Fante. In this they easily succeeded. Pursuing their objective, Asante regiments attacked the little English fort at Abora under the walls of which a number of Fante fugitives had taken shelter. This tough skirmish had no further violent results, however, since the English were far too weak to contrive any (even if they had then wished to, which they did not), while the Asante merely insisted on recognition of their coastal sovereignty. Later on the clash was to repeat itself in different circumstances. An imperialist Britain would invade Asante and bring the greater part of the empire within colonial control.

Asante upheld its widespread peace and power for nearly two centuries. Safe and busy trading trails went out westward through Bonduku and Kong to the cities of the Middle and Upper Niger, eastward through Salaga to Hausaland, southward to the Europeans on the coast; and all these made Kumasi, the capital established 'under the shade of the *kuma* tree', into a market of far-reaching influence and a place of majesty and sure protection. When European agents were allowed to come here – and nine of them came in 1817–20, of whom five have left accounts of what they saw and heard – they were impressed by the king's liberal trading policies, the city's comfortable urban spread, and the agreeable condition of the people there.

'The rubble and offal of each house', noted Bowdich in 1817, 'was burnt every morning at the back of the streets, and the inhabitants were as nice and cleanly in their dwellings as in their persons', a comment that could then have been made with some difficulty of most of the big cities of Europe. Many caravans arrived and left for distant markets. Many visitors came from still more distant countries. A record of 1815, for example, shows a Muslim dignitary as having arrived from Arabia with two companions who left for Timbuktu

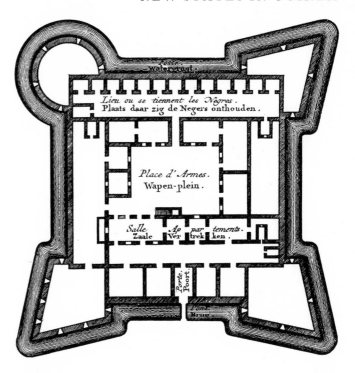

The English fort at Ouidah, now long since vanished, showing the armoury and the slave quarters

and Tripoli in the following year, while the dignitary himself returned to Mecca.

These Muslims who came to Kumasi did not convert the Asantehene and his court, though some of them seem to have tried their hand at doing so. They had freedom to worship as they pleased, and were not without a certain local power, being in command of most of the distributive trades or in service as clerks to the royal administration. A European visitor in 1824 even found that some of their leading men 'enjoyed rank at court, or were invested with administrative powers, entitling them even to a voice in the senate'. The head of the king's civil service, the Gyaasehene, employed a Muslim secretary who was literate in Arabic, while other such men served on government staffs in distant provinces, helped to draw up treaties and maintain political records, and generally formed the skeleton of a literate chancery system.

In these and other ways the Asante empire formed another and outstanding example of the gradual transition of Iron Age subsistence systems, during the eighteenth and nineteenth centuries, to more centralized, modern and expansive forms of power and organization. There is much in this to recall the earlier experience of the centralized states of the Western

241

Sudan. As early as the reign of Osei Kojo (1764–77) there were administrative innovations which opened the way to greater central authority through the growth of the king's civil service. If this bureaucracy affected most of the peasants and villagers of the empire very little, it was none the less increasingly influential at certain decisive points. Household troops recruited from slaves or mercenaries, and designed to bolster the king's power against his chiefs and governors, had become part of this centralizing apparatus by as early as the reign of Osei Bonsu at the beginning of the nineteenth century. So had eunuch officials. A militia called the Ankobia was kept for special service in the capital – a city of some 40,000 inhabitants by the early nineteenth century – and its control reserved for appointed men who could be relied upon, if the need arose, to act against hereditary chiefs. Not only Muslim Sudanese, but also Christian Europeans, were taken into royal employment. Facing British invasion in the 1870s, the Asantehene engaged a German called Nielsen to raise and train Hausa troops for his army. Another early 'expatriate technician' was a Frenchman called Bonnat, co-governor of a province. A third was a Scots American who supplied economic advice.

By the nineteenth century, Wilks tells us, 'the central government had assumed control of a wide range of activities.' Among these was a state trading organization maintained by the king alongside the 'private sector' in trade and mining. Down to 1873, in Caseley Hayford's words, 'a constant stream of Ashanti traders might be seen daily wending their way to the coast and back again . . . The trade chiefs would in due course render a faithful account to the king's stewards, being allowed to retain a fair portion of the profits.' Officials were kept at royal expense, paid for their services, and sometimes given an old age pension. Foreign affairs and other state business were administered by strong central control, while communications were upheld throughout the far-flung empire by a rapid system of messengers across long miles of road. The king in Kumasi, Bonnat could observe, 'knows each day what is happening in the most humble villages of his empire. From all sides he receives reports and minute details . . . [while] conversely, day and night, the orders of the king are despatched in all directions.'

Like Oyo before it, the Asante empire had trouble with its constituent populations. Around 1750 a breakaway group of Akan marched westward into the inland

country of the Ivory Coast, there to found a state under their new name, the Baoulé. Distant peoples tended to revolt or disobey. More important, the early Asante towns established around Kumasi in the late seventeenth century retained a largely autonomous character, so that 'the king's administration', Wilks explains, 'possessed no jurisdiction within the territories of the chiefs of Bekwai, Juaben, Kokofu, Nsuta and Mampong'. Such weaknesses as these counted for much during British invasion. Even so, the empire remained great and powerful throughout most of the nineteenth century. Only the superior firepower and military organization of the British were able to subdue and finally destroy it.

Peasants and Prophets

While Oyo and Asante gathered strength and grew into states and empires, the Western Sudan entered a long period of rebellion and reform.

Under Moroccan rulers the men of Timbuktu lost their old freedom of action and enterprise. Their city dwindled in wealth and prestige. Their trade declined. Their schools of learning shone no longer as in the days of Ahmad Baba and his contemporaries of the sixteenth century. When Europeans came here two hundred years later they would be astonished that so poor a city could ever have enjoyed so wonderful a reputation. The old Songhay capital of Gao suffered even more from Moroccan invasion and occupation. This once dynamic trading centre, where the emperor Askia Muhamad had his tomb, fell to little more than a provincial market-village, dusty and ill-considered, easily forgotten. Jenne, the third of the great Middle Niger cities, remained important as the northern terminal for much of the trade of the forest lands, but slowly fell away in size and wealth.

This shrinking of the cities was fatal to any hope of remaking the power of the Songhay empire. For more than a century they had given Songhay its motive power and cohesiveness. Once they were lost, the empire sundered into pieces. The long-service soldiers of the Askia melted away, returning to their villages or taking service with other lords. The careful edifice of bureaucratic control vanished from the scene. In tune with this collapse the early seventeenth century saw the rebellion of tributary peoples of the empire. Groups thrust into servile status by the lords of Songhay threw off their bonds. There came a time of reassertion for

Nana Owusu Sampa III, Omanhene of Akrokerri,
celebrating the Afahye (Yam) festival on 5 December 1964

all those peasant folk, generally hostile to the cities and to Islam, who had felt the pressure of the Songhay system in wide regions lying on both sides of the Niger.

One by one the gates of urban order and authority were forced or smashed. Out of the northern oases there came the lean Tuareg of the Sahara, battering at Gao and Timbuktu, taking their revenge on the power which had long subdued them or held them at bay. Out of the southern lands, the southern grasslands marked by their lofty baobab trees, there pressed other riders bent on the same looting purpose, Mossi and Dogon and Bambara and their like, men who had long waited their moment and seized it now with fury and the glint of spears. Discouraged and defeated, the Moroccans in the cities lost all heart for further conquest, and far away in Marrakesh and Fez were soon forgotten or abandoned to their fate. Nothing remained of Songhay power but a few centres of resistance in the south from whence, now and then, desperate raids were launched upon what yet remained of Moroccan military strength.

But gradually, from all this tumult and dismay, a new pattern began to emerge. Country folk transformed themselves from raiders into settlers. Having done so, some of them borrowed Songhay traditions and techniques of central government, and began, after their own fragmented fashion, to build new systems of non-Muslim law and order. Among these were Bambara peasants who lived along the Niger west of Timbuktu. Not long after 1600 these farmers founded new settlements beside the river west of Jenne and the Niger lakes. Towards 1650 we hear of them being led by an enterprising chief called Kaladian, probably an historical figure though possibly the traditional name for several 'founding heroes'; and Kaladian reigns until about 1680, founding a little state that is based on the river port of Segu. From here Kaladian sends expeditions against neighbouring folk, obliging them to pay tribute in the manner of the old empire. But this early Bambara 'empire' has no systematic framework of authority to sustain it, and disappears with Kaladian's death.

Yet the process continues. In about 1712 the little Bambara state at Segu comes under the rule of another bold and ambitious leader who is certainly an historical figure, the famous Mamari Kulibaly, Mamari the *Biton*, the Commander, at first the captain of a raiding band but soon a king of substance. Mamari outwits or outfights his rivals and enemies, and lays far stronger political foundations in Segu. It is not for nothing that

he has his military title. He borrows defensive techniques from Songhay tradition, forms a long-service army several thousand strong, adds a long-service 'navy' of canoes to patrol the Niger, using for these purposes men who have been captured in war and thus reduced to servile status.

With these forces Mamari the Commander challenges and defeats his close neighbours, Soninke, Fulani, Mossi and others. In 1730 he beats back an invasion by the Muslim king of Kong, a southern trading state which no doubt disliked this Bambara interference with ancient Muslim channels of trade and influence. Mamari also attacks far down-river and briefly holds Timbuktu. He makes the little state of Segu into a miniature successor-empire of Songhay along the river. In 1753, smarting under his tough rule and monopoly of power, a section of his subjects quit Segu and march north-westward, forming another Bambara state in Kaarta and Nioro, the old homelands of ancient Ghana.

Both of these Bambara states remained important in their region until the middle of the nineteenth century. But their history was a troubled one. After Mamari's death in 1755 there followed eleven years of swashbuckling chaos under the rule of one usurping general after another. Then Ngolo Diara seized the throne in 1766, put an end to army ambitions, and ruled over a reconstituted state until 1795. Two years after Ngolo Diara's death a solitary English traveller made his way to the city of Segu through many hostile boundaries and not unreasonable suspicions, and revealed, by what he found, that Ngolo Diara's reign had done much to regain the old prosperity of the Middle Niger towns. Mungo Park found Segu with a population of about 30,000, as he thought, inhabiting four residential quarters composed of clay-built houses of one or two storeys. 'The view of this extensive city,' he wrote, 'the numerous canoes upon the river, the crowded population, and the cultivated state of the surrounding countryside, formed altogether a prospect of civilization and magnificence which I little expected to find in the bosom of Africa.'

Elsewhere, the accent on reconstruction in the Western Sudan had once more become specifically Muslim. There now begins a long attempt, or series of attempts, to rebuild once more a grand Muslim polity which is aimed at bringing the whole of this vast region, from the Atlantic to the Nile, within the borders of Islamic law and order and thus recovering the power and splendour of the old Western Caliphate. For a hundred and fifty years this vision will glow with varying success and brilliance. It will inspire one bold enterprise after another, sometimes with high success and at other times with none. Often unleashing bitter warfare, always posing the conflict between Islam and the traditional religions of West Africa, now with one people in the ascendant and now with another, the Muslim effort is driven and led by a long succession of outstanding leaders from the early imams of the far west of the Sudan, almost within scent and hearing of the broad Atlantic, to the Mahdi of the Nile and of the wastes of Kordofan.

The earliest exponents of Muslim revival came from an unexpected quarter. They were Fulani and other cattle-driving folk who had given up their old religion together with their nomad habits, had settled in towns and accepted Islam, and had acquired chiefs and political ambitions. Profoundly influenced by the Islam of the western Arabs which had reached them by steady infiltration through Mauretania after the fifteenth century, they set out to build new Muslim states. The first of these was situated in the hills of Futa Jallon, near the middle of the modern republic of Guinea, and was established in about 1725 by a mixture of Muslim peoples under Fulani leadership. These subdued the local Dialonke, who were Mande-speaking farmers; and ruled on military and theocratic lines. They drew their chiefs or Almamys from two senior families, the Alfa and the Sori, and provided for the imposition of armed service on men who served as their *mujahidin*, their warriors of Islam. Other groups also met this call to power through religious revolution. A second imamate was founded in 1776 in Futa Toro along the south bank of the Senegal. This was by a Tucolor group (Tekrur in Arabic: these people were and are in fact Fulani) called the Torobé. They defeated the ruling king of the old Denianke line (itself founded in 1559 after an earlier Fulani-Mandinka invasion), and set their leader, Suleiman Ba, in his place. At about the same time a third Fulani imamate emerged in Bondu, the grassland plains which lie along the modern frontiers of Senegal and Mali.

Something of the depth of this Muslim revival can be glimpsed from the memoirs of Mungo Park, who passed through the imamate of Bondu at the end of the eighteenth century. He speaks of the country's growing trade and farming production, but also of its attitudes of tolerance. 'Religious persecution', he says, 'is not known among them, nor is it necessary; for the system

of Muhamad is made to extend itself by means more abundantly efficacious. By establishing small schools in different towns, where many of the pagan as well as Muhamadan children are taught to read the Quran, and instructed in the tenets of the Prophet, the Muhamadan priests fix a bias on the minds, and form the character of the young disciples, which no accidents of life can ever afterwards remove or alter. Many of these little schools I visited in my progress through the country, and observed with pleasure the great docility and submissive deportment of the children . . .'

With this Muslim schooling of the countryside there now developed, as it would seem, a gradual blurring of the sharp edge of conflict between Muslim towns and non-Muslim countryside, so that later on, during the nineteenth century, it was to become possible for Muslim leaders to raise the religious loyalty of peasants who must often have refused it in the past. The sociology of all this will be better explained as scholars now visit the libraries of the devout, and study the many thousands of documents, some old and some new, which are there collected and preserved. Even at this stage of knowledge, however, a few points stand out clearly.

Penetrating the countryside, Muslim missionaries and teachers gave Islam a broader base. In doing this they prepared the way for a change in their teachings. There occurred a certain process of democratization. The older attitudes had contained an element of exclusiveness well suited to Dyula traders and other Muslim groups who travelled the length and breadth of West Africa; or to city-merchants and rulers for whom Islam offered an ideological basis, both for central government in multi-ethnic states and for the techniques of trade and credit. Relatively new Muslim states like Kong, for example, were built on a hierarchy of privilege that was buttressed by Islam, and from which the rank-and-file were distanced if not actually excluded. Particular forms of West African Islam tended to strengthen these tendencies towards social rigidity. Taking over the characteristically African concept of spiritual power vested in a particular person – priest or wizard or soothsayer – Muslim leaders sometimes acquired a mystic authority denied to them by the orthodox tenets of Islam. After the manner of Sunni Ali of Songhay, for example, they tended to be revered as magicians even more than as Muslims. Hence the very special – and often highly privileged – position of Muslim marabouts in certain regions of West Africa, notably Senegal.

Opposite: Fulah woman with gold earrings, at Mopti on the Upper Niger

Perhaps the most interesting of these changes within West African Islam was the steady political eclipse of the Qadiriyya brotherhood – traditionally conservative, hierarchical and contemptuous of the heathen – by the Tijaniyya, a new brotherhood which became an 'Islam for the poor'. Here, too, West Africa worked its own pattern into ideas whose original content had been very different. The Tijaniyya was founded as a proselytizing movement by a North African teacher, Ahmad al-Tijani (1737–1815), who was himself no revolutionary. Transplanted to the Western Sudan, however, the Tijaniyya was to supply the religious means *par excellence* whereby the later Muslim revolutions of the nineteenth century were carried through. It was to be the instrument for conversion of many peoples of the countryside hitherto inimical to the 'Islam of the towns'.

Yet the reforming movement, perhaps needless to say, was never a simple single-stranded thing. Men's motives were as mixed as in other movements of reform in other lands. Towards 1800, when the influence of religious change was present in one form or another right across the Western Sudan from the Futa Toro to the Hausa states, Uthman dan Fodio led a largely Fulani movement of revolt against the rulers of Hausa-land (*Fodyo* or *fudi* was a senior grade of Muslim teacher in the language of the Fulani). Like his companions, Uthman was a member of the Qadiriyya brotherhood, not the Tijaniyya, the latter wielding influence in the Western Sudan only after the rise of its caliph, al-Hajj Umar, in the 1840s. Here there were many elements, whether of Muslim revival, social reform or political ambition. Yet it is worth noting that Uthman's writings and those of his companions placed great importance on the reform of government and the end of administrative abuse as practised, at least according to Fulani accusations, by the Hausa kings. And the success of Uthman's revolt rested to some extent on his achievement in winning support from many Hausa people. He and his companions preached against autocracy, political brutality, everyday injustice. They denounced the 'collecting of concubines and fine clothes and horses that run in the towns, not on the battlefields, and the devouring of the gifts of influence, booty and bribery'. They set themselves against bad rulers 'whose purpose is the ruling of countries and peoples in order to obtain delights and acquire rank...' They wished, on the contrary, to rule by the principles and teachings of the great Islamic tradition of the Rightly-Guided Caliphate; and there was always in their attitudes, at least at the beginning, a powerful note of personal abnegation and moral regeneration.

But having acquired power, these Fulani reformers in Hausaland were faced with the practical problems of wielding it. They stepped into the place of the Hausa kings and, in so doing, were led to compromise between their ideals and the fruits of office. Religiously inspired revolution could demolish an unpopular and stagnant polity: lacking any new *material* policies, it found the task of building a better social structure altogether another problem. Dissension over the land distribution among Fulani leaders quickly followed; and Uthman's son Muhamad Bello, who became the first Sultan of Sokoto, had to impose his imperial authority by force of arms over dissident leaders like 'Abd al-Salam. Before long the new Fulani hierarchy had taken over the administrative system of their Habe-Hausa predecessors. But they had also been driven, like other usurpers and conquerors elsewhere, to corrupting the representative elements of the system they had seized into something very near autocracy.

There was perhaps nothing else they could do within the limits of their situation. Sultan Bello and his peers had to deal with acute and pressing rivalries among the 'family groups' which had led and largely formed the *jihad*. These 'standard bearers' demanded land and power. Necessarily they were given both. In receiving them, they deepened the social divisions of Hausaland. Hausa rule had evolved in some four centuries of state and city government into a constitutional monarchy hedged about with many checks and balances. The Hausa *sarki* or king could act only when assured of a sufficient consensus of his nobles and officials. This was not democracy; but it was certainly not absolutism. In a city-state like Zaria the king's political control was limited by the power of politically-appointed officials, the latter being in turn limited by the parallel power of administrative officials. In the end the king was sovereign; meanwhile, he had to move in everyday affairs with studious care for the equilibrium of a system of which he was also, in the end, only the elected head. Perhaps the position of Elizabeth I of England, at any rate in relation to her nobles and officials, was not so very different.

Yet the Fulani conquerors, having to impose their minority rule upon this system, could have no such delicate regard for precedent and balance. The exercise of new possession carried its own imperatives. 'After Fulani conquest,' M. G. Smith has explained, 'the

Opposite: Ekpo mask, carved by Ukut Urua of Ukana, Ikot Ekpene, south-east Nigeria, in 1930

government of Zaria changed from a constitutional monarchy to a qualified absolutism'; and this absolutism, at Zaria as elsewhere among the conquered Hausa states, 'grew and persisted as a system, although its personnel changed with each reign as an effect of dynastic rivalry'.

Once again one may note the failure of Islam's utopian illusion. The *mujahidin* of Uthman and his standard bearers might in their better moments wish for a new social and religious equality such as could restore the Rightly-Guided Caliphate of legendary times, Abbasid times, or even the 'golden age' of the Western Caliphate in the Sudan. Reality was different. Great though its civic achievements had often been, that 'golden age' of Mali, Kanem and Songhay had not rested on a growing equality between rich and poor, weak and strong. On the contrary, it had rested on a growing inequality; and this was the intensified stratification of society between rulers and ruled, bond and free, poor and privileged, out of which the political and military triumphs of the past had come. If the Hausa rulers had made themselves oppressive to ordinary folk, forming armies, building palaces, exacting labour services, they had done so only in the wake of their great exemplars of the Western Caliphate, the Askias of Songhay and Mais of Kanem-Bornu. Herein lay the essential and enduring contradiction of this Muslim

revival: in their best ideals, and in their genuine reformism wherever this existed, the revivers of Islam necessarily set themselves against the very patterns of society which had given Islam its strength.

Even so, the new power in Hausaland offered remarkable evidence of what may happen when philosopher-kings ascend the throne, and it was here that the *mujaddidin*, the revivers of Islam, reached their zenith of intellectual distinction. When the British explorer Clapperton had audience of Sultan Bello it was no accident that he found the latter reading Euclid in Arabic, and was then engaged in a difficult discussion on the merits of Christianity. These new rulers in Hausaland were scholars of stature, eager to reform abuse and render justice. To Uthman, his brother Abdullah and his son Muhamad Bello are attributed some 258 books and essays on a variety of theoretical and practical subjects, while the chancery correspondence between Sultan Bello and his rival of Bornu, Shehu Muhamad al-Amin, bears witness to the high level of literate education in which these men were trained.

Their system of training was far from merely local or provincial. It rested on practices of Islamic learning that were centuries old. F. H. El-Masri has described it. 'After having attained a basic knowledge of religion, reading and writing in boyhood, the aspirant scholar (*talib*) would then travel about to learned men and stay with them till he had perfected with each the particular science in which that scholar had gained his fame; having completed his studies to the satisfaction of a master, he would then be given a licence (*ijaza*) to teach the subject he had been taught, on the authority of the master. In this way the *talib* would go round to collect *ijazas* and thus establish fame as a recognized scholar. This process would not normally cease at a certain stage or age, for whenever a scholar was to be found, who had excelled himself in a branch of knowledge no matter whether a local man or a foreigner, others would go to study under him.'

Cities like Sokoto now offered, in this widening community of religious reform and scholarship, this bodying forth of a new *dar al-Islam*, a magnet of attraction for every man who shared their ideals and wished to emulate their distinction. One such arrived in 1826, coming from Mecca, a Tucolor scholar named Umar bin-Said. Newly appointed caliph of the Tijaniyya brotherhood in the Western Sudan, al-Hajj Umar was to build himself a career on the grand scale. Yet he took his time. He settled in Sokoto and lived there for eleven

Left: A letter from the chancery correspondence of Sultan Amin of Bornu, writing on a boundary dispute to his neighbour, Sultan Mu'azz of Sokoto, about 1877–80
Opposite top: Timbuktu as Heinrich Barth saw it in 1853–4
Bottom: One of a number of brick buildings of the Muslim period at 'Ain Farah, in Darfur, that probably dates from the sixteenth century. The triangular niches are common in Muslim architecture from one end of the Sudan to the other

Mali: the Ginna (house of a Dogon priest), occupied by the
oldest man of the village

years, playing some part in public affairs and marrying, among other wives, a daughter of Sultan Bello's. In 1837, pursuing his slow-maturing plans, he went to live in Futa Jallon a thousand miles to the west. And still he waited. Only in 1848 did he launch his *jihad* from Dinguiraye in Upper Guinea, where he had formed a small imamate. But then his success was rapid and far-reaching. Leaving his son Habibu (by Sultan Bello's daughter) in command of his little imamate at Dinguiraye, Umar marched northward with his *mujahidin*, his warriors of Islam, and overthrew the Bambara rulers of Kaarta and Nioro. In 1861 he took Segu from the Bambara successor of King Ngolo, and established there his son Ahmadu at the head of another imamate.

In mastering Segu, however, Umar was launched upon a career of political unification which could take no account of the precept that Muslim must not war on Muslim. Down river from Segu lay the potent little Islamic state of Hamdullahi ('God Be Praised'). Founded by one of Uthman dan Fodio's followers after 1805, and based principally on Fulani people of the torrid grasslands to the south of the great Niger Bend, this Massina state had evolved through half a century of strong Muslim rule into a theocratic imamate of considerable social achievement. In 1862, ruthlessly moving for power in the whole country of the Middle Niger, Umar struck at this state and destroyed it, only to be killed himself, two years later, during an expedition against the people of the Bandiagara hills. For a while, the empire he had built survived him. His son Ahmadu, though with many difficulties and facing many revolts, remained in substantial control of Segu, Kaarta, Nioro and Dinguiraye.

Yet the great vision of social and religious reform and unification had sadly faded by now. Though originating

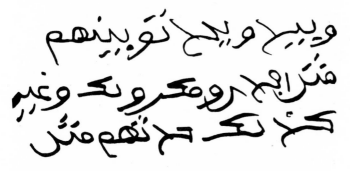

Some West African peoples wrote their languages in an Arabic script. This is from a fragment of local history written in Kotoko, a language of Chad, in about 1900

in that vision, the Tucolor system had become a family business incapable of maintaining the wide popular appeal from which its military strength had sprung. More and more, the wars for Islam degenerated into mere slaving raids and forays after plunder. Perhaps it might have been otherwise in less critical times. As it was, the Muslim revival now clashed fatally with a new power that was to sweep everything before it. As early as 1856 al-Hajj Umar's troops had skirmished with a French garrison, thrust far forward from its base on the west Atlantic coast, at Medina on the Upper Senegal river. Gradually the French now edged their way eastward into the Sudan. In 1890 they forced their way into Segu itself. Soon they had completed the subjection of the Tucolor system and of all rival systems, while the British, marching northward from the Nigerian coast, did the same a few years later in the lands of the Sokoto empire.

Given the balance of wealth, arms and experience of war, this would no doubt have come about in any case. Yet internecine quarrels greatly helped to open the gates of the Sudan. And this characteristic failure, this poverty of political achievement when compared with moral and religious aspiration, reappeared in the Eastern Sudan with the comparable reforming movement of the Mahdi Muhamad Ahmad ibn 'Abdullah. There, true enough, the circumstances were somewhat different. The Mahdia or Muslim Reformation in the Eastern Sudan began in 1881 after a long period of Turco-Egyptian rule aggravated by British and other foreign interventions. In a sense which was not true in the Western Sudan, where no such outside rule had yet existed but for the brief Moroccan interlude after 1591, the Mahdi was also 'Abu 'l-Istiqlal, the Father of Independence. Yet the Mahdi and his companions were no less concerned with religious and moral renewal than their forerunners in the Western Sudan. And Muhamad Ahmad went further than other reformers – than Uthman dan Fodio or Umar bin-Said or Muhamad al-Wahab in Arabia – precisely in that he declared himself the Mahdi, the appointed of God; and his vision was correspondingly wider than theirs. He saw himself as the central figure in a reformed and united *dar al-Islam* that would embrace the whole of West as well as North Africa. His trouble came in translating this highly political vision – and what, after all, could have seemed more worthy of achievement than the unification of the African Muslim world? – into political practice, especially at a time when

European imperialism had already started on its road to conquest.

Looking back on their grand enterprises, one may well think that the Mahdi and his near-contemporaries in the rest of the Sudan were above all unfortunate in their time. Much misunderstood or calumniated in Christian European records, they were undoubtedly men of outstanding vision and memorable purpose. Their tragedy was that they came too late to re-establish the wide Islamic systems of the medieval world, and yet too early to reconstruct any large region of Africa upon a scheme of rational multi-ethnic union. Their vision and their purpose foundered in the greatest crisis that Africa had ever known.

East Africa: After the Portuguese

Having wrecked the Afro-Asian trading system of the Indian Ocean, the Portuguese had made some effort to restore it to their own advantage. In this they failed and were quickly superseded by the Dutch. But the Dutch bothered not at all with East Africa or its trade, finding the Golden East more profitably attractive. From this neglect there followed two developments along the coast in the eighteenth century.

The first was a dwindling or vanishing of Portuguese garrisons and settlements. The effort of those that remained was reduced to occasional expeditions by little groups of armed settlers far up the Zambezi or along the Mozambique seaboard, while most of the gold-bearing country of the central plateau remained, as before, beyond their reach. Stiffly encased within a monopolist system directed from Lisbon by way of viceroys in Goa on the south-west Indian coast, the governors and captains in Africa had a care for little more than the fortunes they could hope to make during the brief periods of appointment they had bought. Those who served in lesser positions understandably followed suit. Indifference and boredom reigned over all. English naval visitors at Mozambique Island in 1812 found themselves greeted at the governor's residence 'by the clashing of billiard balls and the confused clamour of contending voices, so that we at first took it to be a tavern or gambling house.' But the governor, they were told, had gathered a fortune worth £80,000.

The second development, partly a product of the first, brought a measure of African recovery in the wake of Portuguese indigence. This was especially the case among the Somali and northern Swahili cities. These successfully evicted their Portuguese garrisons and destroyed any further obligation to pay tribute to the Portuguese, having for these purposes allied themselves at the end of the seventeenth century with Arab fellow-Muslims from Oman and Muscat in southern Arabia. There could now be at least a partial reforging of old commercial ties with countries beyond the Indian Ocean. It was during this time of recovery that the northern Swahili cities developed a dramatic and richly eloquent literature, writing their own flexible and expressive language in a modified Arabic script.

Along the coast south of Mombasa the recovery was slower. At Mombasa itself the Portuguese continued to garrison their great castle of Fort Jesus until 1729 when they were at last ousted in the wake of many troubles, and were never able to return. Since their early days of piracy they had done little here but maintain themselves and exact such tribute as they could. An English visitor in 1667 had found it 'a place of no great traffic . . . while the inhabitants are so squeezed perpetually by the governor that they seldom or never come to be worth anything of an estate. Nor are they suffered to trade . . . without the governor's licence, which to be sure is never given whenever he can get anything by using it himself.' Yet the people of Mombasa seem otherwise to have been left to their own devices, and the city remained a lively centre of Swahili culture.

The old and once prosperous entrepôt of Kisimani on Mafia Island, off the Tanganyika coast, still existed in the sixteenth century and was then, as often before, a dependency of Kilwa. Natural disaster in the shape of ocean encroachment brought its life to an end not long after that. Nowadays there is nothing to be seen there but the fragments of a few mosques and other buildings and a scatter of broken Persian and Chinese pottery along the beach. Nearby on Juani Island, lying a little to seaward along the coral-paved ocean shelf on which these islands rise, a new town called Kua appeared in the seventeenth or early eighteenth century. Very probably based on older but more humble foundations, Kua became a small but well-built city of some importance until it was ruined, around 1822, by Sakalava raiders from Madagascar.

As at Kua, the ruins of Kilwa Kisiwani – Kilwa of the Island – show that there was still enough wealth and power in the old coastal trade after 1700 to allow the construction of mosques, merchants' houses and quite extensive royal quarters. Compared with the earlier buildings, however, these are relatively crude: the

Opposite: West Africa: figure of a man firing a gun. Though a few firearms appeared in West Africa during the sixteenth century, they became common only later. During the eighteenth and nineteenth centuries large quantities of guns of various kinds were sold to Africa by European traders, and exercised a growing influence on events

mosques have lost much of their fine decoration in carved coral, while there is little in the palace or residential structures to indicate the sophisticated comfort of medieval Kilwa. Life had evidently lost its old self-confidence of earlier days. The trading routes were sorely fouled or altogether cut, and Kilwa had suffered at least one highly damaging raid by people from the interior. Little or no gold came any more from the distant mines. Such Chinese wares as continued to arrive were only of the cheapest kind.

To complete this decline, slave trading and raiding now became an important part of East Coast commerce. In earlier times, so far as all the evidence can show, slaving had never been more than a minor aspect of East African trade. Now it vastly expanded. The Portuguese turned for slaves to the East as well as the West Coast. Others followed them. As early as 1754, a French captain was buying slaves in the Kilwa region both for use in the Mascarene Islands, Mauritius and Bourbon (later renamed Réunion), and for transport to Saint Domingue (afterwards Haiti) in the Caribbean. In 1776 another Frenchman even concluded a treaty with the sultan of Kilwa, a much reduced monarch when compared with his forebears, that allowed the French an exclusive right to purchase slaves from Kilwa as well as to build a fort there if they wished.

Early in the nineteenth century, Portuguese slave exports from the Mozambique coast were running at the rate of about ten thousand a year, very much higher than in any previous period.

A much larger expansion of slaving also developed along the central and northern sectors of the Swahili coast. This followed the growing commercial enterprise of the Arabs from Oman and Muscat. Their Imam Seyyid Said, operating with a small but well-found naval force from his Arabian capital of Muscat, now brought the more important harbours of the coast under his tributary control, claiming a right derived from the Omani share in expelling the Portuguese a century earlier. A man of energy and vision, Said set out to rebuild the old Indian Ocean connexion between Africa, Arabia, India and the Far East. With this he had good success, and in 1840 took the bold and intelligent step of transferring his court from sun-scorched Muscat to the pleasant island of Zanzibar.

By this time Zanzibar was already the greatest slaving port on the whole East Coast, far eclipsing any in Mozambique. A British estimate of 1839 put the total number of slaves who were sold there every year at between 40,000 and 45,000. Seyyid Said pushed it higher. Ceaselessly energetic, he made Zanzibar into the world's biggest producer of cloves, a spice that was sure

A slave market at Zanzibar in 1872

Opposite: Ivory Coast: wooden mask of the Dan people, bearing a clan mark from the nose to the ear (Height of mask: 8 in.)

of a good sale in several continents (The clove tree had been brought to Zanzibar in about 1818 from Mauritius). Local labour proving insufficient for the new clove plantations, the Zanzibari Arabs went into partnership with Swahili traders so as to obtain slave labour from the interior. By the 1850s these Arab-Swahili slaving pioneers had pushed their way far inland from the coast of Tanganyika, and had even made contact with other slaving agents who had come eastward from Angola on the other side of the continent. It was along their trails that European explorers would soon begin to penetrate inland Africa. Meanwhile chaos and havoc accompanied the traders. Slaving fired local wars through Tanganyika and Kenya into Uganda, and beyond Uganda into the forests of the eastern Congo. The tolerant security of the past vanished in these raids and ruthless forays. There occurred here the same kind of political degeneration as in other parts of Africa affected by the warlike search for captives who could be sold as slaves. Peoples ceased to trust their neighbours. Every foreign traveller, whether Arab or European, became a likely enemy to be met with spears or flight.

The zone of crisis broadened rapidly in the 1850s. Between the Arab-Swahili slaving network in the north and similar Portuguese arrangements in the south, no people who lay anywhere near the main caravan trails – eastward from Zanzibar to Lake Tanganyika and beyond, or up the Zambezi and the Shiré into the old lands of Malawi and the vanished empire of the Monomotapa – could now feel itself safe. Here the old Portuguese trading settlements, concerned in the past with the gold and ivory trade and with local plantation farming, fell easy victims to the get-rich-quick temptation of slaving, and came soon to a sorry end. 'When the slave trade began,' commented Livingstone on the situation along the Middle Zambezi in the late 1840s, 'it seemed to many of the merchants a more speedy mode of becoming rich, to sell off the [plantation] slaves, than to pursue the slow mode of gold-washing and agriculture; and they continued to export them until they had neither hands to labour nor to fight for them. It was just the story of the goose and the golden egg. The coffee and sugar plantations and gold-washings were abandoned, because the labour had been exported to the Brazils. Many of the Portuguese then followed their slaves, and the government was obliged to pass a law to prevent any further emigration. . . .'

In such ways as these, and in others closely related to them, many remaining points of inland stability were sucked within a torrent of violence and death. Only further to the southward, in the lands of the Karanga state beyond reach of these rapacious appetites, had life remained much the same as in the past. But even here there came a turning-point. After the beginning of the nineteenth century, the crisis of southern Africa engulfed the peaceful lands of the Karanga as well.

Madagascar lay outside these upheavals. Colonized by Indonesians at the beginning of the central-southern African Iron Age, Malagasy harbours welcomed their shipping for long after that. It was from Java and neighbouring islands, Idrisi tells us in about 1150, that people went to south-east Africa for supplies of iron they could sell to Indian armourers. By the fourteenth century the greater part of the island was divided among a number of peoples of initially Indonesian stock, some of whom, like the Hova, were strongly established in the interior of the island. New immigrant groups, some of them from Africa, were still arriving but their numbers were evidently small. 'Their historical importance derives above all', Deschamps believes, 'from the new political conceptions they brought with them, leading as these did to the foundation of kingdoms' in the Madagascar of the sixteenth century.

Southern Africa: The Wars of Wandering

Two great factors of expansion and collision, one of them very old and the other almost new, now laid the scene for events of terrible and tragic meaning in the far south-eastern region of Africa.

The factor that was old was the continued growth of Bantu-speaking peoples and the onward development of their Iron Age polities in the plains and hills to the south of the Limpopo. By the thirteenth or fourteenth century these peoples were firmly settled throughout the later European provinces of the Transvaal, Orange Free State and Natal, as well as in many of the valleys of the Drakensberg Mountains where Basutoland was to emerge in the nineteenth century. They had likewise pushed further southward into superbly fertile lands along the southernmost coast of Africa. For at least a hundred years before the arrival of the Portuguese in 1488 the Pondo and their neighbours, living now in what is called the Transkei region of Cape Province, were in touch with Indian Ocean sea-merchants who

Fishermen hauling in their nets in the evening, on the
eastern coast of Ghana

bought ivory in exchange for cottons, beads and even Chinese porcelain.

All these peoples prospered. Anyone who has travelled in these wonderful southern lands of Natal and the Cape, perhaps the finest and most generous of all Africa, and can picture how they must have been before the ruinous overcrowding and overstocking of the twentieth century, will have no difficulty in seeing why. Prospering, these peoples multiplied. By the eighteenth century they were beginning to feel short of land. Obeying their traditional customs, they hived off 'junior groups' who went away in search of homes elsewhere. In this they clashed with the native Bushman and Khoisan (Hottentots) as they had often done before. But with the eighteenth century all these peoples were faced with a factor of expansion that was new.

The Bushman and Khoisan of the far south had felt this pressure long before. Those who lived within reach of the early Dutch settlers after 1652 soon found themselves driven out or reduced to slavery. As time went on, and the little settlement at the Cape changed from a mere market-garden for visiting ships to a self-supporting colony of farmers, the collision grew sharper. These newcomers developed an insatiable appetite for land and free labour. Their ideal, stubbornly pursued, was for every farmer to live beyond sight of his neighbour's smoke. Gradually, they pushed inland. Gradually, too, they formed themselves into a nation, no longer calling themselves Dutch but Afrikaner or Boer; and built their farming economy on the curious notion that all Africans, the Biblical 'sons of Ham', were appointed by God to labour as their slaves.

Their progress inland was slow but steady. By 1760 their hunters had already crossed the Orange river into the heart of southern Africa; and in 1779 there came a bitter war with the Bantu who lived near the Great Fish river. It was only the first of many such wars. In 1795, with the end of Dutch Company rule, two little Boer republics were proclaimed near the Cape, those of Graaff Reinet and Swellendam, setting the pattern for all that was to follow. During the Anglo-French struggles of 1793–1815 the government of the Cape passed to a Britain now intent on abolishing the slave trade. Almost from the first, accordingly, the slave-based system of the Boers clashed with the anti-slavery policies of British colonial rule.

Resenting the legal limitations that were placed on their 'right' to enslave Africans, Boer farmers began shifting still further into the interior, meaning in this way to escape British interference. Drawn reluctantly into the raids and wars that inescapably followed along this northward-moving 'frontier of settlement', the British went after the Boers. In 1820 they even planted some five thousand British settlers along the inland 'frontier' in a vain hope of keeping the peace between predatory Boers and retaliating Africans. Nothing availed. The wars went on: 1799 saw the third 'Kaffir War', 1812 the fourth, 1818 the fifth, and 1834 the sixth with others yet to follow. But 1834 also brought a British decision to end slavery in the Cape Colony. Outraged by this invasion of their 'rights', Boer farmers under Louis Trichardt led the largest of all the Boer migrations, the 'Great Trek' of several thousand families during several years across the Orange and Fish rivers into the 'promised lands' of the interior.

With this the inland wars were shifted far towards the north. 'I have myself been an eyewitness of Boers coming to a village', Livingstone wrote of inland South Africa during the 1840s, 'and, according to their usual custom, demanding twenty or thirty women to weed their gardens, and have seen these women proceed to the scene of unrequited toil, carrying their food on their heads, their children on their backs, and instruments of labour on their shoulders. Nor have the Boers any wish to conceal the meanness of thus employing unpaid labour; on the contrary, every one of them, from Mr Potgieter and Mr Gert Krieger, the commandants, downwards, lauded his own humanity and justice in making such an equitable regulation. "We make the people work for us, in consideration of allowing them to live in our country".' The characteristic pattern of Boer settlement was firmly fixed, and it would last for many a weary decade.

As the 'frontier' of Boer expansion thus shifted northward, steadily compressing the land available to its native peoples for pasture and settlement, repeatedly thrusting Bantu peoples back upon themselves, other profound changes occurred in the populous lands of modern Natal. Sections of Nguni long settled in these fertile lands began to reorganize and unify themselves into a military nation on new and aggressive principles. The connexion between these two series of events – northward-moving Boer penetration and Nguni reorganization – was never more than indirect, yet it is hard to believe that it did not exist. Remote and even insignificant at first, the evidence for this connexion becomes clearer with the rise of Dingiswayo and the Mtetwa after 1807.

Opposite: Landscape in Guinea, north-east of Conakry, its capital

The Mtetwa were a branch of the Nguni living not far from the sea in the far north-east of Natal. They seem to have become leaders in their region in about 1780. Twenty-eight years later, in 1808, they acquired a new chief called Dingiswayo, who set out to unify a number of other branches under Mtetwa rule. There was nothing very new about this, for it followed a familiar pattern of Iron Age development. But it occurred at a time when fugitives from the south, or Nguni who had travelled in the south, must surely have brought back news of European penetration and methods of war. Moreover it is known that Dingiswayo, exiled from his homeland before becoming chief, had encountered at least one European during his wanderings, probably a doctor called Cowan, who is said to have become his friend. Elected chief, Dingiswayo deliberately set himself to strengthen the Mtetwa state, and did so with a fuller understanding of his times than previous chiefs had ever had. 'Not only with the mere novelties of horse and gun was it that Dingiswayo had returned from exile,' Bryant tells us, 'but, infinitely more momentous, with the ideas of civilization and militarism which those things signified . . .'

Dingiswayo succeeded in making the Mtetwa paramount in north-eastern Natal. In 1810 he called on a young warrior, then aged twenty-three, to command his regiments and reorganize their warfare. This was Shaka; and Shaka, from the very first, undertook a military revolution. Once again one may infer the continuing pressure of those alarming reports from the south. They showed, if they showed anything, that the old easy-going ways of war would no longer suffice. How far Shaka understood this must remain another matter for conjecture. But he probably understood a good deal, if only because 'through all these stirring times of [Mtetwa] conquest and tribal expansion', as Bryant writes, 'the youthful Shaka passed as enthusiastic participating witness'.

Up till then, and even under the formidable Dingiswayo, Nguni regiments had generally fought in the traditional manner. Bryant has described it. 'A day having been mutually arranged beforehand, each clan turned out *en masse* to enjoy the excitement. A score or two of warrior youths – for single clans were mostly small before the union – bearing assegais and shields, marched proudly and gleefully forth, with as many women and girls to stand behind and cheer . . . Each party, drawn up at a distance from the other . . . would send forth its chosen braves to single combat in the arena. Such a champion falling wounded would become the prize of the victors and be taken home by them to be ransomed, perhaps before sundown, with a head of cattle . . . Over the slain mutual condolences would be exchanged . . .'

Shaka did away with all that. A military genius whose life was to be increasingly bloodstained and embittered, he displaced this Homeric warfare of champions and cheers by the grim Roman discipline and purpose of hard-trained soldiers who relied on skilled manoeuvre and close combat, and who fought to kill. He took over the old 'horns and chest' formation of the Nguni and their neighbours, but insisted on a speed and obedience never known before. With this, moreover, he abolished the throwing-spear in favour of a short stabbing assegai. Had he perhaps observed that throwing-spears were powerless against rifles – now in use by raiding groups like the Koranas as well as by Europeans – and that only by a grapple at close-quarters could the Zulu hope to overcome this new menace? However that may be, his new formations were very much a product of the times. They proved unbeatable by other African armies, and for a long time by European troops as well.

What Dingiswayo had begun, Shaka continued with a grim and fanatical endurance. His own clan, the Zulu, became the heart of a widening empire in Natal. (Bryant thought the population under Zulu dominion after Shaka's accession in 1816 was about 78,000, divided into 46 clans of whom the Zulu themselves numbered only about two per cent of the whole.) Taking over the paramountcy from Dingiswayo four years after the fourth 'Kaffir War' along the frontier of the Cape Province and two years before the fifth, Shaka turned upon his African rivals with the harsh pressures of a long-service army, far better than any seen before, and subdued them, killed them, or drove them out. There began those grim years of warfare remembered by the peoples of Natal and Basutoland as the *Lifaquane*, the 'wars of wandering'. These it was that spread before advancing Europeans a scene of carnage and chaos which they hastened to assume were natural to this land.

Smashed in tremendous hand-to-hand battles during 1818–19, Shaka's main rivals gave up the fight and broke away northward. Soshengane led his followers into the coastlands of Mozambique. Zwandendaba crossed the Middle Limpopo and fell upon the old Karanga empire, reducing its chiefly palaces at Zimbabwe, Khami and elsewhere to empty ruins; and

Opposite left: Vessel of straw and wicker-work decorated with cowrie shells, from the northern Sudan (Height: $11\frac{1}{2}$ in.)
Right: Mali: Bambara head-dress of carved wood with straw and cowrie shell decoration (Height: $22\frac{1}{2}$ in.)

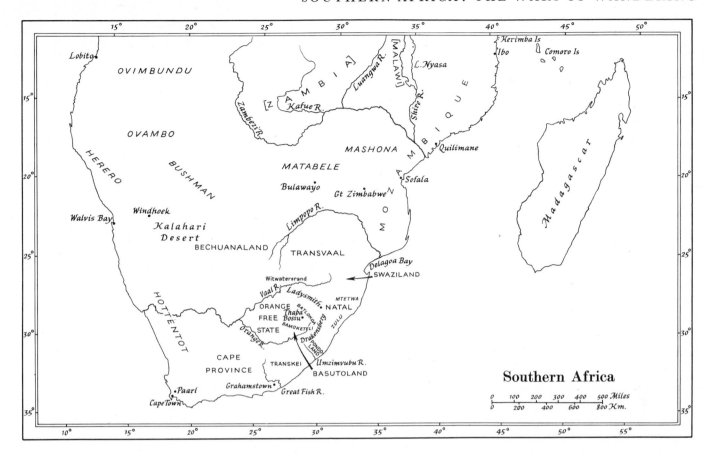

Southern Africa

pursued his bitter course northward until he and his warriors reached the shores of Lake Tanganyika in about 1840. Later again, incapable of pushing south or holding his ground against the rifle-carrying Boers now pressing in across the high veld west of the Drakensberg, in what was to become the Orange Free State, a breakaway commander of Shaka's, Mzilikazi, together with a strong body of Shaka-trained troops, followed across the Limpopo where Zwandendaba had led. Mzilikazi and his men went no further, but settled in the ravaged lands of the Karanga. Fifty years later they in turn were followed by invading Europeans under British leadership.

Yet this was only half the *Lifaquane*. Another bloody series of collisions occurred to the south and west as well. In 1822 a Hlubi group under Mpangazita fled westward out of Natal over the Drakensberg Mountains and clashed in their northern foothills with the Batlokoa and Bamoketeli. The latter, led by another great figure of the times, Mosheshwe, moved to the central area of the Drakensberg. There on the tabletop mountain of Thaba Bosiu and in its nearby valleys, Mosheshwe made a rallying point for fugitive or scattered clans.

Out of these, by outstanding political skill and diplomatic talent, he formed the nucleus of the Basuto nation. Temporizing with Shaka, Mosheshwe carved out a mountain territory in which his followers could be relatively safe. His stronghold at Thaba Bosiu was successively attacked by the *impis* of Mzilikazi, by the Boers, and by the British; but none of them prevailed and some were soundly trounced.

By 1830 the situation at last grew calmer. Yet the ravages had been unexampled in their destruction. Nothing like this had been known before. Crossing the high veld to the Drakensberg in 1833, the French missionary Casalis and his companions were depressed by the 'solitary and desolate aspect of the country . . . On every side we saw human bones whitening in the sun and rain, and more than once we had to turn our wagon out of its course so as to avoid passing over these sad remains . . . Yet as we came nearer to the residence of the chief [Mosheshwe], appearances encouragingly changed. We began to meet fairly big herds pasturing under the care of well-armed herdsmen. We saw fields under what looked like careful cultivation . . .' It was a hard-won peace. But it was not to endure.

Opposite top: Capture of Abdelkader's headquarters by the French in 1844, painted by Horace Vernet
Bottom left: Costumes of the Portuguese artillery in Angola in 1807
Bottom right: British troops led by Sir Garnet Wolseley entering Kumasi in 1874 during the wars on Asante

265

A Continent in Turmoil

When Europeans began invading Africa after the 1850s they were often and understandably impressed by the widespread violence and insecurity they found, and pointed repeatedly to these as a moral justification for their invasion. They came easily to think that all this ravaging and desolation must be endemic to 'savage Africa', and they accordingly argued that outside intervention could alone 'save Africa from itself'. Only a few of them, mainly the French and English missionaries in Basutoland and Natal, saw that the crisis was a relatively new one.

Bryant spoke for these as late as the 1920s when he wrote of the 'wave of political animosity, panic, fear or general unrest [which] seems to have invaded the South African native mind in the earlier decades of the past century – or even, indeed, the whole Negro race mind; for we find evidence of similar upheavals at the same period also in other parts of the Dark Continent.' Not many Europeans applied or were able to apply any such historical judgment. The vast majority had no inkling of having arrived in Africa at a time when wide regions, including several in which these Europeans were most closely interested, had become enmeshed for one reason or another in the turmoil of profound social upheaval.

To this, perhaps needless to say, some reservations should be made. Much of Africa was not in turmoil during the nineteenth century. There were many corners of this massive continent where the old ways held firm and where little or nothing had disturbed the quiet revolving of traditional precedent and custom, firm with the dignity and self-assurance of an old achievement, as one generation after another issued from the loins of its ancestors, accepted its responsibilities, and forged its vital link between the dead, the living, and the yet unborn. 'There is perfect security for life and property', Livingstone found in the lands around the Upper Zambezi, 'all over the interior country.' There were other regions where much had changed in the previous two centuries, but where states like Asante proved strong enough to absorb the shocks of inner transformation. Still other countries, such as Algeria, had shown how the consequences of outside interference or invasion could likewise be assimilated into viable modifications of what had gone before.

Even with such necessary reservations, it remains true that by 1800 or soon after there were few regions where many polities, large or small, old or new, had not clearly felt and reacted to strong pressures of transition. Widely varying in form and power though it certainly was, the impact of change had been constantly and pervasively at work. This continued after 1800. But after 1800 it grew rapidly to crisis. Fifty years later there was scarcely a single region where a majority of peoples were not at grips with new problems whose strains and pressures were too tense or difficult for any kind of traditional solution, and against whose overbearing power the old solutions had become useless and even futile. Old Africa, Iron Age Africa, could no longer meet the challenge of the times, and would now be swept away on a flood of unavailing protest and misfortune.

Part of this crisis of the nineteenth century lay within the dynamics of Iron Age society itself. Even without the northward-shifting frontier of European penetration and settlement in southern Africa, for example, it is obvious that the growing numbers of southern Africans and their migrating polities must sooner or later have raised an acute problem of relative overpopulation. This, indeed, had already begun to happen among the Nguni and their neighbours of Natal. It seems likewise clear that efforts at unifying the Western Sudan on the principles of an earlier age, but in the very different circumstances brought about by long-service armies and musket warfare, must similarly have broken down or at best achieved but a brief and fragile stability, even without the invasion by the French. After the 1820s the wars of Yorubaland were increasingly affected by the sale of firearms from the coast, and later by the growing territorial encroachment of the British. Yet the origins and main course of these Yoruba wars were the product not of foreign influence but of efforts to restore a single system of Yoruba dominion. The times were out of joint. Not even the absence or withdrawal of direct foreign intervention could have set them right.

To these inherent strains of Iron Age growth and transformation, however, others were added with dramatic speed and violence. Africa and her near-neighbour, Europe, were now entirely out of step. If the gap in technological and military power between leading African and European states had been narrow in the Middle Ages, now it was enormous. For at least three centuries Europe had undergone a many-sided development of liberal and scientific speculation,

Opposite: Some leading figures in the resistance to European invasion during the nineteenth century: Muhamad Aly (*c.* 1769–1849) in Egypt (*top left*); Abdelkader (1808–83) in western Algeria (*top right*); King Mosheshwe (*c.* 1795–1870) of the Basuto in South Africa (*bottom left*); King Prempeh (1874–1935) of Asante (*bottom centre*); and the Mahdi (1843–85) in the Eastern Sudan (*bottom right*)

mechanical discovery and industrial expansion. While Africa still relied on handicraft production, Europe had built the factory system. The balance of happiness might not therefore be with Europe. 'If we consider', wrote Heinrich Barth in a well-known passage on the Kano textile manufacture of the 1850s, comparing it with his memory of European sweat-shops and satanic mills, 'that this industry is not carried on here as in Europe, in immense establishments degrading man to the meanest condition of life, but that it gives employment and support to families without compelling them to sacrifice their domestic habits, we must presume that Kano ought to be one of the happiest countries . . .' But the balance of happiness was not the point. What mattered now was the balance of power. And this had shifted far into the European side of the scales. Faced with an expanding and immeasurably more aggressive Europe, traditional Africa in sad disarray was confronted with a process of encroachment and invasion which it could not possibly defeat.

This took many forms. Two were of a peaceful kind. These involved the settlement on the Windward Coast of small groups of pioneers from Britain and the United States, their peculiarity resting in the fact that nearly all the settlers were first- or second-generation Africans liberated from British or American enslavement. A small reach of land in Temne country was colonized in this way during 1797, and another piece of land, further to the eastward, in 1821. Both attempts all but foundered in their early years, yet lived to form the independent countries of Sierra Leone and Liberia today.

A curious story lies behind the ventures of these pioneers. In 1772 an English Chief Justice, Lord Mansfield, was moved to hand down a judgment that no man in England, no matter whence he came, could be a slave. Now at that time there were some 15,000 African slaves in England. Automatically they became free men. Many of them, no less automatically, likewise became destitute. Their numbers swelled as liberated slaves of African origin fled from the United States. The philanthropists took up their cause. Why not send some of them back to Africa? A company was set up for the purpose.

Once established, the little colony soon became for the philanthropists a charge they could not carry. In 1808 the Sierra Leone Company gave up its effort, and the settlement, still numbering fewer than 2,000 souls, passed under British official rule as a Crown Colony. A year earlier, in 1807, the British Parliament had at last declared the slave trade illegal in British ships. Soon the British Navy was attempting to prevent the trade in other ships as well. Sierra Leone became a haven for Africans taken from arrested slave-ships. By about 1850 more than 70,000 liberated captives had been set ashore in Sierra Leone as free men.

Liberian origins were similar. After the American War of Independence many slaves achieved their freedom. By 1790 these free Negroes numbered as many as 60,000. By 1829 they were more than a quarter of a million. Some white Americans conceived the idea of finding a home for them in Africa. This was vigorously opposed by the majority of free Negroes on the grounds that they were not Africans, but Americans. All the same, a few agreed to go. In 1821 their white backers purchased a piece of land on Cape Mesurado, near the eastern extremity of the Windward Coast, and settled there 130 of these unwanted Americans. Like the venture in Sierra Leone, infant Liberia nearly perished of want and poor management. Yet the crisis was overcome. Later their little settlement became Monrovia; and Monrovia became the capital of an American settler-state which eventually began to reconcile itself with the local inhabitants, and grew by slow steps into the Liberia of today.

These were some of the results of the ending of the slave trade. There were many others. To those coastal states which had built their prosperity on the trade, answering for decade after decade the insistent European call for captives and still more captives, the end of the trade signalled a turmoil that was only partially and slowly resolved by switching to palm oil and other natural exports. Challenged by growing competition, European merchants were now eager to displace African coastal monopoly by a monopoly of their own. They began to argue that direct intervention could alone conserve their interests, as well as 'saving Africa from itself'. These merchants, or at any rate the more powerful among them, soon began applying to their reluctant governments for military and political support, for consuls and territorial annexations, for official assumption of European power. Later these demands were amply fulfilled. Yet except for a few points here and there – the Dutch and then the British in South Africa, the Portuguese in the old Congo kingdoms and along the Lower Zambezi, the French invasions of Egypt in 1798 and of Algeria in 1830 – actual territorial seizure remained unimportant until the 1860s or even the 1880s.

Opposite: Tomb of the Mahdi at Khartoum

But European involvement, whether European governments wanted it or not (and generally they opposed it), unrelentingly deepened. The year 1840 saw the French applying a system of regular administration to the scattered points they had long held upon the Senegal coast. In 1849 the first British consuls were appointed to ports like Ouidah and Lagos. And these new authorities found themselves increasingly drawn into neighbouring affairs. In 1860, for example, we find the British naval commander on the West African coast suggesting that British officers should be sent to 'train' one Yoruba army against another. In that same year the French occupied Dakar and began pushing inland. A year later the British occupied Lagos.

Small annexations inexorably continued. But with annexations came the need for revenue, and revenue could best be had by taxing trade. Yet taxation supposed frontiers, and soon it grew clear that the wider the frontiers the higher the revenue could be. So we have Consul Beecroft of Lagos declaring in 1862 that Badagri on the mainland should be brought within the Lagos tariff. A year earlier Consul Foote had got the British navy to bombard Porto Novo, likewise on the mainland, for reasons basically the same. Little by little, coastal encroachment led to coastal seizures; and coastal seizures, deepening the involvement of Europe, led step by step to inland invasion.

Ministers and officials in London and Paris might dislike and oppose this process. Their hesitations made little difference. Though largely concealed as yet, the machinery of imperial expansion was already in gear and could not be stopped. In 1865, a Select Committee of the House of Commons recommended British withdrawal from all parts of West Africa 'except, probably, Sierra Leone'. But nine years later the Gold Coast stations, far from being abandoned, were embodied in a new British colony. Even after the discovery of the anti-malarial properties of quinine, during the 1850s, the Niger river was officially regarded as of little value. But no fewer than twenty-one British firms had stations in the Niger delta by 1864. Within another seven years there were five British steamers in the river.

When considering the records of this astonishing period one is repeatedly struck by how little the men at the top understood the movement of their times. They sat at the controls, thinking themselves in full command, believing they knew the immediate course on which their ship of state was moving; and time after time they were wrong. Only in the 1870s did they begin to understand. Even then the French government was still proposing to the British that most of the French stations on the western coast as far as the Congo should be exchanged for the Gambia. This might seem eminently sensible to officials in Paris and London, but it did not work and it could not work. For now the fury of imperial expansion had become a public fever. 'In the present tone and temper of the public mind,' a British minister regretfully observed in 1873, and it was soon to be true of France as well, 'no abandonment of territory would . . . be permitted by Parliament, or sanctioned by public opinion.' Even the Gambia, though with barely a score of Englishmen living there, must remain British.

This fury carried all before it. The imperial scene was set in western Europe by an atmosphere of frantic national competition for oversea possession. European imperialism acquired a driving power of its own. 'I do not know the cause of this sudden revolution,' Lord Salisbury, the British Foreign Minister, was complaining as late as 1891, 'but there it is.' Others understood better. Pursuing their interests and ambitions, they blew the trumpets of patriotism and banged the drums of national rivalry. Ministers and officials gave way reluctantly; but they gave way. They made concessions, hoping the cost might still be small. There was nothing else they could do. 'Protectorates are unwelcome burdens,' a British official explained to his minister in 1883, 'but in this case it is, if my view is correct, a question between British Protectorates, which would be unwelcome, and French Protectorates, which would be fatal.' A single gunboat in the Bights of Benin and Biafra, he thought, would be sufficient 'to keep the protégés in order'. Little did he know.

If British and French ministers and advisers failed to read the signposts of the times, African leaders were even more at a loss. They watched the erratic course of European policy and action, and could seldom make head or tail of it. They accepted the alliance or friendship of this or that European country, not seeing how they opened the gate for later conquest. Many kept their heads in this most puzzling situation, and tried to draw what benefit they could from European presence and pressure. Others lost their heads and flung the gate still wider open. The ideologies of Iron Age life had provided for many contingencies, but not for an explanation of nineteenth-century Europe. The lesson was to be a hard and often bitter one.

Opposite top: The German missionary Rebmann preaching from the missionary house at Kisulutini, Kenya, sketched by the explorer Richard Burton
Bottom: Boer farmers of South Africa returning with their servants from hunting. Aquatint (1802) by Samuel Daniell

Above: Two Africans carrying a European in a hammock; sculpture from the Lower Congo (Length: 44 in.)
Opposite: Statuette from the Lower Congo depicting a missionary holding a cup and bottle (Height: 29½ in.)
Right: Ivory statuette from the Lower Congo depicting Europeans carried on the shoulders of Africans (Height: 2¾ in.)

7 Conquest and Colonial Rule

*Geographical exploration of inner Africa – New missionary endeavours –
Rise of European imperialism and its meaning for Africa – Rivalries for
African possessions : from coastal encroachment to the continental 'scramble'
and full-scale invasion – Brief history of the colonial period in the first two
of its three main phases : 1900–20 and 1920–45*

Prelude: The Explorers

Systematic exploration of inner Africa may be said to
have begun with Mungo Park's journey of 1795–7 into
the Western Sudan. Park's travels, like those of other
brave men who soon followed him, had nothing to do
with ambitions of conquest, and little with those of
commerce. Rather were they the fruit of philanthropy
and the pursuit of science. The latter, indeed, came
first. When the British African Association was founded
in 1788, what Sir Joseph Banks and his companions
chiefly wished for was an understanding of the shape
and layout of the African continent. Armed with such
knowledge, the philanthropists afterwards worked to
realize a policy of 'Christianity and commerce' that
should finish off the slave trade and 'civilize the
Africans'. Imperialism was still in the future.

   The exploring effort was for a long time understandably spasmodic. The difficulties were immense. More
than thirty years separated Park's confirmation that the
Niger flowed to the east, and not westward, from the
Landers' fixing of the Oil Rivers as the Niger's outflow
to the sea. René Caillié made his great journey from the
Gambia through the Western Sudan and the Sahara to
Morocco in 1827–8, but not until 1889 would Binger
thoroughly investigate the countries which bordered
Caillié's route to the interior. Yet the effort went gradually forward. By the 1860s a handful of successful ex-
peditions had mapped all the main features of the West
African interior, while the beginnings of a systematic
study of its peoples had appeared with the writings of
Heinrich Barth in 1857. Meanwhile in southern and

King Kazembe, ruler of a large Luba-Lunda state in the
Katanga region, as the Portuguese explorer Gamitto
described him in 1831

Opposite: Ibibio funerary sculpture of painted cement,
made under missionary influence, at Ikot Ekpene near
Calabar, eastern Nigeria. The man standing beside the
monument is a descendant of the deceased

central Africa the journeys of David Livingstone, embarked on in 1841 and heroically continued for a quarter of a century, had fired the imagination and ambition of many other explorers, whether missionaries or not. In 1857 Burton walked a thousand miles from Bagamoyo on the Tanganyika coast to Lake Tanganyika, while his companion Speke continued northward to Lake Victoria. With Grant a few years later, Speke reached the upper waters of the White Nile at the same time as Samuel Baker, coming down from Khartoum, was marching into the western uplands of Uganda. After the 1860s it was largely a matter of correcting errors and filling in the map, a work that was finally completed, at least for hazardous and outlying regions such as the Sahara, only in the 1930s.

Nineteenth-century missionary enterprise had the same slow spasmodic growth. Here too the difficulties were very great, not least those of physical resistance to malaria and other fevers. Yet the call for recruits was answered in spite of all attendant dangers. As many as fifty-two missionaries are said to have succumbed to one or other fever along the West Coast in 1825 alone, but the flow of volunteers never failed. In 1804 the British Church Missionary Society began operations in Sierra Leone. Twenty-three years later, marking an important step forward, the Fourah Bay Institution was founded

'Rev. S. Crowther crossing the river in his Bathing Tub'
(From a missionary tract)

for the education of promising pupils. One of the first of its pupils was Samuel Ajayi Crowther, later Bishop of the Niger, an outstanding student of West African languages and translator of part of the Bible into Yoruba. In 1846 mission stations were established in Yorubaland, and in 1865 as far upriver as Lokoja where the Niger and the Benue converge.

Many denominations, Protestant or Catholic, took part in similar ventures in several coastal lands of Africa, gradually pushing their solitary way into the interior. By 1900 there were few large regions where Christian missionaries had failed to arrive and settle. Early Catholic endeavours of the sixteenth and seventeenth centuries were now reproduced on a continental scale. They did much to promote the emergence of a new Christian-educated élite. This was to play a part of some importance, even before 1900, in the formation of anti-colonial trends of thought.

Invasion: 1880-1900

European imperialist rivalries and ambitions culminated in the 1880s in what *The Times*, with a justice that would stick, contemptuously called the 'scramble for Africa'. Looking back on that hasty and haphazard process of enclosure, some historians have detected its driving motive in Anglo-French agreements arising from British seizure of Egypt and the Suez Canal. Others have pointed to the provocative actions of Leopold II of Belgium in carving out for himself an enormous central African colony under the very noses of his far more powerful contemporaries.

Yet to see this astonishing adventure in diplomatic terms is to play Hamlet without the Dane: behind all the diplomatic and political moves lay more decisive pressures. These were released by the tremendous growth of western European capitalism, and were embodied on the African scene by what Mary Kingsley, a shrewd observer of the 1890s, called 'our great solid understuff, the merchant adventurers'. It was above all men like Goldie and Rhodes who ensured that governments in Europe should underwrite imperial enterprise beyond the seas. And it was out of their efforts, consciously or not, that the strenuous ideologies of European imperialism now took shape and action.

When these pressures finally exploded into many sided invasion, the powers of western Europe found themselves with a number of critical advantages. They possessed useful footholds along the coast. They had

Opposite: Yoruba figures from the shrine of Shango at the court of the Temi of Ede, Nigeria. They are made of iroko wood and are displayed in front of the shrine during the annual Shango festival. There are about twenty figures at this shrine (Average height of figures: about 30 in.)

long-standing ties with several coastal peoples. They disposed of overwhelming industrial and military strength against a continent still largely enclosed within the narrow productive limits of subsistence economy, of pre-capitalist production for use and not for exchange. Except for the years between 1914 and 1918, they were also able to control their rivalries in Africa within a general agreement among themselves. No matter how much they might quarrel elsewhere, they were usually careful not to quarrel in Africa. The broad limits of expansion for each of the interested powers – for Britain, France, Germany, Belgium (though as yet only through its king), Italy, Portugal and Spain – were defined with little trouble at the Berlin colonial conference of 1884–5.

An effective agreement on partition had in fact long preceded this conference. In North Africa the French had established their 'priority of interest' as early as 1830 with a sudden invasion of Algeria. This was continued at the eastern end of the Mediterranean by Britain, for whom Lower Egypt and the Red Sea had become of major importance as a channel of communication with the British empire in India. Here the British, following on the revolt of Arabi Pasha, finally asserted their primacy over the French by an invasion of 1882. This was ostensibly aimed at restoring the earlier Anglo-French financial control of Egypt. But having got into Egypt, the British stayed, declaring a protectorate in 1914 and finally evacuating the country only in the wake of the Second World War and the rise of a new Egyptian nationalism. Meanwhile the French had established a protectorate over Tunisia in 1883. Twenty years later, partly as the outcome of a deal with Britain which confirmed the latter's free hand in Egypt, France turned her attention to Morocco. In 1904 this ancient country was divided into 'zones of influence' by France and Spain, and colonial subjection soon followed.

The same process was repeated elsewhere, and often against the same tough resistance. No doubt it may be true that those regions of Africa worst plunged in crisis during the nineteenth century – the East African slaving zone is an obvious example – gained something from an imperial control which could at least stop internecine warfare. Yet a stiff price had to be paid even for this. With every internal war that could be stopped, another and uglier war of invasion or pacification was likely to be started: and the records of all this are dark with slaughter and destruction. King Leopold and his agents of the strangely named Congo Free State might reasonably claim to have put an end to the Arab-Swahili

export of slaves. They achieved this, unfortunately, at the cost in death or misery of no mean fraction of the peoples over whom they set their rule.

Like the British in the lands behind Lagos and the Gold Coast, the French encountered strong peoples who were proud of their independence, and were ready to fight for it. Their resistance failed in the end because they possessed inferior equipment and military organization, and because they could never achieve any substantial unity among themselves. Yet it needed nearly twenty years of warfare for the French to make good their claim to the lands of ancient Ghana, Mali and Songhay.

Gun-train of a British invading force in the Ethiopian mountains, after the defeat and death of King Theodore II at Magdala in 1868

Opposite top: Mali: Gazelle-mask, the head-dress of the Kurumba dancers
Bottom: Nigeria: beadwork jacket from an Eshu figure about 16 in. high. Eshu is the 'go-between' or messenger of the spiritual forces with man. An essential figure in traditional Yoruba households, Eshu's well-being and satisfaction ensure the success of all important communications with the elemental forces

279

Lesser invaders found their task no easier even though their ambitions might be smaller. Protected by Britain, the Portuguese were allowed to assert spheres of influence over inland Angola and Mozambique, countries where until now they had never exercised more than a very occasional power by means of rare military expeditions. Now they set about proving 'effective occupation' for the first time. Stronger but also newer on the scene, the Germans likewise acquired footholds in South-West Africa, the Cameroons, Togo, and Tanganyika. Though sometimes accused of a greater brutality than other invaders, they used methods essentially the same. Like their competitors and partners – for this great imperial share-out had the aspects both of competition and partnership – the Germans moved inland from their coastal footholds by a process of encroachment and aggressive provocation, seizing on every African riposte as a means of extending their military action and thus their 'effective occupation'. In this way, for example, they drew the Herero of South-West Africa into a contest on terms that were almost fatal for any survival of this people. Thousands of them died from wounds or thirst along the margins of the Kalahari desert into which they were mercilessly driven. This was warfare on a scale of killing and destruction scarcely paralleled even in the Natal of Shaka Zulu. While it was by no means only the Germans who practised such methods, there is some ground for arguing that the Germans outdid the others in their bland assumption of being justified in what they did.

Though often prosecuted against long-enduring resistance by many African peoples, colonial conquest was also carried forward by more peaceful means. Of these the most effective was a process of infiltration, steadily advanced until the stage of 'effective occupation' could be reached, behind a screen of 'treaties of protection'. These were 'signed' with one or other European power by chiefs who could seldom or never have understood the intentions of their new 'protectors'. With these and other methods the European powers gradually partitioned Africa. They then drew up a large number of treaties among themselves, especially during the 1890s. These inter-imperialist treaties formalized the recognition of frontiers which for a long time would remain little more than mere lines on the continental map. Having settled their own potential conflicts, the European powers next proceeded to the detailed penetration and subjection of the lands of which they had thus assured each other 'effective occupation'. If the

years 1880-1900 were broadly those of conquest and the 'establishment of presence', the decades 1900-20 may reasonably be defined as the 'period of pacification' during which installation of colonial rule was made complete.

The System Installed: 1900-20

At the European end the consequences of this new form of imperialism were liable to be measured by an accountancy of monetary profit and loss. For Africans, however, they varied by the actual techniques that were adopted. Within the new frontiers a number of different methods of colonial rule were introduced according to the strength, wealth, and particular political tradition of the new rulers. Though at first little more than hand-to-mouth expedients, these methods or 'doctrines' were gradually evolved into different theories of government and were generally collected under the labels of 'direct' or 'indirect' rule.

Much influenced by their experience of governing India through local kings and princes, the British hoped to try the same economical method in Africa. They looked for kings or princes who might be ready to act as intermediaries. Here and there, as notably with the Fulani emirs of Northern Nigeria, they conveniently found them. Elsewhere they tried to create such chiefs by nomination. Both kinds of effort tended to pervert existing institutions. The Fulani emirs, for example, became little more than outright dictators ruling by foreign power, something they had scarcely been before, while 'nominated chiefs' – sometimes called 'warrant chiefs' – either failed dismally to win authority among their people or else reduced themselves to mere agents of the new imperial power. All this helped the long if often partially concealed dismantlement of traditional forms of rule.

The French acted somewhat differently in the wide grassland countries of the Western Sudan. Here they had come into prolonged and hard-fought conflict with the kings and peoples of several states. Like the British with relation to the Mahdi and his troops in the Eastern Sudan, they faced stubborn and intelligent resistance. Neither the kingdom of Segu nor that of Sikasso, nor the strong power erected by Samory Touré in the 1880s, nor most of the lesser states whether Muslim or pagan, gave in without a fight. The wars were bloody and long sustained, and repression was conducted with a harsh and often indiscriminate brutality. Few rulers were

Opposite: Photographs from the Anglo-Boer war (1899-1902). Above, a Boer encampment outside Ladysmith; and below, Boers of three generations who took part in the war

P.J. LEMMER
K^? 1AAR

J.D.L. BOTHA
15 1AAR

S.I. PRETORIUS
67 1AAR

TREE GENERATIONS
IN THE WAR
1900

Top: Photograph of the Republic Gold Mining Company's mines in South Africa in 1888

Bottom left: Boer soldiers swearing the oath of fealty to the Germans, when helping them to put down the Hottentot rising in South West Africa (1904-07)

Bottom right: Rev John Langalibalele Dube, one of the forerunners of the cause of African progress and equality in South Africa. Dube founded the first African newspaper in Natal in 1904, the *Ilanga lase Natal* (Sun of Natal)

ready to act as agents of the French. And the French therefore tended to destroy traditional authority wherever they met it, concentrating all power in the hands of their own commanders or administrators. Even where they felt it wise or found it possible to maintain local rulers, these were deprived of all effective authority. 'In the Mossi country,' noted an official report of 1905, 'indirect rule has produced its expected results. The people have accepted with confidence the substitution of our authority for that of the Moro Naba [king of the Mossi] . . . Stripped of his political powers, [the Moro Naba] Mouméni has nonetheless retained all his religious prestige in the eyes of the natives. . . .'

Yet the difference between direct and indirect rule, the supposedly different methods of colonial government generally ascribed to France and Britain, was far less obvious to the ruled than to theorists in far-away Europe. Both Britain and France were found to rely closely and in almost every case upon a combination of direct rule through a European officer and indirect rule through local collaborators or paid agents. And since the number of European officers could never be large – for their salaries and expenses had to be paid from local taxation, such being the basic rule of all this colonial enterprise – the quality of actual day-to-day government generally varied with the local collaborators or agents even more than with the political or personal attitudes of the Europeans.

Local policemen, nominated chiefs, interpreters, assistants of one sort or another: these were the men to whom 'pacified populations' were increasingly subjected. Where local societies had remained more or less intact, or had become integrated in the colonial system by treaties of protection rather than by outright conquest, this could work in their favour. Many a local chief and his counsellors were able to inform themselves of European intentions, punctually and securely, through the good will of 'boma clerks' capable of reading the local administrator's papers and quietly passing on their information. Often, though, and especially in areas taken after bitter fighting, the intermediaries added to the miseries of conquest. 'Established as masters in the villages,' a French report on the Western Sudan says of such men during the 1920s, 'they are a burden on the inhabitants who must feed them: the favourite wife, the junior brother, the servant and the stableman, all folk with a taste for good living who demand good cooking and chicken at every meal.'

Little real difference, moreover, marked the methods of annexation and pacification. Just as European pioneers had relied largely on signing treaties with chiefs who were then considered to have made over their land, mineral rights, or other attributes of sovereignty to this or that European power, so now the expeditionary forces, plunging ever more deeply into the territories thus 'assigned' to them, were prone to use closely similar techniques of subjection. Inevitably, they tried to split their prospective subjects along the grain of old rivalries or state boundaries, selecting this or that people to support against its neighbours in exchange for promises of later preference.

Characteristic of this was the British attack on Bida in the emirate of Nupe in 1897. This attack proved successful, thanks in part to the help of the Nupe against their Fulani overlords. The rest was done by superior fire power. 'The Fulani cavalry', runs a contemporary British account, 'made repeated charges on all sides, but were utterly nonplussed by the galling fire from the Maxims', machine guns of an early but most effective type in that time and place; and George Goldie, leader of the expedition, could then telegraph to London in the best style of earlier conquests in India that 'Bida is ours'. The Nupe, of course, were left to understand that their allies had intended to liberate them from one imperial rule only to impose another. Having taken Bida, the same expedition repeated its success against Ilorin whose emir also showed fight. 'The guns and Maxims having been brought into action, the [British-Hausa] square reached the riverbank without waiting, and the Fulah force broke up and retired within the city. Nothing now remained but to shell the place. . . .'

Yet there were several important differences in the methods of exploitation. Here the equatorial territories suffered worst through the baleful example of the Leopoldian system in the Congo. This involved the handing over to European concession companies of sole rights not only to land and labour within a given region, often very large, but also to the fruits of the forest and the soil. Huge areas of the Congo Basin (enclosed after 1885 within the Congo Free State, so named because it was supposed to be free of discriminatory taxes for all the interested European powers) were opened to the most reckless despoliation of land and people. Here the concession companies included the Leopoldian administration of enormous 'Crown Lands'. King and businessmen reaped their rich harvest of profits, at least after 1895, from the export of rubber and ivory collected by

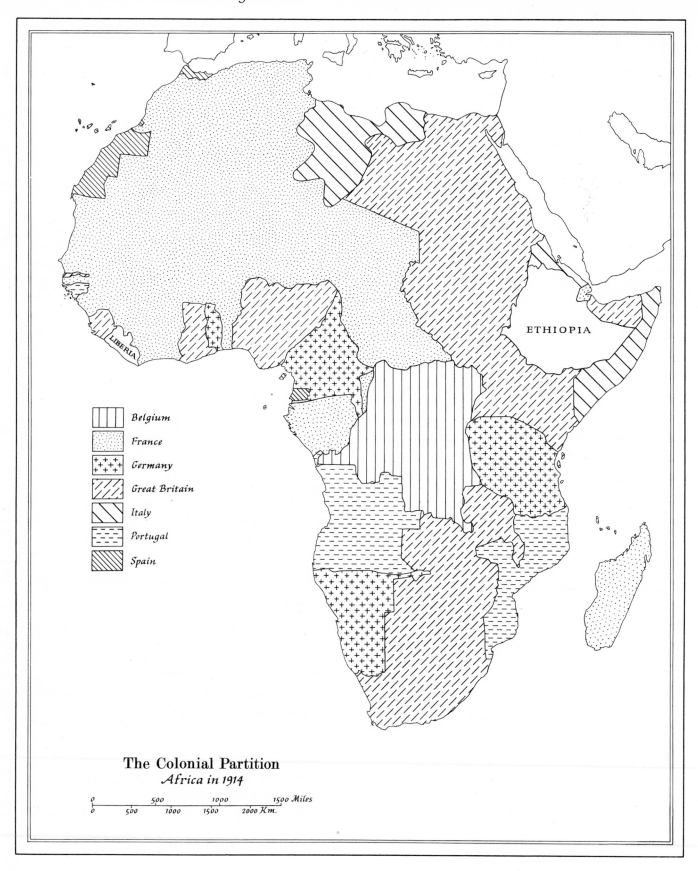

Belgium
France
Germany
Great Britain
Italy
Portugal
Spain

LIBERIA

ETHIOPIA

The Colonial Partition
Africa in 1914

0   500   1000   1500 Miles
0 500 1000 1500 2000 Km.

forced labour and costing little more than the expense of transport and military administration. The results were undoubtedly appalling. An official Belgian commission reporting in 1919 reached the conclusion that the population of the Belgian Congo (transferred to Belgian sovereignty in 1908 after the dissolution of the Congo Free State) had been 'reduced by half' since the beginning of the European occupation in the 1880s. No such losses, we may note, had ever been caused by the East African slave trade, revolting though it was. The cure had proved far worse than the disease.

The same highly destructive system was applied in French and German equatorial Africa a little later. In 1900 the whole vast area of French Equatorial Africa (now the Republics of Chad, Gabon, Central Africa and Congo-Brazzaville) was divided among forty French concession companies which enjoyed a charter of thirty years. 'One idea dominates the system,' declared a relevant French decree: 'All the products of the conceded territory, whatever they may be, are the property of the concession company . . .' These and other colonial interests did as well for themselves, although more briefly, in the German-occupied Cameroons. In 1898 the South Cameroons Company, its chairman the Hamburg financier Scharlach, but its capital mainly Belgian, received nearly twenty million acres where it could collect rubber free of all payment for all eternity. A year later the North-West Cameroons Company was given no less than one fifth of the whole territory. Operations of this kind could not be conducted without brutality and gross abuse. Such were the scandals set loose by the German companies that their activities were largely wound up before the First World War; while the concessions of the French companies, although surviving to their full term in 1930, were mercifully not renewed.

Elsewhere methods varied. Often they were much less 'intense', especially where no obvious natural wealth could be collected by forced labour or where other methods could be successfully applied. Most West African peoples suffered a good deal less, in this period, than those in the central, eastern and southern regions. They were submitted to no powerful concession companies. Their territories were seldom regarded as fit for permanent European settlement. In Southern Africa it was different again. Here the main British drive was for mineral deposits and for good farming land where Europeans could be settled. Here, too, the general method was through concession or chartered companies who were given far-reaching powers of government by their respective countries, but whose interests scarcely included the forced collection of rubber, ivory, and other natural products, and whose impact was therefore less severe. The plateau lands between the Limpopo and the Zambezi were accordingly administered by the chartered British South Africa Company until 1923, when the colony of Southern Rhodesia was formed, ostensibly under Crown rule but, in fact, with a free hand for local European settlers.

Further north the lands between the Zambezi and Katanga, the latter now seized by Belgium, were similarly administered by the British South Africa Company until 1924, when colonial rule was installed. Here and there, as in South Africa, Algeria, and Kenya, especially favourable country was marked out for settlement by Europeans. The African farming lands thus engrossed were simply treated as 'vacant', and therefore as 'Crown property' to be disposed of as the colonial rulers thought fit. South Africa took its present shape in 1910, after the Anglo-Boer war, when the British conceded all powers of government to the white populations of the Cape Province, Natal, Orange Free State, and Transvaal, subtracting from this Union only the protectorates of Swaziland, Basutoland and Bechuanaland.

However various the methods, the results were in one great aspect the same. They brought a new subjection by peoples who, unlike all previous and internal conquerors, regarded themselves as naturally superior to Africans, and who were also able to apply methods of oppression and exploitation of a range and intensity never known before. They evoked revolt after revolt. Some of these revolts, like those of the Matabele and Mashona in the early Southern Rhodesia of the 1890s, or the Herero and Hottentot risings in South-West Africa, or the resistance of the Ovimbundu kingdoms in Angola during 1902-3, or the Maji-Maji war against the Germans in Tanganyika a little later, were on a massive scale. Such revolts were of a kind with the earlier wars of resistance to actual invasion: with the struggles of Arabi in Egypt, with the bitter fight put up against the French by the Algerians under Amir Abdelkader in the 1840s, with the defensive battles of the Asante, with the wars of Ahmadu and Samory in the Western Sudan and of the Mahdi in the Eastern Sudan. Other revolts were 'mere local troubles', little recorded outside the colonial annals. They were none the less numerous, and they continued for a long time.

These wars took their heavy toll. Yet another form of warfare had meanwhile caused more victims in four years than all those who may have died in pre-colonial 'tribal fighting' over twice as many decades. Some 46,000 Kenya Africans are estimated to have lost their lives in British military service between 1914 and 1918, a greater destruction, as a British critic noted at the time, 'than a generation of inter-tribal wars'. From West Africa the French mobilized no fewer than 211,000 Africans, of whom 169,000 were deployed in the fearful battles of the Western Front in France with an officially admitted total of 24,762 killed, this taking no account of a large number of others whose fate was never ascertained. Not even the most minimal effort was ever made to compensate the families of the dead.

The year 1935 brought a last though peculiarly vicious postscript to the chapter of invasion. On 3 October of that year, to the accompaniment of air attack on defenceless villages and a welter of bombastic propaganda, the armies of Fascist Italy invaded Ethiopia. The conquest was no easy one. Not until 1 April 1936 were the invaders able to reach Gondar; only on 5 May could they enter the capital of Addis Abeba. Even then their troubles were not over. Resistance continued. As late as 1 January 1939, the Italian Foreign Minister Ciano was noting that 'Asmara is still in a state of complete revolt.' Two years later the game was up. Beaten by British armies coming up from East Africa, Italy's Fascist legions vanished from the scene. The Emperor Haile Selassie re-entered Addis Abeba on 5 May 1941, almost five years to the day since he had gone into exile.

The System at Work: 1920-45

It was a curious system. The colonial powers – now without Germany, whose colonies were divided between Britain and France in the form of Mandated Territories of the newly-formed League of Nations – possessed far more territory than they knew what to do with. Having seized much of this in order to prevent it from falling to rivals, they were often content with mere territorial possession, a fact which may help to explain their relative willingness to abandon mere territorial possession forty years later. Most colonies were expected to pay for their own colonial government, so that the degree of intensity with which territorial possession could be asserted was often left to depend on local taxable capacity and the attraction of mining or other profitable forms of private investment.

To this there were exceptions in country selected for European settlement. Here the intensity of territorial occupation was far greater. Local populations were driven into farming labour under semi-slave conditions, notably in South Africa.

All this being so, the general character of the central years of the colonial period was of hand-to-mouth administration, political decay, and economic stagnation. Very little could be done to realize the humanitarian promises of 'civilizing Africa' that had sounded and resounded in the parliaments of Europe during the years of conquest. Yet the underlying pressures of European occupation – of occupation by powers which were the emanation of societies geared to industrial production and the search for private profit – were gradually having their profound if planless effect. Little by little, Africans were gripped by the economic system of their new rulers.

Methods of rule which imposed the need for money began to undermine traditional economics of subsistence where money had little or no place. Contrived in South Africa and rapidly applied elsewhere, such methods sought to raise revenue by money taxes. Even more, they sought to augment the supply of cheap labour. Except in the territories ruled by an industrially primitive Portugal, it had come to be accepted that forced labour could not be profitably used in any systematic way. As forced labour practices dwindled after 1920, it became ever more needful to lever the African peasant out of his village and oblige him to work in mines and plantations. He was accordingly mulcted of an annual tax which had to be paid in cash. This could be earned only by going to work for Europeans, while failure to pay could be met, and regularly was met, by visits from the colonial police and spells of 'prison labour'.

Apart from this central method of collecting labour, the sheer impact of European production also had its effect. A wide variety of simple industrial goods, whether clothing or shoes or factory-made trinkets or bicycles or the like, became available for the first time; and men were increasingly willing to work for Europeans in order to earn the cash to buy them with. These diverse pressures, directly coercive or not, led to a continual disintegration of traditional systems of community life, law, and self-respect. Wide regions were annually denuded of a significant proportion of their 'fit adult males', to borrow one of the curiously zoological phrases of the colonial era, and the effects

Opposite: Fragment of a Yoruba bowl, made to hold the palm nuts used for divination, from Shaki, Oyo, in western Nigeria. The bowl, which was supported on the woman's head, is lost

were often disastrous. 'The whole fabric of the old order of society is undermined', noted an official report of 1935 on the consequences of migrant labour in Nyasaland (Malawi), 'when thirty to sixty per cent of the able-bodied men are absent at one time. . . . Emigration [i.e. labour migration], which destroys the old, offers nothing to take its place, and the family-community is threatened with complete dissolution.'

In many other territories, especially in the central and southern regions, the situation was not much better; in South Africa it was generally worse. Nor was it even true that these migrant workers, by moving into the European cash economy, also moved into the European industrial system and learned corresponding skills and an understanding of the new world they had to face. On the contrary, they were almost invariably used for un-skilled or semi-skilled labour under colour bars which prevented them from learning anything but how to use a pick and shovel. Wages were paid at the minimal sub-sistence level for a single man, even when, as rarely, their families could accompany them; and it will never be known how many hundreds of thousands of African families were thereby crippled or destroyed. Not for many years would there be any serious colonial effort to mitigate or mend the damage of this migrant labour system.

Another solvent of traditional stability was the steady destruction of African handicraft industries. Reviewing the past, an official report on Nigeria observed, in 1948, that 'since the growth of European economic enterprise in Nigeria, native mining has been on the decline because of the *de facto* monopolization of deposits by Europeans . . . or through the competition of European products with the final products of native mineral industries.' The once flourishing handicraft industry of the Hausa had tinned its brassware with locally-produced metal. Yet 'by 1923 this indigenous tin-producing industry had completely disappeared.' Much the same was true of Nigerian iron smelting, practised here for some two thousand years: by the 1930s it had 'largely died out'. Traditional guilds of smiths, Forde was noting at about the same time, 'have decayed, leaving their members impoverished, and threatened with social degradation.' And it was no different in many other territories. Ibn Khaldun had reckoned the Algerian weaving centre of Tlemcen to have used some 4,000 hand-looms in the fourteenth century. By the middle of the nineteenth century, after French occupation, there were only about 500. In 1954 Tlemcen was found to have exactly 105 looms.

Under pressures such as these the heart of traditional Africa, its village life and economy, suffered lesion after lesion. Yet the new mining and urban centres had no real alternative to offer. In these it became the habit for countless thousands of migrant workers from the villages to live in barracks or compounds from which all women, married or not, were deliberately excluded. Any hope of earning more than the minimal wages of bachelor subsistence was blocked by colour bars, by bans on trade union organization, and by a more or less complete denial of training facilities. The situation was most obviously bad in South Africa, though the reasons for this may be only that much more is known of South Africa than of other territories in the colonial period. There the expropriation of African land had reached a point by the 1930s where some nine tenths of all cultivable soil was 'reserved' for European occupation. Outside their crowded tenth, Africans lived on sufferance, subjected to a host of petty persecutions, and debarred from selling their labour in anything approaching a free market.

It goes without saying that local conditions greatly varied. In the cities of Kenya, for instance, it was possible for African migrant workers to bring their families to town, and many did. Yet a man's wages continued to be calculated on the basis of bachelor subsistence, it being regularly supposed in the face of all the evidence that his family was happily supported on a farm in the countryside. As late as 1954 an official inquiry into wages paid to Kenya African workers found that these were 'generally insufficient not only to feed, house and clothe their families, but even for their own needs', and concluded that 'approximately one half of the urban workers in private industry, and approximately one quarter of those in the public services, are in receipt of wages insufficient to provide for their basic essential needs of health, decency, and working efficiency', a fairly bleak memorial to the benefits of sixty years of colonial rule.

Conditions tended to be better, even much better, in some of the western territories. There was little alienation of productive land in the French West African Federation (Senegal, Mauretania, Soudan [now Mali], Niger, Upper Volta, Guinea, Ivory Coast, Dahomey; there was also Togo, formally a Mandated Territory of the League of Nations and later, until independence in 1960, a Trusteeship Territory of the United Nations); and none at all in the British territories (Nigeria, Gold Coast [now Ghana], Sierra Leone, Gambia, as well as

Opposite: Wooden statue of a mother and child from Baga, Guinea (Height: 26¾ in.)

the British part of ex-German Togo, another Mandated and later Trusteeship Territory).

In contrast with countries of growing European settlement in eastern and central-southern Africa, the colonial economies in West Africa were effectively dominated by a small number of powerful trading and mining companies. These played a key part in fixing the terms of trade: the prices, that is, which African producers could realize for their products and the prices they were obliged to pay for European goods they might wish to buy. As elsewhere – except in a handful of countries such as South Africa and Algeria which were designed for European settlement on the grand scale – the general level of non-commercial investment remained very low, although movement of raw materials and crops from the interior (and of troops into the interior) was aided by the completion of a few railways. These almost all ran inland from the coast, so that West Africa today lacks any effective inter-territorial network. In Nigeria a line linking points in the north had been completed as early as 1911 and was joined with a line to Lagos on the coast two years later. After 1920 the French carried their rail link through Senegal as far as the Upper Niger at Kayes and then to Bamako, now the capital of Mali. Another line joined Conakry with the plains of Upper Guinea. There were a few others of the same kind, such as the line from Lobito through inland Angola to the Katangan copperbelt, and the East African railroad from Mombasa. Some attention was given to ports, notably Dakar in Senegal, Freetown in Sierra Leone, and Sekondi on the Gold Coast; but systematic construction of wharf and dock-side rail facilities came only during the raw material boom after the Second World War.

Western Africa was often more fortunate in political affairs as well. While the governing ideology of 'white man's countries' like Kenya supposed that it must be 'hundreds of years' before 'the natives could be fit to take a hand in government', the outlook in West Africa was very different. The Gold Coast had enjoyed at least the shadow of a form of self-rule through legislative council from the early years of the colony; and the absence of European settlers could also sometimes mean the absence of an ideology of racialist superiority on the part of the administrators. In Nigeria the Lagos colony had likewise had its advisory council from the 1860s. A new colonial constitution of 1922 provided for advisory executive and legislative councils. If the unofficial members of these councils were almost invariably 'safe men' from the colonial standpoint, they were still Nigerians. Even in early days there existed a Nigerian and Gold Coast political public opinion which repeatedly exercised its influence, however indirectly and partially, on methods of government, not least through energetic newspapers like the *Gold Coast Independent*. One of the undoubted achievements of this public opinion was to prevent the freehold sale of land to Europeans. Generally, the political and social suffocation of the colonial period was felt less severely along the coast of Guinea than in other regions.

French policies of 'assimilation' introduced another variant, but these became important on the political scene only after 1945. Before the Second World War the only 'French West Africans' who had managed to acquire citizenship rights in the French Republic were the inhabitants of the old colonial towns of Dakar, Gorée, Rufisque and Saint Louis along the coast of Senegal. These were admitted to the community of French civilization and allowed to elect an African deputy to the National Assembly of the Third Republic.

How one measures the African balance of loss and gain through the gruelling episode of European colonial rule will depend, no doubt, upon who one is. Most Africans have probably seen in it little or nothing but loss and sorrow for their continent. Many Europeans, even when thinking not solely of their own interests, have claimed for it little but gain. The truth is obviously difficult to reach, and will vary from one territory to another or even from one colonial power to another. Muting the emotional overtones, there is perhaps not much doubt where the judgment of history may be found to lie. It is the negative sides of the experience that will command attention; and for this the reasons are not difficult to see. They consist in the fact that the central consequence of colonial rule was not the reconstruction of Africa on modern lines, on the lines now necessary to Africa's emancipation from the Iron Age limits of the past. On the contrary, the central consequence was merely to undertake or to complete the ruin and dismantlement of the societies and structures which the conquerors found in place. By 1900, beyond any doubt, the greater part of Africa required most urgently a renovation in terms of modern learning, science, production and productive relationships. But it was not the colonial system that provided or ever could provide this renovation. Potent to destroy, the bearers of the white man's burden proved helpless to rebuild. All they could do, whether consciously or

Opposite: A Miango village near Jos in northern Nigeria

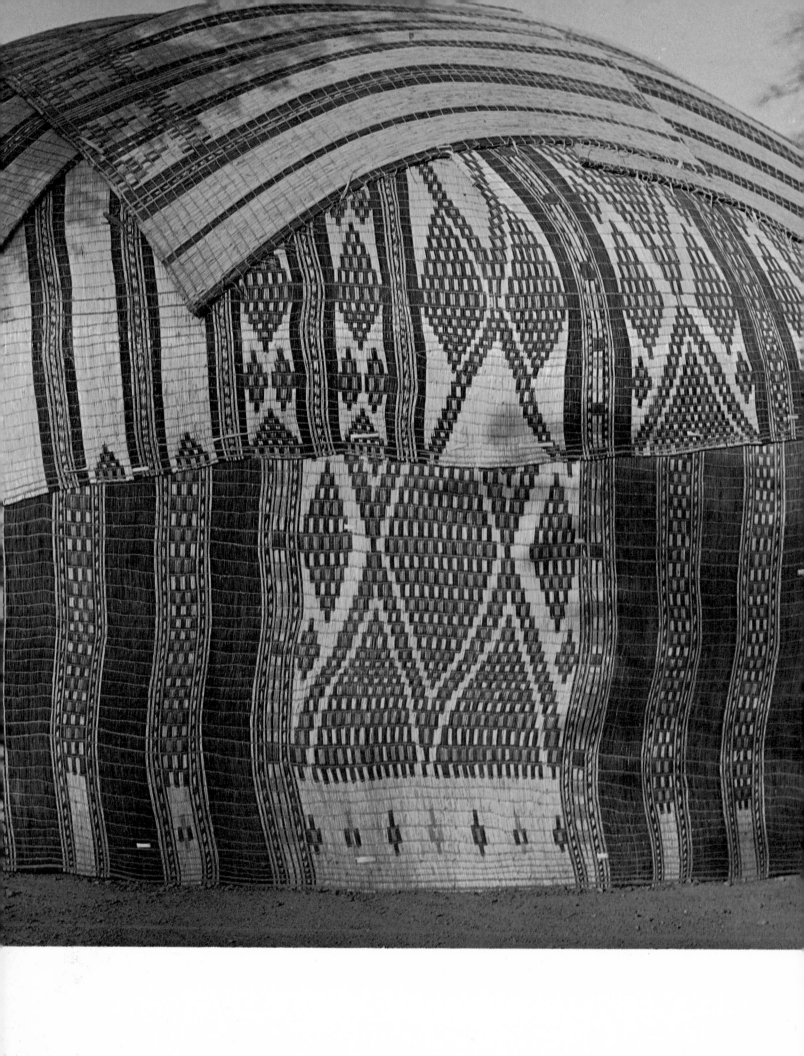

not, was to deepen that developing crisis of change and transformation which much of Africa had already entered before they came upon the scene. They could and did deepen this crisis; they could not resolve it.

Of course there is more to be said than this. Like other great movements in history, the colonial experience was a contradictory thing. To see only its destructive essence is to ignore a number of lesser consequences, side-effects, by-products, that were not negative. While the impact and value of these varied with the nature of the metropolitan society from which the rulers came, they were present even in colonies, such as those of Portugal, that were governed by an attitude almost pre-industrial or even pre-capitalist. Though wastefully and planlessly, with reluctance or contempt, the colonial rulers still opened a few new doors to the outside world. They helped to overcome the comparative isolation of the past. Their paternalist yet persevering Christian missionary endeavour and self-sacrifice – all this being very much akin to the comparable Christian effort among the British working classes of the nineteenth century – became a powerful influence in awakening a minority of Africans to their true situation and in preparing for a different future. A better understanding of the world undermined not only the authority of the colonial regime itself, but also the authority of all those Africans who stood for traditional methods and therefore, in the circumstances, for continued subjection, technological inferiority, and poverty of social power. And it carried on this undermining process so effectively, at least in the limited but important field of African educated opinion, that what really came to matter during much of the colonial period, as Oliver has shrewdly noted, was no longer what went on in the palaces of traditional potentates but what went on in the mission schools.

These are the reasons why the colonial conquest was unique, and why it must be judged as such. Many African empires had arisen in the past, many innovating regimes, many strong reformers. Yet these had remained within their Iron Age framework even though, as the nineteenth century wore on, some of them were beginning to escape from it. Many outside influences and even a few outside invasions had arrived in previous centuries. But these had never been sufficiently large or long-enduring, or launched from a sufficiently different social system, to resist a more or less rapid absorption into the adaptive patterns of indigenous African life. With colonialism it was altogether different. After that,

Africa could never again be the same. The patterns of indigenous life simply could not contain, much less absorb, these eruptive methods and technologies; they wrecked the old framework beyond hope of repair. In this narrow sense the colonial experience may be said to have done some service, however blind and painful. By 1945 the whole complex structure of Iron Age society, so greatly out of step as it was with the world from which the conquerors came, had suffered a collapse so fatal that it could never be put together again.

Even remotely in the continental heartlands, far within the rain forests of the Congo, a skilled Belgian sociologist could find by 1946 a decay in traditional forms so far-reaching that 'nowhere any more, it may be said, does the chief really administer his tribe; nowhere is the traditional grouping still intact.' Just as the industrial revolution had swept away the confining bonds of pre-industrial society in Britain a century and more earlier, and had done this in a comparably planless, violent, and blindly painful way, so too did the colonial hurricane level to the ground every great polity it found, shaking them to their very roots, and leaving in its wake the need not only for new structures, but for structures of an altogether different and expansive type.

Yet there was, as we have seen, one profound difference between the consequences of the industrial revolution in Europe and those of the colonial system in Africa. The first destroyed but also, after its fashion, mightily rebuilt afresh; the second, having gone far to ruin what it found, could only leave for Africans the task of making a new society. No such new society came into being during the colonial period. Little was left behind but an utter impoverishment of the old society, a chaos of ideas and social relationships. This is why it must be fruitless to argue, as some Europeans and Americans have liked to do, that the colonial episode was beneficial and even necessary to the transformation of Iron Age Africa. There is indeed nothing in that episode to show that these peoples could not or would not have worked this transformation for themselves, far less wastefully, far less expensively in life and suffering and self-respect, without the coercion of outside interference. And it was in fact to be the task of Africans during the next phase of transition, the period beginning after the Second World War, both to create the opportunity for rebuilding, and then, during the 1960s, to face at last the direct challenge of reconstruction.

Opposite: Wickerwork tent of the Kurtei near Niamey, Niger

8 Towards Liberation

The forerunners of modern African independence movements, north and south of the Sahara, before 1945 – Outline of the third main phase of the colonial period after 1945 – Growth of nationalism and the emergence of independent states – The legacy of the past and new problems of economic and social transition

The Forerunners

The tides of nationalism have flowed through many fogs and shadows up and down the world. But it may help to explain some of the special features of nationalism, as they developed afterwards in Africa, if one remembers that these furious currents of opinion took their initial rise during a dawn that was in many ways generous and lucid. Up to the time of the Napoleonic empire, at least, European nationalism was the child of the Enlightenment and the Rights of Man: even later, during the middle years of the nineteenth century, it was still the poets and philosophers of the 'submerged nationalities', whether Italian, Slav or Magyar, who sang most potently of human equality and therefore of human freedom. And it was in much the same spirit of emancipation, and even by way of many of the same modes of expression, that the tides of nationalism took their rise in Africa: for in Africa, as in Europe, the driving inspiration was not that all men should be divided by becoming nationals, but that all men should be united by becoming free.

What the 'morning stars' of the African awakening, men like Africanus Horton and Edward Blyden, the latter from Jamaica but long settled in Africa, were concerned to achieve was not the nationalist mosaic of Europe – not the European 'tribal nationalism' of Hannah Arendt's recent lapidary phrase – but the abolition of all those artificial barriers against equality, and therefore against freedom, that racialism and imperialism had imposed. 'Why should not the same race who governed Egypt', wrote Horton in his

Vindication of the African Race, published in 1868, 'once more stand on their legs and endeavour to raise their characters in the scale of the civilized world?'

This was the egalitarian tradition of thought, often markedly Christian in its African expression, that held firm until the very threshold of nationalist achievement and even after the threshold was crossed. 'What is the difference between a white man and a black man?' asked an African missionary in the Nyasaland of 1911 where the difference in power and wealth had become enormous: 'Are we not of the same blood and all from Adam?' And this was the tradition that would inspire new leaders in another generous and lucid dawn, little more than three decades later, during the sharp awakening and release which accompanied defeat of the Nazi-Fascist alliance and its racialist ideologies.

This line of thought may be traced through every phase of the colonial period. Involvement in the First World War gave it a new strength. If the African volunteers who suffered on the battlefields of European conflict 'were good enough to fight and die in the Empire's cause', wrote the *Gold Coast Independent* in 1921 (and the Gold Coast had given 3,000 men to the Empire's cause, as well as the price of eleven aeroplanes), 'they were good enough ... to have a share in the government of their countries.' Others felt the same. Although the period of full colonial installation had scarcely begun, and the last wars of pacification were still in progress, the year 1920 saw a meeting in Accra of African spokesmen from each of the four British West African territories, and the formation of a National Congress of British West Africa. 'We desire,' announced the Gold Coast leader Caseley Hayford in his inaugural

Opposite: Moroccan revolt against Spanish colonial rule in 1924–6. Above, a party of Moroccans on the watch, and below, the Spanish batteries above Tetuan

address, 'as the intelligentsia of our people, to promote unity among our people'; and the aims of unity, however tentatively stated, were equality and freedom.

During the weary years after 1920 more Africans escaped from stagnation at home into a wider world. Some went to Western Europe, where they could compare their own situation and struggles with those of other 'depressed classes'. Others travelled to the United States, where they could learn from the teachings of Afro-American thinkers such as William Burghardt Du Bois and visionaries such as Marcus Garvey. Still others reached the newly-founded Soviet Union, where they could imbibe the stronger medicine of social revolution. By the early 1930s the political awakening had begun to ripen into new and wider forms of thought and action. What now mattered most was no longer what happened in the mission school, but what happened in a host of little centres of political discussion and incipient trade union organization.

Ideas of change had great diversity of form. In Egypt, as in Tunisia and Algeria, national movements became largely the work of middle-class intellectuals acting within the Islamic tradition, even while, as with Egyptians like Ali 'Abd al-Razaq and Taha Husain, they questioned much Islamic doctrine taken formerly for granted or above discussion. Like the nationalist party of the Wafd in the field of politics, al-Razaq opened the way for an ideological rebirth of purely Egyptian nationalism by challenging the right of the Caliphate to consider Egypt merely as a unit of the 'Islamic empire'. Elsewhere the same ferment was at work. Founded in 1920, the Tunisian Destour or 'party of the constitution' aimed at national emancipation from French rule, and was supplanted in 1934 by a new party, the Néo-Destour, under more determined leaders such as Habib Bourghiba, who later became Tunisia's first president. Algeria saw the crystallization of its first modern nationalist movement in 1925, when Messali Hadj formed the Etoile Nord-Africaine, the Star of North Africa. This was displaced in 1934 by the more militant Parti Populaire Algérien, duly banned by the French in 1939 but kept alive underground.

Westward again, the year 1926 saw the great Moroccan revolt of Abdul Karim. But Moroccan nationalism, grounded in a movement of Islamic reform promoted by the Salafis, 'the good or pious ancestors', is usually dated from 1930. Like other Muslims elsewhere, the Salafis had seen the invading French army in the light of a Christian power seeking to suppress Islam. But they advanced to more directly political ground in 1930, when the French caused the promulgation of a *dahir* or sultan's decree whereby the Berber peoples of Morocco were removed from the jurisdiction of Islamic courts. Salafism blossomed into nationalism. Then it was that Allal al-Fassi formed a secret society called al-Zawaiyya which soon became the core of a nationalist movement, the Istiqlal or party of independence.

At the other end of Africa the 1930s likewise saw the spread of new ideas of emancipation among many Africans of South Africa who had previously stood within traditional frames of thought: among peasants now enclosed in squalid rural slums, among migrant workers labouring in the gold mines of the Witwatersrand, and, gradually, among the rural peoples of the countryside as well. In less harried lands the spread was slower, but it stubbornly continued. If ideas of emancipation still lay in the future for most of the peoples of central Africa, this was no longer true in the eastern or western regions. Thus the Kikuyu of Kenya, whose land included fertile and healthy uplands increasingly enclosed by European farmers, had embarked on the politics of protest as early as 1921. This was when the Young Kikuyu Association was formed under the lead of a Nairobi telephone operator called Harry Thuku. Its message, as framed by Thuku, was clear enough. 'Hearken, every day you pay hut tax to the Europeans of Government', was one of the points in his 1922 programme: 'Where is it sent? It is their task to steal the property of the Kikuyu people.'

Now, too, there came a widening breakaway from Christian church communities seen as dominated by Europeans for their own ends. By 1929 there were many independent African churches whose message proclaimed 'Africa for the Africans', and was as much political as religious. Meanwhile the politics of protest in West Africa had continued to assume ever more determined forms of directly political organization. When the Second World War once more shook the prestige and power of the colonial rulers, and thrust many thousands of Africans into new patterns of thought or action, the ground of popular understanding was well and widely laid.

Opposite top: Ethiopian cavalry at Addis Abeba during the Italian invasion of 1935
Bottom: French security troops charging crowds in the streets of Algiers during demonstrations on Armistice Day, 1960

After 1945: New Nations

In its consequences for Africa the Second World War greatly accelerated that general dismantlement of traditional society which had begun with colonial invasion in the 1880s. The evidence, as before, is complex and even contradictory; yet its negative aspects were now increasingly apparent, as the following fairly characteristic piece of evidence may be enough to show. 'For five years', Father van Wing could write of the Belgian Congo in 1945, 'our populations were subjected to a war-effort that was extremely intense and varied. The whole black population was mobilized to produce as much as possible, and as rapidly as possible, in order to export what the Allies needed and to provide what they lacked. That is the dominating fact.'

This 'dominating fact' in mines and plantations was coupled with an often disastrous decline of the indigenous rural economy. Deepening poverty in the countryside drove men and women in ever rising numbers into towns and cities. The flood gained fresh strength as soon as the colonial powers had recovered from their own losses and disorganization. Wartime demand for raw materials was surpassed by a post-war boom in Western European and American production. By the mid-1950s there was scarcely a single city in Africa which had failed to treble or quadruple its population since 1939. Vast numbers of peasants broke away from the misery of rural poverty and braved the different misery of life in hastily-erected urban slums, 'locations' or, in the graphic French term for them, 'tin-can towns'.

Nothing like this had been seen since the British industrial revolution. Thrust suddenly into a cash economy far beyond their control or understanding, these new townsmen made shift as they could. However much they suffered, whether from colour-bar discrimination in South Africa and other colonies of white settlement, or from sheer material and moral inanition elsewhere, the flood continued. Something of the same picture could be painted of these towns as of the English industrial cities of the mid-nineteenth century. 'The evils associated with the absence of family life, drunkenness, prostitution, and venereal disease,' observed a Royal Commission on East Africa in 1955, 'are rife in the towns with large African populations. . . .' One of the most illuminating series of statistics available for these years concerns the rising rate of alcohol import. By 1951 official figures show the French West African colonial federation as importing fifteen times more strong drink than in 1938; and the French territories were not unique in this respect.

As these trends uncontrollably continued it soon became clear, at least to those who cared to look, that much of Africa was now plunged in profound and widening social and economic disintegration, and that none of the old colonial solutions could any longer hope to work. The wiser heads in colonial administrations perceived the way the wind was blowing, and vainly sought for means of subduing its force. For these colonies 'to go back to the subsistence economy of the past,' the East Africa Royal Commission decided in 1955, 'or even to stand still in the dawn between the old institutions which are dying and the new which are struggling to be born, would be to court disaster.' Yet how could any solution along colonial lines prevent this? In a large sense it could be said that the partly latent crisis of the nineteenth century and the colonial period itself had now reached explosion point.

This explosion took the form of struggles for national independence within frontiers drawn by the colonial powers. Earlier demands for equality and emancipation now became nationalism in the narrower sense of the word. Gathering in Manchester in 1945, the members of the sixth Pan-African Congress, including Kwame Nkrumah, afterwards President of Ghana, Jomo Kenyatta, afterwards President of Kenya, and a representative of Nnamdi Azikiwe, afterwards President of Nigeria, still spoke (as some of them would afterwards continue to speak, but with a new authority) of the Pan-African cause, but they sounded a markedly new note. Unlike their predecessors, they demanded not only respect for Africans, but also autonomy and even independence. They took advantage of the fruits of the Second World War. If India could be free – and Burma and Ceylon and still other Asian countries – why not Africa as well?

New and more radical nationalist parties were soon formed in colonies such as the Gold Coast, Nigeria, and French West Africa where the ruling power was prepared, if still with great reluctance, to allow them to exist. The other side of the process of dismantlement – the growth of the politics of protest – became increasingly apparent. In colonies such as Northern Rhodesia the influence of the British Labour Party had paved a cautious but still useful path towards effective trade unions, invariably prohibited in earlier years; and trade unionism now played a part of growing importance in the effectiveness of national movements. Little

Opposite: Kwame Nkrumah, here seen after elections in 1956, led Ghana (former Gold Coast) to independence in 1957: the first big breakthrough in the cause of African independence south of the Sahara
Overleaf left: Mass meeting in the Nyanza region of Kenya addressed by President Jomo Kenyatta
Overleaf right: The gaiety of independence was expressed, as by this market-trader of Accra during Ghana's independence celebrations, in many practical or festive ways

by little, and then with gathering speed, the nationalist cause spread far outside the limits of the educated minority which had first proclaimed it, and assumed mass dimensions as it drew within its orbit ever larger numbers of townsmen and peasants. These movements soon thrust ahead of the few concessions which British or French colonial governors were ready to accept as necessary; and the half-dozen years after 1945 were accordingly full of violent clashes and upheavals, repressions, shootings and imprisonments. Yet the onward drive of African opinion, coupled with a growing British and French awareness that nothing but major political change could meet this crisis, gradually achieved important constitutional changes.

North of the Sahara the decisive point of change came with the Free Officers' *coup d'état* of 1952 in Egypt and the assumption of power by Gamal Abdel Nasser two years later; although, in mere point of time, the former Italian colony of Libya had achieved sovereignty under its Sanusi king, Idris al-Mahdi al-Sanusi, in 1951. Morocco and Tunisia followed in 1955-6. In 1956, too, the Anglo-Egyptian Condominium over the Eastern Sudan was brought to an end, and the Republic of Sudan was proclaimed in Khartoum. The collapse of Fascist Italy had meanwhile restored independence to the ancient empire of Ethiopia, including its Eritrean province, and the new Italian Republic was also ready to pull out of Somalia. South of the Sahara the pace of constitutional change was set by the Convention Peoples' Party of the Gold Coast under Kwame Nkrumah's dynamic leadership. Achieving internal self-rule in 1951, the country that was now to be called Ghana acquired full political independence in 1957. Nigeria quickly followed with internal self-rule in 1952 and independence in 1960.

Everywhere else the pressures for change grew immeasurably stronger during the 1950s. The year 1960 saw the emergence of an independent Somali Republic which combined the former British territory of Somaliland with that of Italian Somalia. Tanganyika followed in 1961, and Uganda in 1962. Kenya, though in the wake of bitter struggles, became independent in 1963, and so did Zanzibar. This East African island followed its independence with an almost immediate revolution against its sultan and land-owning minority, and joined with nearby Tanganyika in a union which took the name of Tanzania. After ten years of strife and frustration the European-dominated Federation of the two Rhodesias and Nyasaland was abolished in 1963;

Nyasaland and Northern Rhodesia became the independent countries of Malawi and Zambia a year later. With Sierra Leone achieving independence in 1961 and Gambia in 1965, little now remained of the British empire in Africa.

The French colonies moved to the same end by a different route. After Germany's invasion of France in 1940 a pro-Nazi regime established at Vichy tried to maintain both the racialist ethos of colonialism and the fact of direct imperial rule. Democratic France could offer little opposition to this until 1943. By then, however, the war had assumed an explicitly anti-colonialist form under the dual if very differently motivated pressures of the United States and the Soviet Union, and these had an increasing influence on the Free French movement led by General Charles de Gaulle. Suspected by the Americans as a British instrument, de Gaulle found himself played off against ex-Vichyist leaders in North Africa. Reacting to this, he spoke more and more sharply for republican ideas in the grand tradition of liberty and equality, and opened the way for cautious change in those colonies where African élites had thrown in their lot with his cause.

Out of these manoeuvres there came the famous Brazzaville declaration of 1944, generally regarded as the beginning of the end of the French empire in Africa. Viewed in the light of later years, the Brazzaville decisions must seem surprisingly timid. 'The nature of the French colonial task', they announced, '*excludes all idea of autonomy, all possibility of development outside the bloc of the French Empire: even the distant establishment of self-government in the colonies is excluded.*' (Emphasis in the original.)

Yet the Brazzaville decisions offered 'participation'. Coupled with the spirit of the times, this helped to pave the way for provisions in the 1946 constitution of the new Fourth Republic whereby the French colonies were to elect, albeit by restricted franchise, a number of Africans who would sit as deputies in the National Assembly in Paris. Grasping this opportunity, a majority of the nascent nationalist parties came together at a unity conference in 1946, at Bamako in the Soudan (later Mali), and formed themselves into a multi-territorial alliance called the Rassemblement Démocratique Africain. It was the leaders of the RDA who now made the running throughout French Africa.

In 1956 one of the last governments of the Fourth Republic proclaimed that each of the territories might

Opposite: The market-place at Mopti on the Upper Niger, a city engaged in river-trade for several centuries

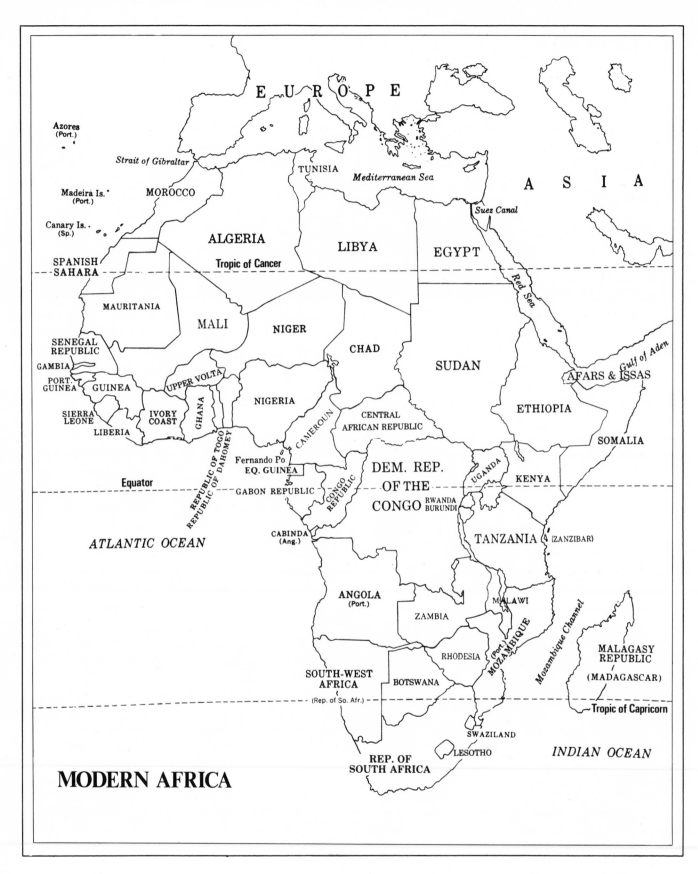

MODERN AFRICA

Azores
(Port.)

Strait of Gibraltar

Madeira Is.
(Port.)

Canary Is.
(Sp.)

SPANISH
SAHARA

TUNISIA

Mediterranean Sea

MOROCCO

ALGERIA

Tropic of Cancer

LIBYA

EGYPT

Suez Canal

EUROPE

ASIA

MAURITANIA

MALI

NIGER

CHAD

SUDAN

Red Sea

Gulf of Aden

SENEGAL
REPUBLIC

GAMBIA

PORT.
GUINEA   GUINEA

UPPER VOLTA

SIERRA
LEONE

LIBERIA

IVORY
COAST

GHANA

NIGERIA

CAMEROUN

CENTRAL
AFRICAN REPUBLIC

ETHIOPIA

AFARS & ISSAS

SOMALIA

REPUBLIC OF TOGO
REPUBLIC OF DAHOMEY

Fernando Po
EQ. GUINEA

Equator

GABON REPUBLIC

CONGO
REPUBLIC

DEM. REP.
OF THE
CONGO

UGANDA

KENYA

RWANDA
BURUNDI

ATLANTIC OCEAN

CABINDA
(Ang.)

TANZANIA (ZANZIBAR)

ANGOLA
(Port.)

ZAMBIA

MALAWI

MOZAMBIQUE (Port.)

Mozambique Channel

MALAGASY
REPUBLIC
(MADAGASCAR)

RHODESIA

SOUTH-WEST
AFRICA

BOTSWANA

Tropic of Capricorn

(Rep. of So. Afr.)

SWAZILAND

LESOTHO

INDIAN OCEAN

REP. OF
SOUTH AFRICA

Opposite top: The repressions of racialist rule in South Africa have proved inseparable from bitter violence. The scene here is the small town of Sharpeville after police had shot into a crowd of demonstrators in 1961
Bottom: After 1960 the Portuguese colonies were increasingly rocked by African rebellions. This photograph, taken in 1964, shows a guerrilla detachment somewhere in 'Portuguese' Guinea, where armed resistance began in 1963 and rapidly gained control of most of the rural areas

Left: Independence celebrations in Algeria, 11 December 1960
Right: Excavating the mineral wealth of Africa: copper-mines in Zambia
Below: Akosombo dam on the Volta river nearing completion in 1964. Political power can mean little without economic power: in 1965 the government of Ghana completed, ahead of scheduled time and under scheduled cost, one of the largest dams and hydro-electric complexes anywhere in the world

have internal self-rule. This *loi cadre* or 'framework law', as it was called, did much to split the budding unity of the French West African movements while giving each of them more freedom of action within its own boundaries. Two years later, newly returned to power in France, de Gaulle offered all these territories a choice between immediate independence or membership of a new French Community run from Paris. Only the Guinea 'Section of the RDA', the Parti Démocrate de Guinée under the leadership of Sékou Touré, was strong enough to take advantage of this. Surviving a subsequent French boycott, Guinea pointed the way for the others, all of whom, including Madagascar, followed in 1960 after another shift in French policy that was greatly influenced by Félix Houphouet-Boigny of the Ivory Coast. With this the French Community was dead, although the hand of Paris was reaffirmed and strengthened by military and financial agreements under which France retained a predominant influence in nearly all these former colonies. Up to 1965 France retained some 20,000 troops in 'Black Africa'. Even after 1965 France continued to influence or control many of its economic and budgetary decisions. Association in the West European Common Market further confirmed these ties with France.

As late as 1959 the Belgians were still asserting their intention of governing the Congo for another thirty years or more. Suddenly in January 1960 they broke away from this traditional policy, and conceded full political independence within six months. This duly came in the middle of 1960 with almost nothing prepared. Not only were there fewer than a score of Congolese university graduates at this time – and not a single one of these with any serious administrative experience – but, far more disturbing, no Congolese national party or movement had enjoyed more than a few months in which to organize and prepare itself for power. Without a single Congolese officer, its mercenary *Force Publique* (a colonial force raised by colonial methods in the days of the Congo Free State, and used ever since for the woeful tasks of pacification) mutinied almost at once. The newly-independent administration collapsed under these and other strains. Its most effective leader, Patrice Lumumba, fell victim to outside pressures and internal intrigues, and was murdered in 1961. Years of chaos lay ahead.

Even so there remained, by 1963, only the embattled 'White South' to carry on the old traditions of direct imperialist rule: South Africa, Southern Rhodesia, and the Portuguese 'oversea provinces' of Angola and Mozambique. Apart from these, Britain still had power in three territories in or around South Africa, Swaziland, Basutoland and Bechuanaland, but each of these was moving towards political independence in one form or another, and soon gained it. Elsewhere the Portuguese held the Cape Verde Islands and their mainland West African colony of Guinea. The Spanish retained Rio d'Oro (Spanish Sahara), the enclave of Sidi Ifni, and Spanish Guinea (consisting of the small island of Fernando Po and a mainland fragment known as Rio Muni). All these enclosed a total population smaller than half a million. France kept her Red Sea enclave of Djibouti with a population of fewer than 50,000.

But it was different in the 'White South'. South Africa saw the rise to power, in 1948, of a National Party of Afrikaner (Boer) extremists for whom any concessions to African equality of rights were abhorrent, and whose racist policies of *apartheid*, or 'separate development', supposed that South Africa's non-white majority (now some fifteen millions out of a total of nineteen) should remain for ever in a servant or servile position. In 1965, following the same road, the very small white minority in neighbouring Rhodesia rebelled against its Crown Colony status, and declared for independence under a system very close to *apartheid*. Last-ditch defence of colonial rule and its corresponding racist assumptions likewise continued in the Portuguese colonies of Angola and Mozambique, where, however, nationalist movements began armed resistance which the Portuguese proved incapable of putting down. By the end of the 1960s it seemed probable that still larger clashes lay ahead as the regimes of the 'White South' gathered arms and foreign aid.

Reconstruction

While most of Africa north of the Zambezi had achieved political independence by the early 1960s, the further progress of these new states was beset with troubles. Many were small or very small in territory or population. Others were tied so closely to the financial or commercial leading strings of their former rulers as to enjoy little but the appearance of sovereignty. Not a few were utterly without reserves of cash, capital and trained personnel; and some of them, having failed to settle acute internal rivalries, were deep in the toils of civil war. Only a handful of these new nations had as yet begun, or seemed able to begin, the tremendously difficult task of reshaping and rebuilding their national life in such a way as to overcome, step by step, the deep crises of economic system and political structure they had inherited from the past.

The period after 1960 was accordingly one of great dispute about the future, of setback and disillusionment, of search for new types of society which could offer genuine economic and social development as well as political freedom. In more than a few of these new states there were rulers who appeared content to relapse into positions of personal privilege and to repress, by convenient arrogation of all power to themselves, every effective criticism or popular movement aimed at regeneration. But even in these countries, abused though they were by political frivolity or personal corruption, the hopes and pressures of liberation continued to exercise an influence towards expansive change. They raised a ferment of new ideas, programmes, doctrines and ideological debate; and all this, however immediately fruitless it might seem, could only promise well for a continent of peoples long deprived of contact with the problems and solutions of the rest of the world, or of any democratic methods of discussing these. It soon became clear that political and economic solutions accepted on the day of independence could be regarded as no more than provisional.

Africans now began to move across barriers which had previously divided them. These were of many kinds, both old and new. Although the societies of Iron Age Africa had possessed profound inner unities of culture and formation, they had known no more than partial and temporary unions imposed by internal conquest. Since very distant times, in this continent of most ancient human settlement, ethnic and language divisions had fissured into a multitude of separate identities, each of which, rooted in the centuries, had grown and flowered within its own ambience. How deep are these roots of different identity has been strikingly shown by the study of language: the three or four 'parent tongues' of most West African languages, for example, may have begun their ramification more than 10,000 years ago. Iron Age history nourished this process of separate growth. And then for seventy years or more the European colonial system, brief but large in its consequences, placed nearly all Africans within a multitude of new compartments above whose walls it was difficult or impossible to hear or see anything of value about neighbours near or far. Many Africans managed to travel abroad during the colonial period, but inter-regional or even inter-territorial knowledge remained minimal: East and West Africa could often seem further from each other than either was from England or France. Even the spread of education had its accompanying disadvantages, since one 'colonial language' was not the same as any other (apart from that of France and Belgium), and there were moments when Africans seemed bound to become divided between English-speaking and French-speaking rivals.

Yet the boundaries and divisions began to be crossed. All these new states were linked to one another, whether they liked it or not, by the same colonial experience. They faced much the same problems, carried many of the same handicaps, often ran the same dangers. This community of experience helped them to come together. Inter-African conferences and encounters turned into meetings of genuine self-discovery. Conceived in the very different circumstances of Afro-American experience beyond the Atlantic, Pan-Africanism began to play a fertile role in Africa itself.

In 1963, overleaping conflicts and divisions, thirty-two African governments agreed to form an Organization of African Unity with joint organs for economic planning, political consultation, and military defence. Though variously interpreted, this move towards systematic unity soon showed itself more than merely symbolic. Its future was, of course, variously interpreted. Some leaders, with Kwame Nkrumah in the van, saw it as the parent of a Union Government for the whole of Africa. Others wished for this but thought the obstacles too great. Others again regarded the new Organization as little more than a useful cover for continued separatism. But very few cared or dared, at least in public, to oppose the trend towards continental unity. For this trend now appeared to have won the support of wide areas of public opinion in many lands.

Along with this, the most influential thought which now gained ground was the broadening conviction that nothing but radical and far-reaching social and economic change along indigenous lines, African lines, could advance these new nations from their fragile and provisional status of the early 1960s. There arose a belief that Africans must complete their transition to the modern world by methods which could not and would not be the same as the methods recommended by their late rulers. This conviction deepened as the true weakness of their political independence grew patently clear. There were many new departures. More and more thoughtful people, tying up with the ideas of Pan-Africanism, argued that foreign policies of 'non-alignment' – meaning, in the language of the day, a refusal to admit loyalty to any other international grouping – must be matched by domestic policies of non-capitalist and socialist development. Efforts at continental unity must likewise go hand-in-hand with new policies aimed at internal unity. By 1965 three basic lines of new thought and action had emerged: those of neutralism, socialism, and Pan-Africanism.

They were, of course, argued sharply and often confusedly; and it could scarcely have been otherwise in a continent so suddenly, but also so partially, embarked upon the steering of its own affairs. Neutralism swung between the interpretations of those who wanted freedom to build socialist economies and those who wished merely to stay outside the military systems of the rest of the world. Single-party political systems, more and more the rule after 1960, everywhere faced the major problem of transforming loosely organized anti-colonial movements into political parties with a positive programme for reconstruction and a democratic structure. Here, too, there was confusion and diversity of aim. Some countries genuinely moved towards a larger measure of internal unity and democratic growth. Others saw the degeneration of their governments into 'group dictatorship' by small conservative élites who had taken over power from withdrawing colonial administrations; and who now used their relatively high degree of education and wealth to grow fat and idle at the expense of the majority of their fellow citizens. Here and there, predictably enough, there were *coups d'état* and popular upheavals.

Ideas about socialism were no less various or sincere.

Some leaders and parties thought of socialism as no more than a mild form of humanitarian restraint, inspired by ancient traditions of communal ownership and co-operation, upon economies that should otherwise become vigorously capitalist. Others used the slogans of socialism as a demagogic fig-leaf for their personal exploitation of the state. Still others took the ideas of socialism seriously. These they saw as meaning a total effort to rebuild society on a new and systematic basis, and now, with Ghana in the lead, reached out for means of doing so. Here it was that the notion of a total reconstruction began to make some headway. Political freedom could be of little value, it was argued, unless it were completed by an institutional freedom from the confining limits of a pre-industrial and anti-scientific past.

By 1965, whether in one way or another, the historical posture of Africa had at all events enormously changed. All these ideas, together with the men and women who defended and enlarged upon them, had gone far to project a new atmosphere and sense of African identity and purpose. Whether they spoke of an 'African personality' which should express the underlying cultural unities of Africa, and endow all Africans with membership in a grouping clearly distinctive to itself; whether they campaigned for an African neutralism which might enable them to chart their course through the conflicts of the world, and promote a continental plan of common action; whether they argued for a socialism which should be specifically African in its forms, and yet open the gate to radical enlargement of every activity of daily life: in this way or in that, with profound conviction or with little, clearly or confusedly, large numbers of men and women throughout Africa were now thinking of their countries and their continent in ways which were entirely new.

With the withdrawal of direct colonial rule, the long period of transition was once more in acute crisis. But now the crisis was felt and analysed far more deeply than at any earlier time. Many pressures drove this awakening to reality; above all, perhaps, the impossibility of things remaining as they were. Preventive medicine had unleashed a population growth which overflowed the capacity of any existing socio-political structure to meet the most elementary demands of modern life. Even the comparatively rich and fertile countries of coastal West Africa were still importing food to the tune of large sums of money they could not afford. Tens of thousands of boys and girls were vainly trying to enter secondary schools. Other thousands were leaving secondary schools with little or no hope of finding skilled employment. Countless urban workers were living on the brink of an extreme poverty. Rural reconstruction after the ravages of the 1940s and 50s was slow or altogether absent.

During the 1960s these things were increasingly seen and understood as the central challenge of the new independence. Deprived of their old securities, increasingly aware that far-reaching reorganization could alone save them from deepening poverty, from social confusion, and from dependence on the charity of others, millions of ordinary people were now launched upon a conscious effort to grasp the nature of their plight and to work their way towards its resolution. In this massive and confused campaign, spread across a continent where one level of post-colonial development often contrasted strongly and even violently with another, they were assailed by contrary advice from every quarter. They were faced by many discouragements, whether in the grim confusions of the Congo, in the gloomy packing of prisons in the 'White South', in the spectacle of self-appointed bureaucracies posing as the heroes of a new order, or in the growing knowledge of their immediate situation.

Yet these discouragements and others like them, though looming large across the scene, were no longer the whole picture nor even the more important part of it. Beneath them and beyond them, pressing forward, there were the healthy pressures of a new dissatisfaction with any halting halfway house to full development. There were new and expensive technologies at work within a changing framework of social power and organization. There were new and outward-thrusting thoughts and policies that promised to be capable, at last, of clothing the aspirations of unity and progress in the armour of a new reality.

The opening years of the 1970s confirmed this diagnosis, but also deepened it. If the problems of systematic transition were increasingly understood, they were still not being solved. But if they were not being solved, this was because they were more difficult than, ten years earlier, they had seemed to be. What was now perceived was that the nature of these problems went to the very roots of social life, whether traditional or 'colonial', and would be settled only by profound and therefore far-reaching changes in political and economic organisation. As men realised

the depth of the difficulties in which they now stood, their earlier illusions began to disappear. Africa's newly-independent countries were not going to be able to rise into the heavens of 'high consumption' by copying the capitalist systems of their former masters. They were not going to be able to achieve an egalitarian prosperity by importing revolutions from outside. Least of all could they hope to flourish on a diet of exhortation. The transition towards truly independent forms of self-organization must be the fruit of hard thought and even harder sacrifice.

These problems arose partly from the nature of African social organization as it had evolved in pre-colonial times, but even more from the circumstances of post-colonial independence. They were repeatedly illustrated, sometimes very destructively, by events that occurred during the second half of the 1960s and in the 1970s. Perhaps the most instructive if also most destructive of these illustrations was the falling apart in 1966 of the first Federation of Nigeria, by a long way Africa's most populous and potentially most powerful country. Reacting from wanton killings of Ibo people, the Eastern Region broke away from the Federation and declared its independence as the Republic of Biafra. In doing so, however, the secessionist régime claimed to include large numbers of Nigerians – perhaps as many as two-fifths of the population claimed as 'Biafran' – who were not only against secession but were strongly opposed to the 'Biafran solution'. War dragged on till early 1970, when the secession was brought to an end under conditions of outstanding clemency shown to the defeated secessionists; and a new federal structure began to emerge.

The Biafran affair dramatised problems common to most of the newly-independent countries, though in varying degrees and under varying appearances. As in Europe, the ideas of nationalism had begotten their natural heir, micro-nationalism, the logical if ultimately vain response of constituent peoples who feel that they can do better 'on their own' than within a multi-ethnic unity of many peoples. In the case of Biafra, ambitious Ibo leaders declared for their own separate nationalism; a little earlier, their Hausa-Fulani counterparts in northern Nigeria had come near to making the same decision; there were others, among the Yoruba in the west of the country, who similarly contemplated a Yoruba secession. Forgetting their own history, Europeans tended to call this 'tribalism' as if, in some way or other, Africans could have ideas only at a lower level of organization or intelligence. Modern Europe has in fact been full of precisely the same ideas of 'tribalism'.

Yet it was clear that micro-nationalism could only be the road to fresh disasters: already, Africa had too many sealed frontiers, not too few. Many of its countries were too small in territory or population or natural wealth to be able to provide the domestic markets necessary to any generalized economic and social growth. Here again the ideas of reformist nationalism appeared to have exhausted their expansive value. By 1970 it had come about that nearly all these sovereign units, however small or stricken with poverty, were the 'possession' of this or that ruling group or 'élite'. Each defended its own sovereignty, however fragile or unreal this might really be; and, as this process continued to unfold, the hopes of organic co-operation vested in bodies such as the Organization of African Unity became increasingly futile. Instead of marching towards a greater internal unity among their many language-groups or nations, Africans were going in the opposite direction. And the further they went in this direction the more completely did they fall back into dependence on non-African powers and interests.

What was required, it now began to be urged, was new forms of organization, both within and between the newly-independent countries, which could central-ize but also, at the same time, de-centralize: which could allow, that is, for the creative exercise of many local autonomies, corresponding to many cultures and loyalties, while, at the same time, welding all these into a small and even very small number of regional units capable of functional co-operation in many crucial fields of life. This was the thinking which helped to promote a new twelve-state structure for the Federation of Nigeria, in place of the three- or four-region structure taken over from the last years of British rule.

It was similarly clear, however (though still difficult to argue in public), that if Nigeria would do better as a federation of twelve or fifteen states, many of the peoples round Nigeria would also do better for themselves by joining in multi-ethnic unities bound together by federal or confederal ties. There were far fewer historical and cultural differences between the Yoruba of western Nigeria and the people of much of neighbouring Dahomey, or between the Hausa-Fulani of Northern Nigeria and many of the people of the neighbouring Niger Republic, than between peoples already enclosed within Nigeria. And other illustra-tions elsewhere could lead to the same conclusion: the key to progress, however hard to grasp and turn, manifestly lay in working towards a close functional co-operation between neighbouring states. Thus Tanzania and Zambia, meeting the pressures of an aggressive 'White South', drew nearer to each other during these years, combining to provide mutual long-range communications by road, rail and pipeline, as well as working together in other useful ways. Both countries gained from this kind of unity of policy and action, although it remained to be seen how far it could survive the stress and tumult of the times.

For there were powerful forces contending against this rational process of continental reorganization; in many cases, they easily carried the day. It was not only that the new 'national élites' or power groupings within each state desired to preserve their fiefs and privileges: it was also that their major foreign connexions desired the same thing. Africa as a whole might undoubtedly require a 'fresh start' that must be revolutionary in the same degree, though not in the same kind, as the English industrial revolution or the French Revolu-tion. But this kind of revolutionary change to entirely new forms of self-organization could not be in the interests of those who saw Africa as a field of profitable enterprise and investment; and it was certainly not to their taste. The harsh fact remained that Africa was still subject to the same forms of wealth-transfer as during the colonial period. Independence had brought many changes, many advances; it had not yet begun, save partially here and there, to alter Africa's relation-ship to the industrialized countries which still domina-ted the fortunes of the continent.

Whether by the play of export and import prices fixed in a world market governed by non-Africans, or by new 'booms' in the extraction of primary products required by non-African industries, or by means less obvious but no less present and potent, most African countries continued to yield wealth to the advanced countries. There was much benign talk of aid for African development; in truth this meant far less than it said, and often it meant nothing at all.

As these trends continued, the consequences became more painful. The rapidly growing cities of the late-colonial period continued to swell their numbers with people coming in from the countryside in search of cash-paid jobs. They found few; and every year during the late 1960s and early 1970s they were finding fewer.

There was the almost certain prospect, and even the actual presence, of huge numbers of urban unemployed for whom the governments could find neither work nor doles. Meanwhile the very emphasis on 'development for export' of farming crops – groundnuts, coffee, cocoa, and so on – bit ever more deeply into the capacity to produce food. Even relatively 'booming' countries such as Ivory Coast were now importing large annual quantities of highly-priced foreign food in order to alleviate desperate domestic shortages. Even the best results of independence, such as the rapid growth of primary and secondary education, now seemed vowed to a deepening frustration.

Under these and comparable strains the problems of transition gathered to a continental crisis. Already difficult to solve, they became more so. They loomed on the skyline of every local situation, terribly menacing, apparently insoluble. Another factor now gave them a fresh urgency and made them still more intractable. For the first time in history, the Africans began to be threatened by a great excess of population over the means of supporting even a minimal standard of life. By 1970 (and probably by a good deal earlier, though the statistics are deplorably defective) there was scarcely a single African country whose population was not increasing by at least 2.5 per cent, and many were increasing at a higher rate. This explosion in natural growth, the general consequence of preventive medicine over several decades, would double the continent's population in about twenty years or little more. It exceeded, and even greatly exceeded, any parallel expansion in the rate of production of food and other necessities.

As in India and elsewhere, this racing natural increase could only be exceedingly hard to slow down. Yet even if it could be slowed down, the existing economies of these countries would remain incapable of preventing a steady lowering in living standards that were already perilously low. Only new economies with a far greater productive capacity – in other words, new productive *systems* – could hope to support these teeming populations. Short of their appearance, much of Africa was heading for conditions of famine which might well reproduce the condition of the Indian subcontinent, where the population explosion had begun earlier but continued without the emergence of new systems capable of supporting it.

The argument in these years returned always to the same point. Further progress, even the retention of

gains already made, called for far-reaching social reconstruction which must, if it were to succeed, entirely change the relationship between Africa and the industrialized countries. Anything less than this would, in the circumstances, be little more than useless. Africa's own historical institutions and ways of life could no longer be recalled; even if they were, they could solve none of the problems which mattered now. Africa's existing institutions, if allowed to continue, could only prolong the process of wealth transfer over which they still presided. These peoples could afford no further transfers of wealth abroad: if they were not to invite and suffer long-enduring disasters on a continental scale, Africans needed every penny they could raise in their own countries, and they would have to spend this every penny to the best effect.

They had reached an historical cross-roads. What were called for now were new institutions of self-organization and investment, production and exchange. And these could be realizable only within new institutions of political and economic unity of action between neighbouring countries. Only a radical break with the past and the present could promise a different future.

The argument continued, leading often to a deep pessimism and sometimes to despair. Wherever they looked, Africans found reasons for discouragement; and the exceptions only proved the rule. The guiding lights of national independence, of cultural resurgence, seemed dim ones now. Caught in troubles of their own, the industrialized countries of the rest of the world had little or nothing to offer save the 'mixture as before', a medicine of pitiably small value, and rendered the more odious for being often labelled with condescension or contempt. Worse still, the advanced countries, or at least many of the more powerful among them, seemed locked in stubborn partnership with the racist régimes of the 'White South'. Thus American and British and other capital continued to pour into a South Africa whose ambitions now, as proclaimed by successive governments in Pretoria, reached out towards a hegemony over the whole continent south of the Equator. French and other helicopters continued to be sold to the armed forces of Portugal, thus providing the Portuguese imperial régime with its only real arm of military superiority over the nationalists of Portugal's colonies, whose wars of resistance were now a decade old. Among the African states themselves, disunity prevailed and grew more damaging to their common interests.

It would of course be naive to imagine that a continent so vast and various, emerging to political independence under conditions so generally disadvantageous, could reach the dry land of reconstruction without a period such as this. Now in midstream, with the waters running hard and threatening at times to close above their heads, Africans have many immediate reasons for pessimism. Yet a period of twenty or forty years is little more than a moment in the long perspectives of history. A wider view can show a different picture. This particular period can make matters worse, even much worse. If merely endured, it can open the way to catastrophe. But if used constructively, it can also prepare the way for the major changes without which the Africans can never, under any conditions, expect to prosper. The need to use these years constructively was increasingly seen as the central challenge of the 1970s. And this insight, in itself, was no bad measure of the great distance covered since the colonial flags were furled.

Brief Guide to Further Reading

Those who wish to know more about Africa and its peoples may like to have a short list of new or fairly new books. Nearly all of the following have more or less specialized bibliographies which can take the reader a long way in many African directions and deeply into many African subjects.

On the geo-physical and ecological background four general works made a good starting point. They are:
  W. Allan, *The African Husbandman*, 1965.
  G. H. T. Kimble, *Tropical Africa*, vol. 1, Land and Livelihood; vol. 2, Society and Polity, 1962.
  L. D. Stamp, *Africa: A Study in Tropical Development*, 1958.
  E. B. Worthington, *Science and the Development of Africa*, 1953.
A more specialized discussion of tropical farming problems and solutions will be found in:
  P. H. Nye and D. J. Greenland, *The Soil under Shifting Cultivation*, 1960.

The last twenty years have seen great advances in the understanding of Stone Age African cultures. Here the reader will be well advised to begin with J. D. Clark's brilliant synthesis, 'The Prehistoric Origins of African Culture' in the *Journal of African History*, 2 of 1964, p. 161. Four specialist works may be mentioned:
  J. D. Clark, *The Prehistory of Africa*, 1970.
  J. D. Clark, *The Prehistory of Southern Africa*, 1959.
  S. Cole, *The Prehistory of East Africa*, 1954 (revised edition 1964).
  C. B. M. McBurney, *The Stone Age of Northern Africa*, 1960.
Especially important for the rise of farming and metal-using cultures is:
  V. G. Childe, *New Light on the Most Ancient East*, latest edition 1954.
Carrying on from there, good introductions to the history of Pharaonic Egypt are:
  W. B. Emery, *Archaic Egypt*, 1961.
  W. A. Fairservis, Jnr., *The Ancient Kingdoms of the Nile*, 1962.
  A. Gardiner, *Egypt of the Pharaohs*, 1961.
The history of Kush, of Christian Nubia, and of other Sudanese achievements up to 1821 are well surveyed in:
  A. J. Arkell, *Short History of the Sudan*, revised edition 1962.
The latest findings in Kushite archaeology and history, at present a field of active and many-sided work, are regularly reported in the journal of the Sudan Antiquities Service, *Kush*, published annually in Khartoum under the editorship of Thabit Hassan Thabit. See especially *Kush 1962*, F. Hintze, 'Preliminary Report on the Excavations at Musawwarat', and *Kush 1964*, W. Y. Adams, 'An Introductory Classification of Meroitic Pottery'. The best available chronology of Kushite rulers is that of F. Hintze, *Studien zur Meroitischen Chronologie*, 1959; see also F. Hintze, 'Nubien und Sudan – ihre Bedeutung für die alte Geschichte Afrikas' in *Spektrum*, vol. 7–8 of 1964. The best overall study is that of P. Shinnie, *Meroe: A Civilisation of the Sudan*, 1967. Anyone who wants to taste the excitement of modern archaeological discoveries in Kushite culture should also read J. Vercoutter, 'Un Palais des "Candaces" Contemporain d'Auguste' in *Syria*, vol. 39 of 1962.

On Ethiopian origins, especially Axumite, a sound introduction is still that of A. Kammerer, *Essai sur l'Histoire Antique d'Abyssinie*, 1926, but later discoveries require it to be supplemented by newer work. A useful general survey is J. Doresse, *L'Empire du Prêtre-Jean*,

vol 1, Ethiopie antique, 1957; but those who wish to be up with the latest discoveries should consult *Annales d'Ethiopie*, 1955 onwards, and a brilliant essay by J. Leclant, 'Frühäthiopischer Kultur' in *Christentum am Nil*, 1963.

Basic works on the Berber bronze age and historical beginnings are:
  G. Camps, *Aux Origines de la Berbérie: Monuments et rites funéraires*, 1961; *Massinissa et les Débuts de l'Histoire*, 1961.

For Phoenician and Roman Africa see:
  G. and C. Charles-Picard, *La Vie Quotidienne à Carthage*, 1958.
  B. H. Warmington, *Carthage*, 1960; *The North African Provinces*, 1954.

For the general history of Iron Age Africa, mainly of Africa south of the Sahara, there is now available a small number of introductory surveys, including:
  R. Cornevin, *Histoire des Peuples de l'Afrique Noire*, 1960; *Histoire de l'Afrique*, 1962. (Both are full of much valuable detail.)
  B. Davidson, *Old Africa Rediscovered*, latest impression 1965. (An overall survey, based mainly on the archaeological record. Published in the United States as *The Lost Cities of Africa*); *Black Mother: Africa, the Years of Trial*, 1961. (On African-European connexions in the period 1450–1850 and the consequences for Africa of the slave trade.)
  H. Deschamps, *L'Afrique Noire Précoloniale*, 1962. (A very good pocket guide to the subject.)
  R. Mauny, *Les Siècles Obscurs de l'Afrique Noire*, 1970.
  B. M. Fagan, *Southern Africa During the Iron Age*, 1965.
  G. P. Murdock, *Africa – its Peoples and their Culture History*, 1959. (A stimulating but controversial inquiry into cultural beginnings.)
  D. A. Olderogge and I. I. Potekin, *Narodi Afriki*, 1954. (This comprehensive work of Soviet scholarship is also available in German translation, *Die Völker Afrikas*, 1961, 2 vols.)
  R. Oliver and J. D. Fage, *A Short History of Africa*, 1962. (This excellent short synthesis contains a valuable reading guide.)
We also have two good atlases of African history:
  J. D. Fage, *An Atlas of African History*, 1958.
  R. Roolvink, *Historical Atlas of the Muslim Peoples*, 1957.
and, so far, one cultural and historical encyclopedia with a vast amount of detailed information on a multitude of subjects:
  I. I. Potekin (ed.), *Afrika: Entsiklopedicheski Spravochnik*, vol. 1 A–L; vol. 2 M–Ya, 1963–4.

Some idea of the wealth of the written records of African history may be had from a number of modern anthologies, including:
  C. Coquery, *La Découverte de l'Afrique*, 1965. (A brief but attractive collection of extracts, beginning with Herodotus.)
  J. Cuvelier and L. Jadin, *L'Ancien Congo d'après les Archives romaines (1518–1640)*, 1954.
  B. Davidson, *The African Past*, 1964. (Chronicles from Antiquity to modern times: Africa south of the Sahara.)
  G. S. P. Freeman-Grenville, *The East African Coast*, 1962. (Select documents from the first to the early nineteenth century.)
  C. Fyfe, *Sierra Leone Inheritance*, 1964.
  T. Hodgkin, *Nigerian Perspectives*, 1960.
  F. Wolfson, *Pageant of Ghana*, 1959.

315

As well as these, there are four anthologies of European exploration in Africa:

E. Axelson (ed.), *South African Explorers*, 1954.
C. Howard (ed.), *West African Explorers*, 1951.
M. Perham and J. Simmons (ed.), *African Discovery*, first published 1942.
C. Richards and J. Place (ed.), *East African Explorers*, 1960.

and one anthology of especial value for early European voyaging:

J. W. Blake (ed.), *Europeans in West Africa, 1450–1560*, 2 vols, 1942.

Of great importance, the early Arabic sources for African history, otherwise available in out-of-date translations or not available at all, are now being published in new translations with up-to-date introductions by V. V. Matveev and L. E. Kubbel of the University of Leningrad. Two volumes covering the seventh to twelfth centuries have so far appeared with extracts from 39 authors:

Arabske Istochniki VII–X Vekov, 1960; and *Arabske Istochniki X–XII Vekov*, 1965, the latter beginning with al-Makdisi, whose principal work dates from AD 966.

This may be the place to mention a few introductory works on the side of language, religion, or social and political ideas:

P. Bohannan, *Africa and Africans*, New York 1964, published as *African Outline*, London 1964.
M. J. Field, *Angels and Ministers of Grace*, 1971.
J. Goody, *Technology, Tradition and the State in Africa*, 1971.
D. Forde (ed.), *African Worlds*, 1954. (Studies by a number of specialists in the cosmological ideas and social values of African peoples.)
M. Fortes and E. E. Evans-Pritchard (ed.), *African Political Systems*, latest edition 1958.
M. Fortes and G. Dieterlen (ed.), *African Systems of Thought*, 1965. (Studies by a number of specialists.)
J. Greenberg, *The Languages of Africa*, 1963. (A concise survey of basic importance.)
P. Tempels, *La Philosophie Bantoue*, 1948. (Also available in English, this is now generally accepted as a work of pioneering value.)

The plastic and other arts of Africa south of the Sahara have been variously and sometimes curiously described. Scholarly and well illustrated works on the subject include:

A. Diop (ed.), *L'Art Nègre*, 1949.
E. Elisofon and W. Fagg, *The Sculpture of Africa*, 1958.
W. and B. Forman and P. Dark, *Benin Art*, 1960.
E. Leuzinger, *Africa, The Art of the Negro Peoples*, 1960.
E. de Rouvre, with D. Paulme and J. Brosse, *Parures Africaines*, 1956.
L. Underwood, *Bronzes of West Africa*, 1949; *Masks of West Africa*, 1952.

Returning to the more narrowly historical field, the following is a brief list of basic or introductory works confined to one or other region or country:

NORTH AND NORTH-EAST AFRICA:

N. Barbour, *A Survey of North West Africa*, 1959.
H. I. Bell, *Egypt from Alexander the Great to the Arab Conquest*, 1948.
P. M. Holt, *A Modern History of the Sudan*, 1961.
A. H. M. Jones and E. Monroe, *A History of Ethiopia*, 1955.
C-A. Julien, *Histoire de l'Afrique du Nord*, 1951.
E. Lévi-Provençal, *Histoire de l'Espagne Mussulmane, 710–1031*, 3 vols, 1950–67.

B. Lewis, *The Arabs in History*, 1950.
E. Ullendorff, *The Ethiopians*, 1960.

WEST AFRICA:

J. F. Ade Ajayi, *Christian Missions in Nigeria, 1841–81*, 1965.
D. Birmingham, *The Portuguese Conquest of Angola*, 1965.
E. W. Bovill, *The Golden Trade of the Moors*, 1958.
R. Cornevin, *Histoire du Togo*, 1959.
M. Crowder, *The Story of Nigeria*, 1962.
B. Davidson, *A History of West Africa to 1800*, 1965.
K. Onwuka Dike, *Trade and Politics in the Niger Delta 1830–85*, 1956.
C. Fyfe, *A History of Sierra Leone*, 1962.
J. D. Hargreaves, *Prelude to the Partition of West Africa*, 1963.
A. Ihle, *Das Alte Königreich Kongo*, 1929.
G. I. Jones, *The Trading States of the Oil Rivers*, 1963.
D. Kimble, *A Political History of Ghana, 1850–1928*, 1963.
M. Last, *The Sokoto Caliphate*, 1967.
R. Mauny, *Tableau Géographique de l'Ouest Africain au Moyen Age*, 1961.
C. Newbury, *The Western Slave Coast and its Rulers*, 1961
K. Polányi, *Dahomey and the Slave Trade*, 1966.
J. Rouch, *Contribution à l'Histoire des Songhay*, 1953; *Les Songhay*, 1954.
A. F. C. Ryder, *Benin and the Europeans, 1485–1897*, 1969.
M. G. Smith, *Government in Zazzau 1800–1950*, 1960.
J. Suret-Canale, *L'Afrique Noire Occidentale et Centrale*, vol. 1, Géographie, Civilisations, Histoire, 1961; vol. 2, L'Ere Coloniale, 1900–45, 1964.
L. Tauxier, *Histoire des Bambara*, 1942.
Y. Urvoy, *Histoire des Populations du Soudan Central*, 1936; *Histoire de l'Empire du Bornou*, 1949.
W. E. F. Ward, *A History of Ghana*, 1958.

SOUTH AND SOUTH-CENTRAL AFRICA:

H. Deschamps, *Histoire de Madagascar*, 1960.
C. W. de Kieweit, *A History of South Africa*, 1950.
P. Mason, *The Birth of a Dilemma*, 1958. (Conquest and settlement of Rhodesia.)
H. J. and R. E. Simons, *Class and Colour in South Africa*, 1969.
L. Thompson and M. Wilson, *A History of South Africa*, 2 vols, 1970.
A. J. Wills, *An Introduction to the History of Central Africa*, 1964.

EAST AFRICA:

E. Axelson, *South-East Africa 1488–1530*, 1940; *The Portuguese in South-East Africa 1600–1700*, 1960.
B. Davidson, *A History of East and Central Africa to the Late 19th Century*, 1967.
G. S. P. Freeman-Grenville, *The Medieval History of the Tanganyika Coast*, 1962.
V. L. Grottanelli, *Pescatori dell'Oceano Indiano*, 1955.
J. Iliffe, *Tanganyika Under German Rule 1905–1912*, 1969.
B. A. Ogot, *The History of the Southern Luo*, vol. 1, 1967.
R. Oliver and G. Mathew (ed.), *History of East Africa*, vol. 1, 1962.
J. Strandes, *Die Portugiesenzeit von Deutsch- und Englisch-Ostafrika*, 1899. (English translation 1961, as *The Portuguese Period in East Africa*.)

The books cited above are concerned mainly or entirely with the pre-colonial period. On the colonial period itself there is a vast bibliography of very diverse value, whether of published official papers, individual memoirs, polemics, journalism or, latterly, analytical scholarship; and I shall make no attempt to cover it here. But a few pointers may be useful. The administrative record from an orthodox imperialist standpoint is most effectively set forth and described in Lord Hailey's *An African Survey*, first published in 1938 but reprinted and revised in 1945 and again in 1957. A standard work on the French side is R. Delavignette, *Service Africain*, 1946 (English title, *Freedom and Authority in French West Africa*). A valuable short survey of French attitudes is contained in H. Brunschwig's *Mythes et Réalités de l'Impérialisme Colonial Français 1871–1914*, 1960. Readers may also consult the *Encyclopédie de l'Empire Française*; *Encyclopédie du Congo Belge*; and the *Grande Enciclopédia Portuguesa e Brasiliera*, all of which present many articles on the philosophy, motivation, and claims of European imperialism in Africa as seen by the imperialists themselves.

At the other extreme there is a small number of highly critical works dating from the colonial period, notably H. W. Nevinson, *A Modern Slavery*, 1906 (Angola and São Thomé); E. D. Morel, *Red Rubber* (Congo Free State), revised edition 1919; N. Leys, *Kenya*, 1926; and my own *African Awakening*, 1955. Between the extremes of acceptance and rejection there is a large number of works of varying merit from many standpoints.

The background to the South African situation of today may be found from a number of points of view, more or less critical, in B. Bunting, *Rise and Fall of the South African Reich*, 1964; G. M. Carter, *The Politics of Inequality*, 1958; B. Davidson, *Report on Southern Africa*, 1952; L. Marquard, *The Peoples and Policies of South Africa*, 1952; and H. Tingsten, *The Problem of South Africa*, 1955; while many statements in justification of *apartheid* may be had by application to the Government Publications Office of the Republic of South Africa, Pretoria. Further north the most useful surveys of white-settler situations in south-central Africa are those of C. Leys, *European Politics in Southern Africa*, 1959; C. Leys and C. Pratt, *A New Deal in Central Africa*, 1960; and T. M. Franck, *Race and Nationalism* (in the Rhodesias and Nyasaland), 1960.

For East Africa the second volume of the *History of East Africa*, 1964, edited by V. Harlow and E. M. Chilver, carries on the story into colonial times; while the *Report* of the East Africa Royal Commission, 1955, is of basic importance among British Government policy papers. R. Oliver's *The Missionary Factor in East Africa*, 1952, has many valuable insights; as does F. B. Welbourn's *East African Rebels*, 1961. The white-settler viewpoint is well expressed in J. F. Lipscomb's *White Africans*, 1955; while a contrary view may be found in P. Evans's *Law and Disorder in Kenya*, 1956; in J. M. Kariuki's '*Mau-Mau' Detainee*, 1963; and in D. L. Barnett's and K. Njama's *Mau Mau from Within*, 1966. The West African bibliography is capacious for this period; aside from the books listed above under *West Africa*, all of which have good bibliographies, the reader may follow the story from the imperialist attitude in M. Perham, *Lugard*, 2 vols, 1956 and 1960 (the first covering Lugard's ventures in East Africa, the second in Nigeria); in J. E. Flint, *Sir George Goldie*, 1960; and in R. Oliver, *Sir Harry Johnston and the Scramble for Africa*, 1957. On the Congo Free State, R. Slade's *King Leopold's Congo*, 1962, may be compared with E. D. Morel's *Red Rubber*, mentioned above, and with P. Joye and R. Levine, *Les Trusts au Congo*, 1961 (dealing also with the Belgian Congo). A penetrating study of relations between the Belgian Parliament

and King Leopold will be found in J. Stengers's *Belgique et Congo: L'Elaboration de la Charte Coloniale*, 1963.

German colonialism forms another chapter in this many-sided affair. The best overall introduction is H. Brunschwig's *L'Expansion Allemande Outre-Mer du XVe Siècle à Nos Jours*, 1957. Since the Second World War German scholars have published a number of important works based on the German imperial archives now collected at Potsdam: these include K. Büttner's *Die Anfänge der Deutschen Kolonialpolitik in Ostafrika*, 1959; F. F. Müller's *Deutschland-Zanzibar-Ostafrika*, 1959; and H. Stoecker's *Kamerun unter Deutscher Kolonialherrschaft*, 1960. For South West Africa see, for example, K. Schwabe, *Der Krieg in Deutsch-Südwestafrika*, 1907; H. Loth's *Die Christlichen Missionen in Südwestafrika*, 1963; H. Dreschler's *Südwest-Afrika unter deutscher Kolonialherrschaft*, 1966; and for a report on the current situation and background, R. First, *South West Africa*, 1963.

On the economic consequences of the colonial system the bibliography is still remarkably deficient, but S. H. Fraenkel's *Capital Investment in Africa*, 1938, makes an important starting point for analysis. Apart from books listed above which touch on economic questions from the imperialist angle, the reader may also consult a critical study written from a Marxist approach, that of J. Woddis *The Roots of Revolt*, 1960. An attempt at some conclusions will be found in my *Which Way Africa? The Search for a New Society*, revised edition 1971, chs. 6–12, and bibliography.

For the rise of modern nationalism and the campaigns that led to political independence the best short guides are T. Hodgkin's *Nationalism in Colonial Africa*, 1956, and his *African Political Parties*, 1961. More detailed studies of importance include D. E. Apter's *The Gold Coast in Transition*, 1955; J. S. Coleman's *Nigeria: A Background to Nationalism*, 1958; G. Shepperson's and T. Price's *Independent African*, 1958 (origins, setting and significance of the Chilembwe rising in Nyasaland of 1915); and, for the Maghreb of North Africa, C. A. Julien's *L'Afrique du Nord en Marche*, 1952; while an essential documentation on the Algerian independence movement and war is that of A. Mandouze, *La Révolution Algérienne par les Textes*, 1961. A number of books by African leaders are of key importance: these include Sir Ahmadu Bello's *My Life*, 1962; Kenneth Kaunda's *Zambia Shall Be Free*, 1962; O. Odinga's *Not Yet Uhuru*, 1967; while Kwame Nkrumah's *Autobiography*, 1957, and his *Africa Must Unite*, 1963, are both essential, as are all the works of Julius Nyerere, beginning with *Freedom and Unity* (*Uhuru na Umoja*), 1966.

Lastly, mention may be made of four useful handbooks to the current African scene. These are C. Legum's *Africa: A Handbook to the Continent*, 1961 (revised edn., 1969); H. Kitchen's *A Handbook of African Affairs*, 1964; and R. Segal's *Political Africa: A Who's Who of Personalities and Parties*, 1961; and, latest and largest, *Africa South of the Sahara*, Europa Publications, 1972.

For nationalism in the Portuguese colonies, see:
A. Cabral, *Revolution in Guinea*, 1969.
B. Davidson, *The Liberation of Guiné: Aspects of an African Revolution*, *1969*.
B. Davidson, *In the Eye of the Storm: Angola's People*, 1972.
J. Marcum, *Revolution in Angola, Anatomy of an Explosion 1954–62*, 1969.
E. Mondlane, *The Struggle for Mozambique*, 1969.

Acknowledgments

To Professor Roland Oliver I wish to record my thanks for his patience and generosity in reading the typescript, and helping to correct the errors, of an historical synthesis whose structure and interpretation are of course my responsibility alone. This, too, is the place for me to express my deep admiration to Werner Forman, who travelled in Africa for more than eight months as well as visiting European collections in order to reap his brilliant harvest, and did all this with the energy, determination and scholarly approach that are characteristic of him; and to Bedřich Forman, who faced the problems of design with a sensitivity and understanding whose results also speak for themselves. The three of us feel that we are fortunate in our publishers, and wish especially to thank Mr Michael Raeburn of Weidenfeld and Nicolson for unfailing help and enthusiasm. Altogether this has proved a highly co-operative enterprise, arduous but enjoyable; and such success as we may be thought to have achieved comes in no small measure from our having been able to work so well together.

BASIL DAVIDSON

Werner Forman would like to record his special thanks to all those who helped him during his work in Africa, and in particular to His Highness Oba Akenzua II of Benin; His Highness the Temi of Ede; M. Bubu Hama, President of the National Assembly of the Republic of Niger; Dr Gabriel Camps, Director of the Bardo Museum, Algiers; Mr Neville Chittick, Director of the British Institute of History and Archaeology in East Africa, Nairobi; and Mr Hamo Sassoon, of the same Institute at Dar es-Salaam; Dr K.O. Dike, Vice-Chancellor of the University of Ibadan; Mr Yao Eduful, of Flagstaff House, Accra; Mnr Herman Haan and Dr René Wassing, of the Ethnological Museum, Rotterdam; Dr Rauf Habib, Chief Curator of the Coptic Museum, Cairo; Mr A.T. Hammond of the National Museum, Accra; Professor B. Holas of the Centre des Sciences Humaines, Abidjan; Mme Lalande Isnard, of the National Library, Conakry; Mr Festus V. Izevbigie, of Benin City; Mr J.D. Kirkman, Keeper of the National Museum, Fort Jesus, Mombasa; Dr Kurt Krieger and Dr B. Menzel, of the State Museums, Berlin-Dahlem; Dr E. Krysa, of Conakry; Dr A.A.Y. Kyerematen, Director of the Ghana National Cultural Centre; M. Sampil Mamadou, Curator of the National Museum, Conakry; Professor D.A. Olderogge, of the Institute of Ethnography, Leningrad; Dr Mohammed H. Abd-ur-Rahman, Chief Curator of the Egyptian Museum, Cairo; Dr Jean Rouch, of the National Museum, Niamey; Mr D. Simmonds, Curator of the Trenchard Gallery, Ibadan; M. Moussa Oumar Sy, Director of the National Museum, Bamako; and Sayed Thabit Hassan Thabit, Director of Antiquities, Republic of Sudan.

The author, photographer and publishers also wish to thank the directors, trustees and authorities of the following museums, who allowed objects from their collections to be photographed for this book and who, in many cases, also provided much useful information (References are to pages):
Accra, Ghana National Cultural Centre, 125 (*bottom right*), 232 (*top*), 240; Accra, Ghana National Museum, 123 (*top*), 124, 125 (*top left and right, bottom left*), 126, 174, 175 (*bottom*), 176, 180, 189 (*bottom left*), 231 (*top left and right*), 239, 256; Addis Abeba, Musée Archéologique, 61, 62, 63; Algiers, Musée de Préhistoire et d'Ethnographie du Bardo, 19 (*top and bottom right*), 23; Algiers, Musée National Stéphane Gsell, 73 (*bottom left*); Bamako, Musée National du Mali, 120 (*bottom*), 278 (*top*); Benin Museum, 190 (*bottom*), 196; Cairo, Coptic Museum, 129, 130, 133; Cairo, Egyptian Museum, 38 (*top*), 39; Conakry, Musée National, 227; Dar es-Salaam, British Institute of History and Archaeology, 19 (*left*); Dar es-Salaam, National Museum of Tanganyika, 88 (*top*); Ibadan, Trenchard Gallery, 164; Ife Museum, 106, 109, 111, 112; Jos Museum, 101 (*left*); Khartoum, Sudan Museum, 38 (*bottom*), 46, 49, 51 (*bottom*), 52, 55, 56, 57; Lagos Museum, 100, 101 (*right*), 110, 119, 120 (*top*), 123 (*bottom*), 189 (*top*), 190 (*top*), 191 (*bottom*), 192, 248, 287; Livingstone, National Museum of Zambia, 169 (*bottom*); Tunis, Musée du Bardo, 67 (*left and top right*), 73 (*bottom right*), 79.

Berlin-Dahlem, Museum für Völkerkunde, 179, 272; Leningrad, Museum of Ethnography, 173, 175 (*top*), 189 (*bottom right*), 197, 201 (*bottom left*), 231, 263, 288; Lisbon, Biblioteca da Academia das Ciências, 205 (*bottom*); Lisbon, Museu de Artilheria, 264 (*bottom right*); London, British Museum, 127, 178, 201 (*top*), 202, 206, 208, 212 (*top and bottom*), 226, 251 (*top*), 264 (*bottom left*), 267 (*top left, bottom left and centre*), 271, 275, 276, 279, 282 (*bottom right*); London, Museum of the Institute of Archaeology, University College, 134 (*top left and bottom right*); Modena, Biblioteca Estense, 211; Paris, Bibliothèque Nationale, 198; Paris, Musée de l'Homme, 163, 244; Prague, Národní Galerie, 218 (*bottom*); Rotterdam, Museum voor Land- en Volkerkunde, 255, 273; Versailles, Musée National, 264 (*top*); Warsaw, Muzeum Narodowego, 134 (*bottom left*); Washington, Library of Congress Collection, 221, 224 (*bottom*).

The objects illustrated on page 277 are reproduced by courtesy of His Highness Oba Laoye II, Temi of Ede; that on page 218 (*bottom*) is from the collection of Mr D. Simmonds; and those on pages 115–16 are from a private collection.

The photographs on pages 85, 86 (*top*), 134 (*top right*), 236, 251 (*bottom*) and 301 are by the author, and those on pages 24 (*top*) and 169 (*top*) are by Miss Ruth Lazarus. Other photographs were obtained from the following sources; Alinari, 212 (*centre*), 264 (*top*); Archive de la Présidence, Algiers, 306 (*top*); Mr David Attenborough, 167 (*bottom*); Dr A.D.H. Bivar, 250; Camera Press, 300; Central Press Photos, 296 (*top*), 299; Dr Brian Fagan, 169 (*bottom*); Messrs John Freeman, 134 (*top left and bottom right*), 201 (*top*), 251 (*top*), 264 (*bottom left*), 267 (*top left, bottom left and centre*), 271, 282 (*bottom right*); Keystone Press, 296 (*bottom*), 305 (*top*); Kodansha Ltd, Tokyo, 167 (*top*), 168; Professor J.-P. Leboeuf, Centre tchadien pour les Sciences humaines, Fort-Lamy, 253; Professor J. Leclant, 53; Mansell Collection, 257; PAIGC, 305 (*bottom*); Radio Times Hulton Picture Library, 267 (*top and bottom right*), 281, 282 (*top and bottom left*), 295; Rapho-Lajoux (Editions Duchêne), 12, 24 (*bottom*); Rhodesia High Commission, 17, 18; Sr R. Valadão, Secretariado Nacional da Informacão, 177, 201 (*bottom right*), 264 (*bottom right*); Mr Barney Wayne, 159; Zambia High Commission, 307 (*top*).

The author and publishers also wish to thank the following who have given permission for copyright material to be reproduced: Dr W.Y. Adams, 48 (from *Kush*, vol. XII); Dr Gabriel Camps, 59 (from *Aux Origines de la Berbérie: Monuments et rites funéraires*); Dr Gertrude Caton-Thompson, 172 (from *The Zimbabwe Culture*); Mrs Sonia Cole, 15 (from *The Prehistory of East Africa*); Professor R. Mauny, 103 (from *L'Ouest Afrique au moyen age*); Mme O. du Puigaudeau, 90 (from *Décor Mural de Walata*); Professor P. Shinnie, 132 (from *Medieval Nubia*); Sudan Antiquities Service, 47, 48 (from *Kush*, vols VII and XII), 132 (from P. Shinnie, *Medieval Nubia*); Oxford University Press, 30 (from A. Gardiner, *Egypt of the Pharaohs*), 172 (from G. Caton-Thompson, *The Zimbabwe Culture*).

The maps were specially drawn by Mrs M. Verity.

Index

Index